RECEIVED

LI.

Desk

D0257867

REFERENCE
ONLY

THE POETRY LIBRARY

WITHDRAWN FROM THE POETRY LIBRARY

THE POETRY LIBRARY

THE
Writer's Guide
TO
SELF-PROMOTION
AND
PUBLICITY

POETRY LIBRARY
SOUTH BANK CENTRE
WITHDRAWN FROM THE POETRY LIBRARY
LONDON
SE1 8XX

THE
Writer's Guide
TO
SELF-PROMOTION
AND
PUBLICITY

ELANE FELDMAN

Writer's
Digest
Books

CINCINNATI, OHIO

The Writer's Guide to Self-Promotion and Publicity

Copyright © 1990 by Elane Feldman

Printed and bound in the United States of America. All rights reserved. No part of this book may be reproduced in any form or by any electronic or mechanical means including information storage and retrieval systems without permission in writing from the publisher, except by a reviewer, who may quote brief passages in a review. Published by Writer's Digest Books, an imprint of F&W Publications, Inc., 1507 Dana Avenue, Cincinnati, Ohio 45207. First edition.

94 93 92 91 90   5 4 3 2 1

Library of Congress Cataloging in Publication Data

Feldman, Elane.
    The writer's guide to self-promotion and publicity / Elane Feldman. — 1st ed.
        p.   cm.
    Includes bibliographical references and index.
    ISBN 0-89879-399-8
    1. Authorship — Marketing. 2. Assertiveness (Psychology)
    I. Title.
PN161.F4   1990   90-42504
808'.02'0688 — dc20   CIP

Edited by Chris Dodd
Designed by Cathleen Norz

• ACKNOWLEDGMENTS •

There are so many terrific, helpful people to thank in publishing and the media that citing each person by name would require a listing the size of the New York City phone book! I'll have to just extend a blanket "thank you" to all of them. But, a special word of appreciation must be extended to Miriam Phelps, *Publishers Weekly* librarian, for her gracious help. And to my editor, Jean Fredette, a sincere thanks for her attentive and keen comments and advice.

Special thanks to dear friends Abraham and Barbara Habenstreit for their support, encouragement, and generosity. Also my appreciation is extended to our conscientious U.S. Post Office mailmen: our regular carrier, Mr. Santos Caraballo, and substitute, Mr. Bob Latterman, both of whom consistently, diligently, and carefully brought me the many pieces of mail I received. A special thank you to the hardworking and dedicated librarians at the Cadman Plaza Branch of the Brooklyn Public Library—they were always able to speedily provide just the right help!

As for the obligatory thanks usually seen on Acknowledgment pages for one's spouse, I cannot find an adequate way to succinctly express my love and appreciation to my dear husband Daniel—I hope this book's dedication says just some of what I feel.

THE POETRY LIBRARY

• ABOUT THE AUTHOR •

Elane Feldman's knowledge of the interrelationship between publicity and promotion and the writing life is born out of many years' experience. She has been Director of Marketing, Public Relations, and Promotion at several New York trade book publishers, and has served as a consultant for a variety of clients both in and out of publishing. She has worked on many different books, including those of four Nobel Laureates in Literature.

As a writer, Elane has published more than 150 articles in major national publications. She is currently an adjunct assistant professor of public relations at New York University, and regularly creates and leads seminars and workshops for publishing executives, college students, and writer's organizations.

For my husband Daniel,
without whom much of
what I accomplish would
be impossible.

**"Man is not the creature
of circumstances,
circumstances are the
creature of man."**

—Benjamin Disraeli

• CONTENTS •

Introduction   1

1 Begin at the Beginning 6

How to prepare and package your personal press kit with background sheets, professional credits, and photographs.

2 Tools of the Trade 16

How to choose and use the writer's tools, from stationery and mailing labels to answering machines and personal computers, to your most valuable tool of all: time.

3 The Basics of Self-Promotion   26

Basic strategy for generating publicity using pitch letters, news releases, and your telephone.

4 Protocol and Etiquette for Writers 48

The right ways (and wrong ways) to contact and establish rapport with editors.

5 Establishing and Enhancing Your Reputation 56

Becoming a "household-name" by being a syndicated columnist, an op-ed writer, a "noted expert," and other venues.

6 Networking for Writers 70

Getting the most out of writers conferences, seminars, workshops, and writer's groups.

7 Taking Your Show on the Road 79

Self-Promotion through public speaking, store appearances, autograph sessions, and press conferences.

8 Working with TV and Radio **96**

Securing radio and television interviews and using them to your best advantage. How to work (and not work) with media people – some writer's Golden Rules.

9 Understanding Publishing Realities **127**

Getting the best possible publicity through your publishing company, including book meetings, author's questionnaires, and publicity parties.

10 Especially for Authors **140**

What you need to know about galleys, blurbs, book reviews, and more; selling your books directly; the vanity press.

11 How to "Make" Your Own Luck   **159**

Creative approaches to promoting yourself, including promotional items, newsletters, and "coattailing."

12 Should You Hire A Personal Press Agent? **172**

Deciding if you need professional assistance. Selecting and working with a press agent or publicity consultant.

1 Appendix: Book Publicity Action Plan **185**

A timetable of activities that takes you from prepublication to the bookstore shelves.

2 Appendix: Sample Publicity Forms **189**

Examples of a tip sheet, advance notice, media alert, and confirmation slip to help you prepare your own successful publicity forms.

3 Appendix: Resource Section **193**

Listings of organizations, books, periodicals, directories, and catalogs that can help you write and sell.

Index   **209**

• INTRODUCTION •

Why This Book? . . . .

In this book, we will not spell out the many reasons why people choose to be writers. If you are reading this book you have obviously chosen to write, and are seeking ways to advance yourself and to enhance your reputation. What we will do is explore the various ways writers of general interest books and articles — whether they are just starting out or have been writing for a time — can undertake publicity and promotion activities that will bring results.

For many creative people the words "publicity" and "self-promotion" strike a sour note. It is anathema to even mention the subject, yet for the wise writer these are words that speak to today's realities:

- There are three quarters of a million books already in print.

- Some 70,000 books go out of print annually.

- The number of book publishers continues to shrink yearly due to mergers, reorganizations, or to those who simply close shop.

- The number of magazines available to freelancers has also shrunk. As *Time* magazine reported, "For most freelancers, magazine writing has become the slum of journalism — overcrowded, underpaid, littered with rejection slips."

- The Authors Guild estimates that in 1988, the average annual income for writers was a paltry $8,000, and other estimates have placed it even lower.

Given the many problems inherent in being a writer, whether of nonfiction or fiction, it is the wise writer who knows and capitalizes on the many aspects of self-promotion. But having said that, no matter how obvious the need for self-promotion and for reputation enhancement, it's startling how few writers undertake such activities.

My knowledge of the interrelationship between publicity and promotion and the writing life is born out of many years' experience. I've been director of marketing, public relations, and promotion at several New York trade book publishers, and have served as a consultant for a variety of clients both in and out of publishing. (I have been privileged to work on many different books, including those of four Nobel Laureates in Literature.)

As a writer, I've had more than 150 articles published in major national publications. I'm currently an adjunct assistant professor of public relations at New York University, and regularly create and lead seminars and workshops for publishing executives, college students, and writers' organizations.

In teaching writers workshops in publicity, promotion, and related areas I am continually amazed at how few creative people understand publishing realities and how many are horrified by the very thought of undertaking any self-promotion. The ill-placed optimism that merit alone will carry them to the pinnacles of success, or that publicity is "tacky" (that it means undertaking gimmicky stunts and indulging in hype) and requires a personality long on ego, or that it is a very costly undertaking, are often prevalent attitudes. It is, however, just such beliefs that usually mean grave disappointment and precede failure. It is truly surprising how many writers believe creative people cannot undertake self-promotion without somehow compromising their artistry.

But, in light of today's competitive world, it is patently foolish not to continually work at appropriate self-promotion. ("Appropriate" is a key word here.)

For those who dread the concept of self-promotion, and who persist in thinking it's at great odds with being a creative writer, F. Scott Fitzgerald's comment, ". . . the test of a first rate intelligence is the ability to hold two opposing ideas in the mind at the same time," is especially relevant!

This book will explore ways that writers can publicize and promote themselves—how (if they aren't already being represented by a literary agent) they can be taken seriously by the agenting community; how they can keep themselves in the minds of newspapers or magazine editors; how they can do likewise with book publishing company editors; and how they can best work with book publishing personnel if they have a book scheduled for publication, or one that is already in print.

We will also explore various ways writers can bring themselves to the public's attention, particularly, how to attract the attention of the print and electronic media. This is no mean feat given the huge numbers of individuals, organizations, and companies seeking media coverage.

The overall theme of this book is that the notion that self-promotion equates self-aggrandizement, or that publicizing yourself always means being involved in hype and hoopla simply isn't true. We will provide help and offer ideas on the ways writers can position themselves in a world that is seemingly oversupplied with writers and glutted with people in all fields who are clamoring for attention.

Throughout the ages, many writers have pithily expressed themselves on the subject of the writing life. Gustave Flaubert said, "Writing is a dog's life, but the only life worth living."

It must be so. According to the Authors Guild, in the last poll taken (1986) the Department of Labor indicated that approximately 61,000 Americans identified themselves as freelance writers. This group ranged from those who had written many books and articles, to those who had written a few pieces.

If those numbers seem daunting, don't despair. With the right type of self-promotion and publicity you may well bring yourself to the attention of a book publisher or to one of the general interest, or small or special interest magazine publishers. If you've already been published, you'll learn to capitalize on your "expertise," to build your reputation. So that editors, agents, the media, and readers will seek you out.

Where You Fit In . . . .

In this book, as we are addressing ourselves to a broad spectrum of writers—those who are well established and those who are fairly new to the field—at times it may seem that some of the topics we explore are simplistic. But, we have endeavored to cover all the bases and hope, therefore, there is something here for each of you.

We have provided information to help published authors, as well as those of you who hope to write in varying formats, and those who are currently writing magazine and newspaper pieces. (We're touching all the proverbial "bases," as it has been our experience that writers cross back and forth between writing for periodicals and for book publishers.) Therefore, in addition to offering information that can be used by all writers, we have also provided specific details on self-promotion for writers of books, and for writers of magazine and newspaper articles.

Advertising is *Not* Publicity . . . .

It is important that we understand the differences between publicity and advertising. Simply put: Advertising is what you pay for—either space you purchase in a printed publication (newspaper, magazine, or journal) or "airtime" on radio and television.

Publicity is "free." It involves all types of coverage by the print and electronic media, whether it is space garnered in print, or radio or TV exposure. Thus, generally speaking, the only cost involved is what you spend for mailings, and possibly for the creation of printed materials: news releases, photographs, press kits, and for any and all expenses and materials to support your interview or appearance.

Don't Think, "I Have an Agent, I Needn't Be Concerned about This" . . . .

If you are represented by a literary agent, you may feel you do not have to undertake any self-promotion as you are already taken care of in this area. It is important to keep in mind that while your agent will be trying to sell your work—or working with your publisher on contract details—more often than not, she cannot also be your personal press agent. While it sometimes is the case that agents will try to stimulate publishers into some publicity or promotion activity, they cannot themselves undertake publicity and promotion campaigns for their writers. First, that is not their specialty; second, if they were to do so, it would seriously erode the amount of time they could devote to all their other tasks.

If you work with an agent, you should certainly discuss this subject with him or her early on, but be realistic about your agent's role in this aspect of your career. Be prepared to help yourself.

If you fear that means you'll be viewed as a "beginner," Eleanor Blau reports in the December 11, 1989, *New York Times* that more and more authors are taking charge of their own publicity:

. . . One might think that [Dan Greenburg] does not need to [do his own publicity/promotion]. But he has been . . . for 20 years. . . . Because . . . the number of new books . . . has soared . . . sales representatives are overburdened . . . promotional budgets have been cut back, and besides, [he says] it's "grown up" to take responsibility for your career. . . . He is hardly alone. Wayne Dyer bought up the first printing of his book, *Your Erroneous Zones* . . . before it became a best seller, and drove around the country placing them in bookstores, on consignment.

One Author's Major Success Story. . . . .

One much-heralded success story is centered on the best seller written by Minneapolis businessman Harvey Mackay. Mackay, who runs a successful envelope company, decided to write a "big-time book." Leaving nothing to chance, he created a plan for success that catapulted this business book onto *The New York Times* best-seller list. Tapping his business successes and being possessed of time and capital, he used every technique he could to fly in the face of the odds.

He reportedly visualized seeing his book in the windows of Manhattan's big Fifth Avenue bookshops and on a best-seller list as he wrote. (He went so far as to tape a copy of a best-seller list on his office door as a graphic motivator.)

He also enrolled in a publishing course at Stanford University, persuading the program's director to make his book's first draft mandatory reading at the course. Doing so meant he received feedback from eighty-five editors and publishers who attended the program.

His well "vetted" manuscript was then sold to William Morrow & Co. He wrangled with his editor about the book's title and proved his idea for the title was "right" by paying a major product-naming firm $6,000 to test his name concept against 800 others. Hence *his* chosen title, *How to Swim with the Sharks without Being Eaten Alive,* prevailed.

Mackay also undertook his own marketing research, spending a year and a half visiting 150 of the country's bookstores. He concluded that most books failed, not due to subject matter, but due to their unavailability in stores. To prevent his book from suffering this fate, he demanded and won from Morrow an almost unparalleled 100,000 first printing. To convince the publisher of the wisdom of investing this heavily in a first-time author, he held motivational seminars for the company's sales force and paid for a twenty-six-city promotional tour on his own. He also talked over forty noteworthy Americans from every walk of life into writing blurbs for the cover.

And, even though his publisher was not happy with the idea, he insisted on attending the prestigious Frankfurt Book Fair, where deals for international subsidiary rights sales are struck. After three days, he had sold rights on his book for distribution in thirty countries and in twelve different languages. He continues to plug the book by visiting U.S. bookstores. It's his belief—based on his research—that it was the personal effort that propelled his book to best-sellerdom.

While most writers are unable to undertake anything like the type of self-promotion that Harvey Mackay undertook, nor can they *afford* to, we provide this information as an example of what can be done by an energetic author. And, we offer it as a case in point: *There is something to be learned here for each of us.* For, as in women's fashion magazines, where the editors expect few women will adopt the pictured looks *en toto*, one can always find something to emulate.

You may not have the funds, or the time, to emulate Harvey Mackay. But, as a writer, persistence, imagination, and a strong belief in your "product" are tools you should have — and they're free!

As the anonymous pundit opined, "Triumph is just 'umph' add to 'try.' "

1

Begin at the Beginning

The Press Kit. In undertaking self-promotion, there are things you must do before you do anything else. To be taken seriously you have to present yourself as a professional. It is, therefore, vital that you assemble a personal press kit.

Professional public relations agencies use the press kit as a means of packaging their clients. "Packaging" is *not* a dirty word. You do want to present yourself to the world in a professional manner! An all-purpose press kit has a variety of uses, as we'll see in the pages and chapters that follow.

Most writers are familiar with the book author's press kit, and we'll offer suggestions for putting together these attractive, inexpensive kits. But even magazine writers will find that having such a promotional tool well organized, well executed, and *at hand* (whether used as a whole or for its component parts) is an invaluable aid to their writing careers.

In this chapter, we'll discuss the components of a basic personal press kit, as well as some ideas for presenting your materials in a professional manner.

The Background Sheet. . . . .

This differs from a traditional resume in that, with some exceptions, it excludes educational and personal information (unless it's relevant) and concentrates on your writing career and achievements. If you write in one or more specialized areas, it should crystallize your expertise by listing all the relevant articles or books you've published on the subject(s). As we'll see, it can be used in a variety of ways. Take a look at the sample on the next page.

Here's how to put a background sheet together:

On your letterhead, type the words "Background on:" insert your name, then just below this line, type in the names of all the publications you have appeared in, each article's title, and a description of your piece (if the article's title is not descriptive of the article). Do the same thing for any books you have authored. List any writing-related honors or awards separately, as well as any relevant organizations you belong to. If, for example, you specialize in pieces on wildlife and are active in organizations that are concerned with animal life, indicate this information.

In other sections you want to indicate whatever information is part of your

• SAMPLE BACKGROUND SHEET •

Your Letterhead Here

Background on Joan Smith

Joan Smith is a Contributing Editor to *Today's Budget Traveler*

Articles Published:

Travel Today Magazine
- "Hawaii Yesterday, Today & Tomorrow"
- "Fiji Art & Artifacts"
- "Beautiful Hong Kong"

Diversion
- "Ten Tips for Travelers"
- "New Guidebooks for Disabled Travelers"

Traveller's Diary, Great Britain
- "Venice—In Search of Marco Polo's Roots"
- "New York's Great Italian Restaurants"
- "America's Ten Top Scenic Cities"

St. Louis Post Dispatch (Sunday Travel Section)
- Local Area "B&B" Choices—New & Venerable Establishments

New York Times Book Review (Sunday)
- New travel books (Covering South Pacific)

Organizations:

Joan Smith is an active member of the National Travel Writers Association of America. She is past president of the Society of International Travel Writers.

Awards & Honors:

Joan Smith is the recipient of the "Distinguished Travel Writers Award" from the Center for Travel Writing at the School of Journalism, UCLA, Irvine, California.

She has twice been nominated, by the Society of Travel Writers, USA, for the "STW Annual Award" for writing outstanding travel articles.

Joan Smith lectures on the subject of travel and travel writing and has been a guest speaker at the annual meeting of the Guild of American Travel Writers in 1986 and in 1987.

writing life. If your background material runs to several pages, that is acceptable.

What you don't want on your background sheet, unless you are fairly well known and you know the media will need such information, are *fulsome* details about your personal history. If, however, you will often use your background sheet for publicity in a locality where this information will be useful, you might want a second version of your background sheet—one that contains information relevant to your personal life, such as where you currently live, where you were born, where you were raised or attended school.

Extra Articles . . . .

Keep a supply of clean, legible photocopies on hand of all the articles you have written and that have appeared in print. (Your mailings will rarely include manuscript copies of typed articles that haven't yet been published.) When you contact editors with book or article ideas, you can draw from this supply. If you have published many pieces, it's usually not necessary to send copies of all your articles. Send only what is relevant. Usually three or four of your pieces will suffice.

If you are an author, it is not always necessary or cost effective to send copies of your books as part of your press kit. But there are times you might decide to—namely, if you will be contacting major media to secure an appearance, or to set up an interview, or if you are seeking to establish an on-going relationship, possibly as a columnist. If you do not, make certain that titles and publisher's name(s) for all your books are included in your background sheet.

Offprints of Personal Publicity . . . .

Be sure to keep photocopies on file if you have been written about, been an award recipient, or if your books have received favorable reviews. If need be, set off your segment of any mention using a bright yellow marking pen. And, if it's not immediately apparent how you relate to the item being sent, type or handwrite in the margin of the photocopy—or on a Post-It® note—why this piece is included in your press kit. If any organizations have mentioned you in their press releases, have copies of these available to be included in your mailings.

Photographs . . . .

Most writers, especially book authors, will find a glossy, vertical black-and-white photograph of themselves a vital part of their press kit. Such a photo should be no smaller than 5×7 inches. (We specify a glossy vertical shot, and a minimum size to be mindful of the way most publications use pictures.)

If you do not have a good black-and-white *professional quality photograph* of yourself, now is the time to get one. It is especially important if your physical appearance is germane to your work—and if you will frequently use your press kit to try to set up personal or television appearances.

TIP: If you will frequently use your picture as part of a press kit to send to

TV shows, you might want to also send them a good-quality color picture.

Please note that we emphasize the words *professional quality*. Not only is it important to have a high quality photo, you want one that presents you in the best light—literally and figuratively. The poorly lit, badly shot snapshot in which you look your worst is a waste of your time and money. And one that is not professionally done will reflect poorly on you.

Some writers get attacks of the "cutes" while having their photos taken. One woman who comes to mind had written a novel that was set in a war-torn country. She dressed herself in camouflage fatigue clothing and had herself photographed lurking in the bushes of what was obviously her suburban backyard. (One could easily see the neat houses behind the bushes.) Completing what she no doubt felt was going to be a winning picture, she held an obviously fake toy gun!

What is needed, in most cases, is a good head and shoulders shot, against a light background. If your writing is singularly themed, a photograph that relates to your writing would be fine. For example, if you write mainly about the outdoors and hunting, then a picture of you in an outdoor setting would be a good idea. But, however proud you may be of them, spare your recipients a picture of you proudly displaying your kills—some people may not share your joy for the hunt.

If your writing is mainly about cookery, then a picture of you in a kitchen setting would be suitable. Travel writers could be pictured with an interesting locale as background; education writers could be pictured in a classroom. If you are a generalist-writer or if you are a poet or novelist, a natural-looking, flattering photograph is acceptable. But in all cases, keep uppermost in your mind that you need to be photographed against a light background, which facilitates newspaper use.

It is important not to scrimp on what you spend on your picture. Work with a professional photographer—you are investing in yourself! If you cannot afford the services of a professional, speak with the photographer about a barter arrangement. Your skill as a writer can probably help the graphically inclined photographer create copy for his or her promotional pieces. Gauge your time and you can estimate how the trade off would work.

A word to women: Think carefully about the makeup you will use before you have your picture taken, and consider the clothing you will wear. This might be the time to invest in a good makeup consultation. Tell the consultant what you need help with when you make your appointment. Everyday makeup and makeup to wear for a photo session are very different.

As to your clothing, you want to project a professional image. Unless you write about fashion or need to put forth a glamour image, do not aim for a "drop dead" glitzy, glamour shot. (Romance writers can forget the above points, however. It suits their image to strive for a glamour look.)

Speaking of image, Truman Capote's first novel, *Other Voices, Other Rooms,* bore what has become a classic author's photograph. Capote was shown lounging on a sofa in a decidedly sybaritic fashion. And according to the *New York Times*

Sunday Book Review (June 4, 1989) this photograph worked wonders for the fledgling author's reputation. His biographer, Gerald Clarke, wrote in *Capote*: ". . . Photographs had always served him well . . . and if that one made him both a target and a figure of fun, it did at least achieve its primary purpose: It gave him not only the literary, but also the public personality he had always wanted."

The *Times* said, "Frequently, the most successful [author] photographs are those consonant with the book's subject matter." For *The Bonfire of the Vanities,* author Tom Wolfe was pictured in front of the Bronx County Courthouse [a major site in the novel's plot]. To convey the Russian setting of her novel, *Zoya,* Danielle Steel was pictured wearing a fur hat; P.D. James posed in front of an abbey for her book, *A Taste of Death.* The late Louis L'Amour's books frequently carried a picture of him in a cowboy hat leaning on a saddle — but not always. His publisher's publicity person remarked that to convey the writer's serious side, he was sometimes pictured in his study.

Many publishing people, though, decry the ubiquitous use of the "serious writer pose" (i.e., authors at work on their typewriter or word processor, or posed seated at their desk peering meaningfully, and frequently, somberly, at the camera).

I've taught clients and students a number of ways to produce "interesting" and relevant author photographs:

• For the author of a book aimed at sparing travelers the discomforts of "jet lag," I suggested the author be pictured looking fresh and rested as she de-planed.

• For a trio of women writers who'd produced a work advising families on how to comfortably effect an overseas transfer, I suggested a group picture showing the three perched atop a large steamer trunk.

• For a man who wrote a book on square dancing, I suggested he be pictured suitably attired in western wear, at a square dance.

Ordering Photos in Quantity

To obtain quantities of your photos, see if it would be less expensive to have your photographer provide these or if you can obtain a better price from a reliable photo house. (The Yellow Pages in most towns should have listings for such companies.) Make certain to examine the photo houses' work before you buy their services.

How to Caption Photographs

Before you order quantities of your final photos decide what manner of caption you will be using on each photograph.

Each must bear an identification known as a "photo caption." (This is also called a "cut line.") If the photo house or your photographer can imprint your name and other information onto the bottom white segment of your photo (see illustration page 11) this is a neat and efficient way to create a "captioned

Photo Credit: Andrew Kline

GINNY CALLAN

Author of HORN OF THE MOON COOKBOOK
Published by Harper & Row in June, 1987.

This is a fine example of a writer's photograph. Here the caption (a.k.a., the "cut line") is printed directly onto the bottom of the photograph. We reprint this with the permission of Ginny Callan, author of: Horn of the Moon Cookbook, *published by* Harper & Row, *with photography credit given Andrew Kline.*

photo." If you will be using your picture as part of a press kit publicizing a new book that you'll be promoting, you should add this book's information onto this segment of the photo.

If it is not possible to do this (or if cost prohibits your creating printed photo captions), then caption your photo in the following manner: Type your name, and all other pertinent data, on a sheet of plain white paper. Then, using removable adhesive tape, paste it onto the back of the photo. Fold the unused portion up and over the *front* of the photo. (see illustration page 12)

TIP: If you will frequently mail out your photograph without accompanying material (which provides information on who to contact for more

This is a copy of the caption one would place onto a separate sheet of paper that is pasted or rubber cemented to the back of a photograph. It is then folded up over the photo for mailing purposes. In this case, as this photo will be used to publicize a book, the caption bears specific information about the book.

ELANE FELDMAN
Author of
*THE WRITER'S GUIDE TO
SELF-PROMOTION AND PUBLICITY*
Writer's Digest Books
October 1990
Photo: Karen Zebulon.

back of photo

back of caption

information) make certain your caption always contains the name, address, and phone number of a contact person.

For Group Photos

There may be times when you will use a photograph picturing you with other people.

If so, the caption must always indicate:

• the complete name of each person in the picture, indicating where they are placed in the picture, reading left to right;

• complete details on any event pictured;

• as previously mentioned, a name and telephone number for a contact person.

Folders for Mailing . . . .

If you mail out large packets of material, rather than folding and jamming your items into a standard number 10 business envelope, consider using file folders and larger envelopes. This will make an especially good initial impression on editors.

Do you want to present a really professional look? Then consider using colored, dual-pocket folders. Many of these have a slotted space to hold your business card. (If you plan to use these folders, be consistent and always use the same color in your correspondence.) These inexpensive, colored folders can usually be found at stationery or office supply houses. If, however, they are too expensive or are unobtainable in your area, you can use plain manila folders. In the latter case, paste your business card or address label onto the front of the folder.

> **TIP:** To obtain a stationery/office supplies catalog where you will find these folders and other supplies at good prices, contact Quill Corporation, P.O. Box 4700, Linconshire, IL 60197-4700 (if you live in the Rockies or east of the Rockies); or P.O. Box 50-050, Ontario, CA 91761-1050 (if you live west of the Rockies).

Inexpensive Book Press Kit Folders . . . .

If you are publicizing a book and your publisher cannot create printed press kit folders for you that feature only your book, you can still craft attractive but inexpensive press kit folders. (See sample illustrated on page 14.) Publishers rarely, if ever, create an expensive, printed, individual book press kit folder on a midlist title. Therefore, if your publisher isn't planning to do printed press kit folders for your book, ask them to create the type of press kit folder we describe here, or to provide *you* with a quantity of your book's dust jacket or, if a paperback, its cover.

WRITER'S MARKET BUSINESS SERIES

THE

Writer's Guide

TO

SELF-PROMOTION

AND

PUBLICITY

- Get publicity for your writing
- Launch your own promotion campaign
- Establish credibility via contests and awards
- Develop your résumé, letterhead, & business cards
- Keep your name in front of editors, agents, and readers
- Plus much more

Here is how to use these to create cost-effective press kit folders: Cut your book's cover (or jacket) so its front cover fits neatly onto the front of your plain, pocketed press kit folder. Using rubber cement, firmly glue the book jacket or cover onto the folder's front cover. And each time you mail out publicity material on your book, use this folder in lieu of your plain press kit folder. It's an inexpensive but effective way to put your name—and your book's—before an editor, booker, interviewer, etc.

Your Mom Was Right—Neatness *Does* Count!

Whenever you correspond with anyone in your promotional efforts, always do so in the neatest, most professional manner. Recycled, grimy manila folders and used envelopes are definitely out. If you *must* recycle envelopes, make certain they are in good condition.

What about a Direct Mail Brochure? . . . .

While graphic artists and other types of freelancers frequently use direct mail brochures—finding these a particularly effective way to attract new clients—for those seeking magazine, newspaper, or book writing assignments, or publicity for same, brochures usually aren't necessary. (For those writers seeking commercial writing assignments—that is, for corporations, or advertising or public relations agencies—using brochures describing their work and undertaking direct mail activities might be warranted.)

Freelance creative writers will find, however, that a personalized letter, background sheet, or a personal press kit will suffice. Glossy brochures describing their careers are unnecessary.

2

Tools of the Trade

For use with your press kit mailings and for general correspondence, you will need letterhead stationery, envelopes, labels, and business cards.

Letterhead Stationery . . . .

If you do not have a supply of good, standard-size business stationery (imprinted with your name, address, and phone number) now is the time to order some in quantity. You do not want flashy, multicolored stationery, nor do you need to spend a large sum of money on expensive letterhead paper or business cards with raised print. If, however, you can work with a professional graphic artist, see if he or she can create an attractive and inexpensive multipurpose letterhead "pasteup" for you (A pasteup is an alternate name for the "mechanical" which is the term artists, printers, and production people use for material ready to be photo-offset by a printer.) You will want to use the same letterhead for all your stationery and on your business cards.

If you will be working with an artist versus having a printer do up your stationery—and here again you might be able to barter with an artist exchanging services—make certain to tell the artist that you need a traditional letterhead. Before the artist creates your paste up, ask to see the typeface that is under consideration in a type book or on a sample type sheet. Make certain it is one you feel comfortable with and one your recipients will easily be able to read. While graphic artists might—when creating their own or a corporate client's stationery, for example—choose an eye-catching letterhead and "logo" (a symbol), or artwork that graphically displays their talent or conveys a corporation's message, you as a writer want a less "artistic" representation.

A word about what *not* to have printed on your stationery: Do not print the word "Writer" or "Freelance Writer" or any such term on your letterhead. Also, do not have a list of the publications you have appeared in printed on your stationery. At best this smacks of amateurism, and at worst it indicates you are so out of the mainstream you must use this device. You will, depending on the nature of your correspondence, either provide this information in your cover letter or you will be enclosing your background sheet. And don't use a logo that symbolizes the "writer's life." Overcome the urge to use pictures of pens, computers, or antique printing presses as your logo.

Marion Zimmer Bradley, an editor with many years' experience, related in the September 1988 issue of *Writer's Digest* magazine her aversion to juvenile or unprofessional stationery:

> Writing is a business; I want what [writers] send me to be business-like. ... Your business stationery—even in this business where no one wears a tie or high heels except to have lunch with an editor or to go on the "TODAY" show—must be Dressed for Success; simple, business-like and, if you say so, dull. Remember Joan Wilder in *Romancing the Stone* in her flannel bathrobe finishing her novel? This is really what most women writers wear to the typewriter or the computer keyboard—it's probably the main fringe benefit of our profession; we work in our own rooms and usually own one pair of pantyhose—for autograph sessions and lunches with editors. ... The editors don't see us when we're writing, so they judge us solely by what we send them. ...
>
> But don't go to the extreme; one of the worst manuscripts I ever had to reject came from a writer whose expensive vellum stationery was embossed with gold letters. (He also sent me a resume about three pages long, including movie credits.)

About Paper

Once you have determined if you will have a pasteup made by an artist or will have your printer create your letterhead, select your paper. (Paper is also known as "stock.") As mentioned above, you do not want to use vividly colored paper; if you feel this will make your correspondence stand out, you are mistaken. Using such off-beat paper, unless you are a well established name, will only reflect poorly on you. If you are a well-known person—one who can exhibit such individualism—this type of stationery might be more acceptable.

What you do want is a good quality white (or possibly off-white) bond paper. If you will be ordering from a local printer the type of paper to ask for is twenty-pound bond. If you want to spend a bit more money, ask your printer about either "laid watermarked paper" or "rag content bond," both of which are premium quality stock. You *definitely* never want to use what's called "erasable bond" for any of your typed material.

Envelopes

You will also want a supply of matching number 10 envelopes (i.e., standard business-size envelopes) with your return address imprinted on them. You will probably also need a supply of 9×12 envelopes, or others in various sizes to accommodate your larger mailings (for example, your press kit folders and other sizable packets). The most commonly used—and least expensive—versions are the tan colored ones known as "Kraft envelopes." And, depending on the bulkiness of your mailings, you may want to also buy larger, *padded* envelopes to protect the contents of your packages. If you cannot find these, or do not want to buy them, you can always take a chance that the post office will follow your hand-written instructions. Use a brightly colored felt tip pen and mark your thick Kraft envelope "Do Not Bend or Fold."

Labels . . . .

Also consider having larger mailing labels imprinted with your return address in the corner. If you use a computer printer that accommodates these or if you type your labels you might find these convenient. Barring having these printed, you can always use plain white gummed labels for addresses and have small sized, inexpensive return address labels printed for use on your large envelopes. (These small return address labels are widely available at many catalog mail-order houses such as Miles Kimball or Sunset House.)

Business Cards . . . .

Standard-size and -shaped business cards with your name, address, and phone number(s) will also serve you well in a variety of situations. (Here again you want to avoid off-beat shapes or outsize cards.) In Unusual Ideas for All Writers (page 159) we'll discuss prenotched business cards that fit onto rotary telephone directories.

Other Equipment . . . .

As much as you may dislike them, having a telephone answering machine is a virtual necessity nowadays, especially if you are carving out a career in magazine or newspaper freelancing. And to keep life simple, don't succumb to the temptation to have an outgoing message that is amusing or clever—forget the impersonations of famous voices or Tarzan jungle yells. A polite, friendly, and brief statement asking that your callers leave their name, phone number, and the time of day and date they are calling is what you want. You will find that these machines are practical helpers. And, for those times when you are on a tight deadline—especially if you have but one phone that must do double duty for your business and personal calls—buy a machine that allows for "call screening" (meaning you can listen to what the incoming call is about and decide whether or not you have to immediately pick up or can call the party back at a later time). Also select a machine that allows for "remote pickup," meaning that you will be able to pick up your messages when you are away from your phone.

To help you find an answering machine right for your needs, look into the *Annual Buying Guide* issue of *Consumer Reports*. For that matter, regularly reading *Consumer Reports* magazine is a virtual must for any writer considering purchase of many different kinds of items. The 1990 *Annual* had fine recaps of articles from their monthly magazines. In addition to the article on answering machines, they reported on laptop computers and telephones. There was a whole chapter on "TV and Audio," which included information on VCR's and also one on photography, with detailed advice on acquiring all types of this equipment.

Publicity in the Computer Age . . . .

Today, increasing numbers of writers are using computers with word processing programs to write, to carry out correspondence, and a variety of other tasks. Even if you have a dread of such machines, you really should consider investing in one. Rather than rejecting the subject out of hand, if you have never tried working with a computer, do take the time to learn more about the subject. A good book—specifically geared to the needs of writers—is *Word Processing Secrets for Writers,* by Michael Banks and Ansen Dibell, published by Writer's Digest Books. This $14.95 paperback is full of information—blessedly written *sans* jargon. And it's one that is helpful no matter what word processing system you're considering. Another thing you can do to familiarize yourself with the uses of computers is to take a non-credit adult education course on the subject.

Before you go whole hog into the purchase of a computer, you should understand some basics. The best advice seasoned writers and computer experts will give you is: *First decide upon your applications* (that is, will you use your computer solely to write, or will you want it to also handle accounting, your taxes and other financial functions). A computer, of course, can ease a lot of the chores associated with publicity and promotion. As we'll see in future chapters, you can use it to compile and store mailing lists, print mailing labels, and, if you select a software program with a "mail merge" feature, you can even create customized letters for your press mailings.

If you are completely out of your depth discussing software, hardware, peripherals, and the like, first research the personal computer magazines, such as *PC Magazine* or any of the many other computing magazines you'll find at your local library or on the newsstand, or seek the advice of a knowledgeable salesperson at a computer store in your area.

> TIP: **If you will be writing articles or books on a computer and are using fan-folded, continuous form paper, make certain you use plain white twenty-pound paper with perforated end strips that are completely and cleanly removable. This paper is often called "micro perf." or "clean edge paper."**

Incidentals . . . .

Varied sizes of "Post-It" style self-stick pads are great for affixing notes to anything you mail. They're a neat and efficient item to use in lieu of bulky paper clips and slips of paper. Also helpful are Post-It's self stick, removable (and small size) tape "flags," available in several bright colors as well as white. These flags do just that: They offer a way to mark specific portions of printed material without fear of damaging the paper. (If your local stationer doesn't have these, check the Quill Company, which sells dispenser packs of fifty flags.)

A similar label item is called Redi-Tag®. These removable indicator tags are also reusable, and come in solids and stripes in varied colors and sizes. They are available either blank or pre-printed with messages such as "FYI," "Revised," "FAX," "Copy," "Please Initial," "Sign Here," "Rush," "Please Sign & Date," and even (and may you rarely need it) "Past Due." These tags can also be custom designed for you. They should be found at stationers, or you can contact: Redi-Tag, %Barbara Thomas Enterprises, Inc., P.O. Box 3239, Seal Beach, CA 90740. Or call toll free: (800)421-7585.

Indelible felt tip markers in different colors should also be part of your promotional supplies. Yellow is especially good for highlighting portions of printed material. Red or other brightly colored markers are very helpful, particularly for use on envelopes. You might, for example, use them to pen in "1st Class Mail," "Photos—Do Not Bend," "Time-Dated Mail," or such to help speed your mail and to preserve its contents. And it's always a good idea—if it's the case—to boldly mark envelopes *"Requested Material."* We specify *indelible* ink pens because, come a rainy or snowy day, using non-indelible markers might quickly turn your package into an impressionistic painting!

Date Books, Appointment Calendars, et al.

While it might sound a tad simplistic, we want to say that having *two* date books or calendars can be a plus: a small pocket-sized date book with all your appointments noted to carry with you, and a larger version on your desk or at your work area. Both should contain all your appointments, deadline reminders, and notes on when you should do your follow-up letters and calls. Some writers—who have the wall space to accommodate these—prefer using the large 2×3 feet (so-called) "write-on and wipe-off annual planner." These giant-sized wall planning guides allow you to quickly see all your upcoming deadlines and calls to be made. Notations can be wiped off and the space reused, making these additionally useful. Most stationers—especially the mail-order stationer suppliers—sell these in several versions: dated "Year-at-a-Glance" and undated "Month-at-a-Glance." (*A suggestion for using these*: Color-code your activities. That is, use red for follow-up calls you have to make, blue for letters you have to write, etc.)

News from the Electronic Front. . . . .

Today, increasing numbers of companies and individuals are using fax machines for instant data transmission. While these are presently fairly expensive you might want to investigate the world of "fax" and familiarize yourself with the uses and possibilities these can be put to. Any writer on deadline can attest to the desirability of being able to instantly receive and transmit data. If you think you will need one, you can purchase stand-alone fax machines or install a fax board on a personal computer. The technology is moving so rapidly that, as we write this, virtually every day brings new versions of the fax. One that has recently debuted in America is a combination phone, answering machine, and fax, from Panasonic.

Barring purchase of your own fax, many print shops, copy centers, and even some stationers offer fax service. Check prices beforehand. Some of these services can be expensive.

To learn more about the subject, you might want to read: *Book of Fax* by Daniel Fishman and Elliot King, $12.95 from Ventana Press, P.O. Box 2468-A, Chapel Hill, NC 27514; phone: (919)942-0220.

Other Time Savers from the Stationer's . . . .

Rather than sending letters in a variety of situations, especially when you'll be doing a widespread mailing bearing a *brief* message, consider using postcards. They cost less to mail and have the advantage of being more quickly read by your recipients. If you're thinking, "What a laborious time-waster" — think again. Nowadays you can type one master and have these photocopied, using what are called "three up postcards." You type one master sheet bearing your message and photocopy your original onto the postcards. Commercial stationers should have these, though I've seen them on sale for as little as $5.98 a package through discount mail-order houses. And, with 501 cards per pack, you'll have more than enough to contact many people.

If You Hate Repetitive Typing Chores

Speaking of time-savers, if you often write the same people, consider using self-adhesive address labels that can be fed through your printer's photocopy machine. For repetitive mailings, these are a wonderful idea. As in the postcard idea above, you merely type your list onto a master sheet and use the sheet of labels like copy paper. Check with your stationer first to see if they sell these, then make certain that your local photocopy house has a machine that can take them. These labels are really helpers if you will be creating a newsletter or a regular mailing to the same people. (They also have the advantage of allowing you to quickly change labels when people move.)

A computer and printer, of course, are a quick way to produce mailing labels, too.

Stationery and Envelopes That Save Time for Computer Users . . . .

If you use a computer and a word processing program that allows you to "mail-merge" you don't have to sacrifice the look of letterhead stationery. In other words, you don't have to use plain white computer paper. Nor do you have to spend a great deal of time and effort typing individual letters and envelopes. Instead, use continuous-form letterhead stationery and matching continuous-form envelopes. You have your letterhead printed onto both stationery and envelopes and when you separate each letter and remove the perforated strips from the letters, and the perforations and backing sheets from envelopes, these are virtually indistinguishable from individually typed pieces. These can be a terrific time-saver when you are doing large, multiple mailings. (And, possibly more important, your recipients won't feel like "one of the herd" that you are writing!)

Continuous-form envelopes imprinted with your return address come in particularly handy—for example, if you'll frequently be mailing news releases to the same group.

Another time-saving option would be to purchase continuous sheet shipping labels, imprinted with your return address, for times when you'll be doing multiple mailings of larger packages (e.g., press kits, review copies, etc.).

Whichever way you decide to use these computer generated items, they can really save you time and energy—time that you can better spend on your writing. Here again, if your local printer or stationer cannot supply any of these items, many mail-order computer-supply firms have catalogs where you should find all of these items at good prices.

A Freelancer's Tips . . . .

In an article, "Cutting Corners Without Cutting Quality," written for *Fiction Writers* magazine, freelancer Micki Perry gives a number of helpful tips about saving time and money on large mailings.

Ms. Perry suggests paying a $60 annual fee for a bulk mail permit. (Bulk rate requires that you send more than 200 pieces in zip code order.) She notes there's also a one-time fee of $60 if you use a printed or rubber-stamp permit on your envelope rather than individual postage stamps.

While you're having envelopes printed with your return address, she suggests you consider having the printer include your bulk rate permit in the upper right-hand corner as well.

"The big drawback with bulk mail is the *time* it takes to sort the bulk mailings according to zip codes," she pointed out, adding that some computer programs will facilitate this by printing out labels in zip code order.

Bulk rate does not provide for automatic mail forwarding or return on misdirected letters unless you stamp "Return Postage guaranteed" on the mailings, she notes, "and then you will have to pay first-class rate for those returns. This is the way to keep your mailing list current, but it does cost."

Stuffing Envelopes

What if you can't afford to hire a high schooler or a secretary to do your envelope stuffing, or can't press your family into "forced slave labor"? Ms. Perry suggests that you can, of course, save money by doing it yourself. She adds, though, that before you decide to take on all these clerical tasks, "you should analyze the time [they may take] away from your writing." (More about this later.) Preparing a very large mailing, she pointed out, may take several days.

To expedite sealing and stamping a large number of envelopes, do as follows:

1. Layer the envelopes on a flat surface that you have protected with several layers of paper toweling.

2. Have all the flaps open—facing you.

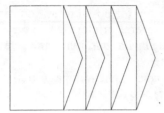

3. Moisten the glue and seal.

4. Fan envelopes out across the desk.

5. Use stamp strips.

6. Moisten the stamp strip, affix the first stamp with your left hand, and with your right hand, tear off the remaining stamps.

7. Continue until all envelopes are stamped.

Folding versus Envelopes

Another money-saver Ms. Perry suggests is to fold your promotional flyer into the shape of a legal-sized envelope, staple it, then stamp and address the back-side. "You'll save the cost of an envelope, plus time for stuffing and sealing.

"However," Perry says, "unless your flyer is on card stock paper, which is an additional cost that must be figured, these trifold flyers don't always arrive in any shape to be used as posters in the stores, and the staple often tears a hole in the worst possible place—like in the middle of your face if you've put a picture on the flyer."

Postcards

Using postcards, she noted, is an even cheaper option than bulk mail, as long as you don't use oversized cards (larger than the 4×6 inch maximum).

"The problem with postcards," Perry explained, "is that they can easily get lost or go unnoticed in the . . . mail, not to mention how they look by the time the Post Office has stamped all over both sides of your gorgeous artwork. . . ." On the plus side, though, "you can have a larger quantity printed and use [them] as bookmarks, cutting not only a second layout cost, but extra printing charges, too."

Though you can't very well comparison shop for postal rates, you can—and should—compare the services and fees of several printers, Ms. Perry added. "Just because the printer printed my wedding invitations, if he can't give me the best price, I'd better consider using someone else."

She also saves money by buying her own paper and envelopes (often from the same wholesaler the commercial printers use) and contracting out typesetting on her own.

"If you know someone who will barter their desktop publishing abilities, this is a huge savings, and it's great for designing your layout and copy."

Decide before you commit to a printer what portion of the job you can do yourself (and what portion someone else can do for you), she suggests. Many "full-service" printers actually contract out certain portions of a job, adding, besides a markup, additional time in getting the job done. An added bonus in doing some of the work yourself, she noted, is that you frequently get your materials "while you wait, rather than in several days."

Time: Your Most Important "Tool" . . . .

The entire purpose of writing, unless you write solely for your own enjoyment and care not one whit about ever being published, is to reach others. Self-promotion and publicity are tools to help you do this. But it is important that you strike a comfortable balance between time you allot for your creative writing and time when you will be actively pursuing publicity.

It is important that you realize you must set special time aside to do self-promotion. Attempting to squeeze time for self-promotion in between your writing will simply not work!

Finding time can be difficult, especially if you hold down a full-time job. But there are ways to carve out time for yourself. You might see about working through several lunch hours, putting in overtime or getting to work earlier. You could then take the time you have thus accumulated and use it to pursue personal publicity. If you have an understanding employer—or circumstances allow—you might be able to use your desk as a place to undertake this type of activity. (Don't be tempted to conduct these activities "on the sly." It will not only reflect poorly on you, but probably make you exceptionally nervous if you attempt to "cheat." Your employer's phone or equipment are not meant to further your writing career.) Your goal is to create a comfortable, uninterrupted period of time in which you can devote yourself to promotional activities.

If you are self-employed, the same concepts apply, but as you are your own "employer," you have an easier time—simply make a contract with yourself to devote x number of hours monthly to your publicity activities.

If you write full time, finding time to undertake self-promotional projects should be even less of a problem. But it is vital that during these times you literally "go to work." Do not allow yourself to be distracted or interrupted by any other personal or business chore. Make an appointment with yourself, note it in your calendar, and work solely on publicity. If you are on a writing deadline, obviously this is not the time to undertake time-consuming publicity activities.

Decide ahead of time how you will spend this time—whether on sending out pitch letters, press kits, or doing phone or mail follow up. Work from your file, or your records, and don't rely only on your memory of what you have previously accomplished in this sphere.

If you are working at home, put your answering machine on. If you don't own one, and the phone rings and you can't resist answering, tell your caller you are busy and will have to call back. You simply must take this self-promotion work time seriously. (I have even called certain people, so determined not to be interrupted, that they have pretended to be other people, willing to take a message for the person I'm calling.)

> **TIP:** Use a kitchen timer, set to remind you when to begin and end the time period you have set aside for "your" work time. This is especially helpful if you must break your work period into segments.

3

The "Basics" of Self-Promotion

If you are interested in doing self-promotion, but are concerned that you don't know how or where to begin, there are some basic terms and principles with which you should be familiar.

Actually, all of them—the "hook," the "pitch," and the news release that follows the "KISS" formula—can be applied to many aspects of your writing career. And developing workable lists of just who to send your pitches and releases to—and learning how to follow up on these approaches by "scripting" them beforehand—are valuable skills for all freelancers.

Start with a "Hook" . . . .

Whether you will be approaching the media or other people you would like to interest in working with you, it is necessary to be able to quickly sum up what you have to say. We discuss here how writers can create one sentence "hooks," that is, statements that encapsulate their subject in an easy to understand manner. Hooks, also referred to as angles or "tag lines," can be used in a variety of situations. If you are the author of a new book, a tag line will help your publisher in a myriad of ways, particularly in presenting your book to sales representatives, who in turn can use the hook to present your book to bookstore buyers. A hook can be used to entice the media to cover your press conference or public appearance.

No matter what type of writing you do, particularly in working with media, you will find it much easier to describe yourself if you have prepared an angle or tag line ahead of time. No matter how complex your subject, you must strive to reduce it to easily grasped hooks.

In the first example that follows, you can see what this writer will work from, and how he creates his tag lines. All the other examples are self-explanatory.

Example #1. William Pickering is a retired army officer who lives in Hilo, Hawaii. His first book is an action adventure novel set in Hawaii (in December '41) just before the attack on Pearl Harbor. His hook plays up his first-hand knowledge:

Tropic Calm is a new novel by William Pickering, a retired army officer, describing the lives of three people in the weeks and days leading up to Pearl Harbor Day. Mr. Pickering, a lifelong resident of the islands, was stationed at Hickam Field in this period.

Example #2. Jane Goodings, who operates Middletown's "Fixit Shop," has written a new paperback book, *Home Owners Fix-It Fast,* which tells readers how to save thousands of dollars on home repair projects.

Example #3. Maury Morrison, art critic and author of *My Kid Can Paint Better!,* offers museumgoers advice on enjoying modern art.

Example #4. Barbara Smithson's article in October's *Woman Today,* "Jobs + Home + New Baby," offers today's woman help on managing multiple careers.

Example #5. Bicycle Travel Across the U.S.A., by Fran Carter, president of Wheels U.S.A., is an informational book for teens seeking inexpensive vacations.

Example #6. LouAnn Williamson's article, "I Ate My Way Around the Globe and Didn't Gain an Ounce!," to be published in the July issue of *Watch Your Waist* magazine, is an amusing and factual article that will help dieters enjoy travel while dieting.

Example #7. Auto mechanic and writer Jim Jameson discusses how to save money on major car repairs in the February issue of *Car Owner.*

Example #8. Local writer Frank Merriman Jr., author of *City Hall—for Sale?,* has been named to head the city's Better Government Committee for 1990-94.

Understanding Media Needs . . . .

Overall, it's important that whenever you're thinking of approaching the media yourself you understand what the media seeks. *Namely, you should be able to provide (1) news, (2) information, or (3) entertainment* (or combinations of these three). In the first example, the novel, there's an entertainment angle. Numbers two through seven offer information. Example number eight is pegged to a news item.

Establishing a Game Plan . . . .

If you have not yet established a national reputation and want to generate publicity, you should establish a *written* plan. This will be particularly helpful for those who have never had any media coverage. Keep in mind how you can supply the news/information/entertainment the media seek.

For those who have had scant publicity exposure it is best to start modestly. If you have had little to no publicity exposure and if your subject is not one of broad general interest, rather than immediately approaching the major TV and radio talk shows and the national print media, start in your own backyard. And try only those shows where your topic makes sense. If, for instance, you specialize in cookery don't try shows that only cover urban matters or politics.

To begin your written plan, draw up lists of names of target markets in the varied media. For radio, try locally or regionally broadcast shows and for television try the public access cable shows or, depending upon your subject, locally broadcast commercial channel TV shows. Even if you live in an area where there are few local commercial TV stations, you might find that the public access channels (which at this writing number some 600) are available to you.

Next on your list would be the local radio talk shows aired in your town or region. Then try for the weekly and then the daily newspapers in the same geographic areas. If there are any locally produced magazines, ones concerned with people and events in your area, try them. (For specifics on whom to contact at various places see "Media Lists," later in this chapter.)

If you succeed in these markets, build to the national markets. As you go, you should have accumulated either a file of your newspaper and magazine clips or tapes of your radio and TV appearances. (See the Radio/TV chapter for information on where to get these.) These are excellent door openers in building towards national appearances.

When you finish your list of local and regional publicity outlets, focus on nationally aired radio and TV shows. Then try for national magazines and writers who contribute to nationally syndicated publications and national newspapers (for example, *USA Today,* and if suitable, the *Wall Street Journal*).

When you attempt to sell yourself, be it to the media or other people who can help you create promotional events, you will want to create atttention-getting "pitch" letters. In the parlance of public relations, the pitch letter is used to do just that. Namely, you want the recipient to "catch" your message and respond favorably.

At times you'll send your pitch with your press kit or a book or an article you are publicizing; then it becomes a cover letter. Other times your pitches will go out alone. In either case you must write a focused, hard-hitting professional pitch to sell yourself and your idea. Remember that the person to whom you write probably receives hundreds of such letters monthly. You want yours to stand out.

Note: We'll be talking here in general about pitching for publicity but, as most writers are aware, the same principles apply in "pitching" story and book ideas for publication.

Pitch Letters — The How-To . . . .

Given the huge quantity of mail editors, news directors, and others in the media receive, you must immediately gain your recipient's attention and pique his or her interest. More important, you want that person to act!

Pitch letters must always include information on where and how you can be reached. It's also a good idea — if you're not going to be available at all times —

to include information on when you will be available for interviews. (Never offer only one day.)

Clearly present the topic you are prepared to discuss. And, for general consumer media, especially the electronic press, limit yourself to one or two areas of your subject.

Examples of Pitch Letters

Please note that the following letters are "provocative" ones. Namely, they are ones that will most probably gain the recipient's attention and interest them in setting up interviews.

In some cases, we have not said up front just what it is we are pitching. The theory here is that after an editor reads the pitch letter he or she will be interested in pursuing the subject.

The following are examples of media-oriented pitch letters. You should find these examples helpful. Use them to focus your thinking on how you can present yourself.

Pitch Letter #1. This was a tough sell, as attracting attention for fictive works is always difficult. This pitch was created to help publicize a novel and was sent to national and regional media—both print and electronic.

Dear (name inserted):

PICTURE THE SCENE . . . as the early morning mist lifts, the City awakens . . . preparations begin. This day the City's most powerful and its most powerless will share in the excitement of the spectacle. The City itself is the world's most famous urban area . . . a magnet . . . a place where the deeds of the rich and famous are grist for gossip mills . . . one where corruption, crime, and brutality vie with lavish entertainments as topics of conversation. From crowded tenements and elegant homes the citizens take their places . . . as thousands of naked runners set off in marathon competition.

NAKED marathon runners? Yes. It's *not* New York City in October we are discussing . . . it is second century Rome.

It is this milieu that is the setting for *Between Eternities,* by Robert H. Pilpel.

This book is set for publication the week of the New York City Marathon, [here we inserted publication date, publisher's name, et al.]

We believe that the author will offer you a fresh new Marathon-themed interview possibility. He will be available in your city on [we inserted dates]. Please call me at the number on this letterhead to arrange an interview.

At this point, we sketched in the novel's story line and thus indicated its newsworthiness related to the upcoming race. We also outlined the author's credentials and quoted favorable advance comments on the book. For visual media, we indicated that we had a good amount of visual material to offer.

Given the New York Marathon's always strong media coverage, we had an excellent angle to play. We offered the by-then jaded and story-poor media an offbeat way to peg another Marathon story!

We used this same pitch in other cities holding marathons, and we skewed the letter according to the recipient's interest area. That is, for radio, newspaper, or magazine. We also targeted ethnic media given the Italian "angle" inherent in the novel's story line.

Pitch Letter #2. This letter was sent to various print and electronic media; the author was only going to be in the U.S. for a brief time and we indicated this.

Dear Colleague:

Kaizen: The Key to Japan's Competitive Success by Masaaki Imai is already being called "remarkable." It is the first book that clearly explains just how the Japanese have become a major force in international industry in the post-World War II period.

Kaizen will be published by Random House Professional Business Publications on November 3, 1986. ($19.95 hardcover.) The author will be in several United States cities [here we inserted dates] to discuss this important new book.

Unlike the plethora of "how the Japanese did it" and/ or "how the U.S.A. can do it, too" tomes and the proliferation of prescriptive good manager volumes, *Kaizen* is a singular work. It is one that has stimulated superb pre-publication comment. [Here we inserted the blurbs we had accumulated and then went on.]

Kaizen is *not* a once-over lightly describing Japan's remarkable renaissance . . . nor is it a quick fix "how-to" for American industry. It *is* an engrossingly written work that clearly explains the Kaizen concept—which is the foundation for Japan's success in the international marketplace.

Kaizen offers practical, easy-to-grasp information for anyone interested in learning how the Japanese employ Kaizen. Throughout the book, the author provides clear-cut and instructive examples of Kaizen in practice. More importantly, *Kaizen* is a guide . . . one stimulating awareness of how this philosophy might be employed in the United States. While Kaizen is a deeply ingrained way of life in Japan, it may well be one of that nation's most intriguing "exportables."

Masaaki Imai is one of our era's leading international management experts. (Please see attached Biography.)

If you are interested in interviewing the author and/or doing a feature on this important new book and need added material call me at: [here we inserted our number, etc.]

Pitch Letter #3. This was used to offer the author only to media in his home city, as his work precluded his traveling.

Dear _____ :

(Title and author here, with price and publisher's name) is a new, bound-to-be controversial book. It's one whose author is eminently qualified to speak on the entire subject of skyjacking and the page one problem of international terrorism.

We thought you would like to keep the enclosed material in your working file should you:

(1) Have need of expert comment for fast-breaking news coverage, or

(2) Be planning a special report on the subject.

(The author named) lives in (home city named) and has agreed to make himself available on fairly short notice, should you be interested in setting up in-person, or phone interviews.

Of course, if you would like to set up an immediate interview, tied into the book's publication, (author named) would be pleased to speak with you. He is able to discuss the many complex aspects of this troubling problem, and to offer pertinent suggestions.

Advance reviews of (title) point up the importance of this controversial, groundbreaking work.
[Here we inserted quotes from advance trade reviews.]

(Title and subtitle) is a unique work by a psychiatrist who has specialized in work on aberrant behavior generally, and on understanding the mindset of terrorist/skyjackers. [Here we inserted titles of his earlier books.]

If you would like to discuss setting up an interview now, please contact us at: (give number.)

Pitch Letter #4. For a magazine writer with a forthcoming article geared to radio and/or TV shows that feature such subjects.

Dear _____:

Take a look at your desk, or those of your colleagues, and you're likely to see what was once a forbidden substance. This item, now a virtual "must have" for millions of us, has a long and intriguing history.

• It's been used by mankind for something over eleven centuries.

• A 17th century English king forbade his subjects to congregate where it was sold.

• Before Pope Clement VIII, it was not permissible for Christians to use it — it was deemed suitable only for "infidels."

• Frederick the Great of Prussia employed a special "secret service" to root out, and penalize, users.

• Songs (and an opera by J.S. Bach) have been written about it.

• It played a special role in Revolutionary America's early history.

If you've guessed it's coffee—you're right! And, if you would like to discuss my forthcoming article in (magazine name) which details the fascinating history of coffee, I would be pleased to speak with you. I would be happy to discuss and/or demonstrate new and interesting recipes using the beverage. This is my schedule [Available dates are given here. The letter goes on to provide information on how, when, and where pitch letter recipients can contact the writer.]

Media Lists . . . .

Throughout this book, we've mentioned "media lists," and, for the novice, it's probably necessary to add a word here on how to develop these.

The simplest way to compile lists of newspaper and/or magazine editors or radio and TV personnel is to consult one of the media directories listed in the Resources section at the end of this book. These directories, many of which are available at larger libraries, list the names, addresses, and key personnel at publications and stations across the country.

Target your mailing to the person most likely to handle the type of information or request you're sending—e.g., a general news release sent to a newspaper is best sent to the city editor or (if it's a small paper) the managing editor. An announcement of a press conference for which you'd like coverage is best sent to a radio or TV station's assignment desk editor—preferably by name.

The most important thing in your compilation is to make sure your list is up to date and accurate. (Be sure the contact person's name and title are correct. You don't want your press release going to someone who left that job five years ago!)

An excellent way to keep up to date on key personnel moves is to read the trade publications such as *Publishers Weekly* (for books) and *Editor and Publisher*.

No Time to Develop Your Own Media Lists? . . . .

If you've scant time, and little inclination, to create your own media lists, you can always turn to specialist companies. One such widely used organization is Media Distribution Services-PRA Group, with twelve offices in the U.S.: Atlanta, Boston, Chicago, Detroit, Los Angeles, Minneapolis, New York, Orlando, Philadelphia, Pittsburgh, San Francisco, Washington, DC and also London, England. MDS (as they're often referred to) says they're the largest media, mailing, and printing service company in the nation, maintaining names and addresses of over 150,000 U.S. and Canadian editors at daily and weekly publications, business and trade journals, consumer magazines, wire services, radio and TV stations, and the like. Contact MDS directly for their information. Another such company is Bacon's PR & Media Information Systems — see our Resources section at the end of this book for their address.

These companies provide help in implementing press mailings. To find other companies, you can check books such as *Literary Market Place* and also the Yellow Pages in most large cities. But it's imperative that you always make certain the companies have current names for *editorial* people. You don't want your pitch or mailing to wind up on the advertising director's desk!

Many of these companies provide "full service," meaning they will take your typed draft, create professional-looking news releases and captioned photos, then do complete assembling and mailing. Others will sell you pre-addressed mailing labels. And of late, several companies have announced they sell personal computer-based data discs containing this type of information. *Note:* We're not providing specific recommendations on the computer disc sellers as we're unable to verify the quality of the lists. The one company that did provide us with a "Demo Version" of their publicity database was helpful, but their disc wasn't usable. Even with the repeated help given us via their phone "technical support," we were completely unable, after several tries, to get this up and running on our PC! Thus, if you consider purchasing such a software setup we strongly urge you to obtain a demo version first, and see if it works.

Should you opt to do it partially yourself, you would process and mail all your materials. Obviously, the more service you purchase, the higher your cost. But, in the long run, it might be both cost- (and time-) effective to buy complete service. Before you proceed, however, request the companies' descriptive brochures. You want to see the types of lists they have, the services they offer, and naturally, compute the costs.

To obtain information about pre-addressed labels for book promotion mailing lists (magazines, newsletters, and newspapers with book review columns of all types) you can contact: ParaLists, Attention: Dan Poynter, Box 4232-116, Santa Barbara, CA 93140-4232, phone: (805)968-7277.

An excellent way to determine some media people's specific needs (for interview subjects and such) and to reach a large number of people in communications is by regularly reading the *PR Party Line* newsletter. (Yearly subscriptions are $145.)

Here are some prototypical (fictive) listings of the type you would find in this valuable *Newsletter:*

Anything in *medicine*? Dr. Jack Jones, medical reporter to ITV's *Hello America* talk show is seeking material on all health-related subjects. Contact his producer, Don Downs, at the show, %ITV, 3 Center Building, Chicago, IL 60611; phone (312)555-9120.

Anything on business travel for lawyers? Starting in April, editor Jane Doe will be writing a monthly travel column for the *Lawyers Journal/ Bulletin* which will highlight travel industry news, specific destinations, and travel books for lawyers. Send information to Ms. Doe % the publication at 2 Astor Place, NYC 10001. No calls, please.

Anything in personal finance or real estate advice areas? Here's the upcoming six-month schedule for major topics in personal finance and real estate being published at *The Money Manager* magazine.
Note: send material—no calls—at least four months ahead of publication dates shown to: Jim Gray, Editor, %*The Money Manager,* 50 Front Street, New York, NY 10011.
January—mutual funds
February—buying/evaluating collectibles
March—IRA's, municipal funds
April—investing in condominiums; also: vacation time shares
May—buying overseas real estate
June—children's education costs: from preschool to postgraduate school.

If *you* are seeking information for an article or a book, you can also place a "call for information" in an issue of this weekly newsletter. This last service is free of charge and will reach many readers who are public relations practitioners and can thus help you in your research. For added information, contact: *PR Party Line Newsletter,* 35 Sutton Place, New York, NY 10022; phone (212)755-3487.

Creating News (Press) Releases . . . .

Another "basic" in self-promotion is knowing how to craft a news release. A release of this kind is writing *about* your writing—an announcement of a new book, controversial information you've uncovered in research for an article, information on autograph parties, public appearances, etc. The subject matter for these releases is almost endless.

The "KISS" Formula

Most professional public relations people are well aware of the acronym "KISS" used in conjunction with the writing of news releases. You should be, too. The acronym "KISS"—in less than polite circles—is interpreted as "Keep It Simple—*Stupid!*" We prefer, however, to interpret it as "Keep It Short and Sweet."

News releases, often also called "press releases," are generally of two types: ones that contain a timely story, an announcement, or information about an event; or ones that are not as timely, unless angled to a special event, season or holiday.

What is important is that in doing the first type, a true *news* release, you realize the word "news" in "news release" means just that. If you have nothing to say that is somehow newsworthy, then do not send a news release. If this is the case, think of *creating* an interesting event, one that merits this form of announcement. We'll see later how to do this.

If you keep the acronym "KISS" in mind when writing news releases, it should help you create a succinct, factual, and well written piece of work.

Know Your "Ws" and "H"

Unlike the pitch letter, which can have a "teaser" lead, the news release conveys information to be used by the media. Consequently, a news release must immediately answer questions posed by the five *Ws* (Who, What, Where, When, and Why) and sometimes also the *"H"* (How).

In the sample news releases shown at end of this chapter, we have provided examples of how the five *W's* and the *H* are used.

While there is no specific guideline on the exact length of every sentence you write for your press release, it's a good idea to vary the length of your sentences. To maintain your reader's interest, make some sentences short and others a bit longer. Never use jargon or technical language in news releases geared to the general public.

Pyramid Power

It's important that you understand how editors generally edit news releases. When preparing material for newspapers and magazines, realize that editors usually cut from the bottom up, that is, from the end of your story first. Therefore, it is important that you always begin your release with the most important information. Material of decreasing importance follows. The term for this type of writing is the "inverted pyramid."

General Ground Rules for News Releases

Attention to the following general rules will give you professional looking, well organized news releases. (You should realize, however, that you will see differences, from one publishing house to another, in the style and graphic design of their own releases.)

Stationery. Unless you plan to produce many news releases—for which you would want to create special letterhead stationery prominently printed with the word "News" (or "News Release") across the top of the paper—it is acceptable for you to use your regular letterhead stationery. Always use plain white bond paper in standard (8½ × 11 inch) or legal (8½ × 14 inch) size. Use both sides of the paper. If the release runs more than one page, staple them.

If the material in your release should not be used before a certain date, specify this on the release. This is typed at the left margin approximately four to five spaces below the top of plain paper or your letterhead.

<u>ADVANCE</u>
<u>FOR RELEASE AT 1 P.M. EST</u>
<u>TUESDAY, DEC. 1</u>

If your material is not "time sensitive," that is, timed for specific release to the media, a date is not necessary and you simply type in:

FOR IMMEDIATE RELEASE
Be sure to use all caps and underline.

Contact Person. Always be sure to include the name and phone number of a contact person on your release. This person is someone the recipient can contact to obtain additional information. If you are uncomfortable blowing your own horn by listing yourself as a contact, you might ask an articulate friend or family member to act as your contact person. Make certain, however, that this person is fully versed in what you will be announcing in your release and keep them updated on any other relevant "newsworthy" information that relates to the material in the news release. Type your contact name on your paper, either placing it two lines below the release date, flush left with it, or, as is sometimes also done, at the top right, about two to three spaces below the line containing the date your material can be used.

Layout. The physical layout of your release is important. Set it up so you allow sufficient room for an editor or reporter to pen information directly onto it. Allow four to six spaces between your release dateline/contact person line and your headline. And allow a similar amount of space between your headline and body copy. Always double-space. You can use single-space for quotes or to set off important material. Allow generous margins—at least 1 to 1½ inches—all around your paper.

Headlines. You must always have a succinct headline on your release, so a busy editor can see at a glance what it's about. Generally, headlines are set in all caps. There are no hard and fast rules as to length of headlines. Many professional press release writers try for sixteen to twenty characters, including spaces. They do so knowing that newspapers, for example, often favor headlines of two lines of sixteen characters each, including all spaces. If your story can be briefly encapsulated, try for a short headline, although it is often difficult to do so in the type of situations we are discussing.

Use colorful, descriptive words in headlines. You are trying to interest both the editor and the ultimate reader, listener, or viewer in your story. And if you are doing individual targeted releases, always keep that publication's readers and publication's style in mind.

Writing Your Release. The body of your release begins with a reiteration of the headline in a tightly written lead sentence (or several sentences). A lead sentence can take several forms: You can summarize facts or you can pose a question that you immediately answer. If you choose a humorous lead make certain it makes sense!

The balance of your release is set up in the "inverted pyramid format," with vital information first and material of decreasing importance following. (While you might be tempted to put much personal data—things that are important to you—right up top, unless it is central to the facts you are imparting in your release, this information must go further down in the release.)

If your release must run onto a second page, indicate this by inserting

"-more-" at the bottom of your first page. If you *need* a third page, staple pages together. Never paper clip them. But please remember our advice to keep it short and sweet.

Ending Your Release. Always indicate the conclusion of your release with an end mark. Today the symbol "#" is widely used. This is usually typed as three "#" marks, placed at column #45, #50, and #55.

You might also notice that occasionally the number "30" is used to signify the end of text. (This dates back to an earlier time when "30" always indicated that this was the end of copy being transmitted.) The "30" end symbol should be centered on the bottom of your page.

A special note to authors: If you are writing a news release about a book, you should always reiterate all of the book's bibliographic data at the end of your release, just before your end symbol. This data is generally placed at the left-hand margin. Your publisher will provide you with the data concerning how to list Library of Congress information and they should also give you their ISBN (the industry-wide identification number followed by the special number assigned to your book).

Enclosures. If you will be enclosing other items (photographs, fact sheets, background sheets, et al.) type the line: "Accompanying Material" two lines *below* the end symbol, flush with the left-hand margin. Then use single-space to list what you enclose. (If you are only enclosing one piece of material, use a phrase such as "Accompanying Matter" or "Accompanying Photograph.")

Final Steps. You want to present as professional a picture as possible with your news release, so have it either photo-offset or photocopied. Never mimeograph a news release.

Mail your release in an envelope no smaller than the standard number 10 envelope. Make certain to "accordion fold" your release (see illustration on page 38) rather than using a standard business fold. You want recipients to see immediately that you are sending "news," thus "copy out" is the standard.

Examples of News Releases . . . .

Here are hypothetical news releases (pages 39-43) that illustrate the points we've outlined. For each, we have indicated the reasons why the writer has written the release, and the ways it might be used.

While specific to the situations cited, the following examples, except for #1, are skewed to media recipients. We explain what each writer hopes to accomplish in each case. These examples should help you begin to focus on where to send *your* news releases. In other words, how to devise a list that is appropriate to the media you hope to attract.

Example #1. This is a press release that will be used in a national publicity campaign. Jean Jones, the writer described in the release, will be mailing it to travel editors at the magazines she would like to write for. (She could also mail

WRITER'S DIGEST BOOKS
PRESS RELEASE

For additional information contact:
Publicity Coordinator
(513)531-2222
TOLL-FREE 1-800-289-0963

1990 WRITER'S MARKET®
Edited by Glenda Tennant Neff
Price: $23.95, hardcover
Pages: 1056
ISBN: 0-89879-374-2
Publication Date: September 1989

This shows how a news release is folded into an "accordion fold." That is with "copy out," so that the recipient immediately sees this is a news release.

it to announce her "news" to those editors she has previously worked with.) She could also mail the release to book editors whom she would like to familiarize with her name, since she has an idea for another travel book that she feels a commercial publishing house would find of interest. (If Jean is unknown to the book company editors, this might be her strategy: She would mail the release, first-class mail, of course. Then after a week or two, she would mail another copy of the news release along with her press kit and a covering query letter outlining her book idea. At this point she would ask the editor if the company would be interested in seeing her book proposal.)

Example #2. The writer will be mailing this release to editors of many general interest publications across the nation, so they will stay aware of his work. He'll also mail this to key people at the major daily and Sunday newspapers in the area in which he lives, hoping it will lead to interviews in local newspapers.

This mailing will be followed up with phone calls to a select group of publications he targets. He would ask these people if they would like to speak with him, and if they would also like to see advance copies of the *Journalism Review* article. This enhances the possibility of his being interviewed, as he's provided a good news "peg."

If he would like to establish a reputation as a "muckraking, hard-hitting journalist," he will mail the release—along with copies of the article it mentions—to the people responsible for booking guests on the major national radio and television shows. Appearing as a guest on these shows would give him widespread national visibility. It is this visibility, he believes, that will open doors for him and lead to other lucrative freelance writing assignments and possibly a book contract. And to bring himself to the attention of book publishers, he will mail the press release and his *Journal* article to editors at appropriate book publishing companies.

• SAMPLE NEWS RELEASE •

Letterhead Here

FOR IMMEDIATE RELEASE
Contact: John Jones
(213) 624-1123

JEAN JONES WINS 1990 "FLORIDA BEST" AWARD FOR BOOK: *FLORIDA: AN ILLUSTRATED HISTORY*

Jean Jones, a lifelong resident of Florida who presently lives in Fort Myers, has been awarded the 1990 "Florida Best" Award for her book, *Florida: An Illustrated History.*

The award is given annually by the Association of Florida Colleges and Universities to honor a writer for an outstanding contribution to the field of writing about Florida.

Ms. Jones will receive a cash prize of $500 and be honored at an Awards Dinner on March 15th at the Breakers Hotel in Palm Beach. At the dinner, NBC television personality Willard Scott, who wrote the book's Introduction, will present her with the award.

In announcing its selection, the Award Committee cited Ms. Jones' book as "a superb example in both pictures and text of the best that Florida has to offer today," and as one that "graphically portrays the colorful history of the State."

The Association of Florida Colleges and Universities is a 250-member organization that was founded in 1947. The Committee that grants the prize for best writing about the state began giving out the prestigious award in 1957.

Florida: An Illustrated History by Jean Jones. Published by the University of Florida, Gainesville. $19.95 hardback, 245 pages, with 156 color illustrations; 32 maps. Introduction by Willard Scott. Index.
(LC # and/or Library of Congress Cataloging in Publication Data)
ISBN # 0-1234-0909

# # #

Accompanying Material: 3 black/white photographs
 #112—Collins Avenue, Miami Beach, ca. 1954
 #113—Kennedy Space Center, ca. 1987
 #114—The Breakers Hotel, Palm Beach, ca. 1941

• SAMPLE NEWS RELEASE •

Letterhead Here

<u>**FOR RELEASE: NOVEMBER 24, 1989**</u>

Contact: Ben Black
        (405) 687-1234

BEN BLACK, FORMER *NATIONAL DIRT* REPORTER, WRITES EXPOSÉ OF TABLOID JOURNALISM FOR *COLUMBIA JOURNALISM REVIEW*

Ben Black, who for fifteen years was a reporter for the *National Dirt*, one of the nation's best-selling supermarket tabloids, has written a scathing exposé of tabloid journalism for the *Columbia Journalism Review*'s Spring 1990 issue. (The *Review* will be on newsstands nationally December 11, 1989.)

In the *Review* article, titled, "Fact or Fanciful Reading at the Checkout Counter?" Mr. Black draws on his firsthand experiences. Often, he reports, when facts for his stories were nonexistent his editors "created them to fit the occasion." His experiences were not unique, he says, and extensively quotes from interviews he conducted with other tabloid writers who are "more than familiar with how to play the game."

Mr. Black states that he has interviewed thirty-five other reporters (all of whom are quoted anonymously) who presently work at tabloids.

To lend credence to his assertions, Mr. Black provides numerous examples. He cites the original notes and interview results he turned in when he was writing stories. He then gives examples of the published stories which he says "completely prove his case . . . fabrication is routine!"

Ben Black is a former Neiman Fellow and a graduate of Duke University. He is presently a resident of Durham, North Carolina, and is currently writing a book on the subject of his article. He says that it is one that will "definitely blow the lid off of the world of the supermarket tabloids."

# # #

• SAMPLE NEWS RELEASE •

Letterhead Here

ADVANCE
FOR IMMEDIATE RELEASE

Contact: Barbara Flynn
(717) 284-3300

LOCAL RESIDENT, BARBARA FLYNN, WILL AUTOGRAPH COPIES OF HIGHLY PRAISED FIRST NOVEL—APRIL 12TH AT COTY'S BOOK- STORE IN BLUE LAKE

Barbara Flynn, a resident of Blue Lake, Indiana, whose first novel, *Jane Smith- ers—Hollywood Star?,* was published by Smyth & Smyth Publishers on March 15, 1990, will autograph the book on Tuesday, April 12, at Coty's Bookstore, 2900 Elm Street, Blue Lake, from 3 to 7 P.M.

The book is 340 pages in hardcover. It sells for $21.95.

Ms. Flynn's book has been called "a delightful evocation of small town Americana circa 1955" by *Publishers News & Reviews,* and, "a factual, yet delightful read" by the *Indiana Historical Society Bulletin. The Blue Mountain Times Sunday Book Review* included the book in its roundup of "New & Noteworthy Books by Area Novelists."

Jane Smithers—Hollywood Star? is the story of a young woman's less than trium- phant return to the Indiana town she was raised in after a failed attempt at becoming a Hollywood actress.

Ms. Flynn says, "Everyone asks if the book is actually autobiographical, and while I—like my central character—attempted and failed to achieve movie stardom, I have created as central characters composites of young women I met in Holly- wood, some of whom did go on to great success." She adds, "It is really gratifying that I have received so many complimentary reviews of the book."

Jane Smithers—Hollywood Star?, by Barbara Flynn. Pub. Date. March 15, 1990. 340 pages. Hardcover—$21.95. LC#   ISBN#

# # #

• **SAMPLE NEWS RELEASE** •

Letterhead Here

<u>FOR IMMEDIATE RELEASE</u>
Contact: Jack Norton
(203) 767-8997

SALEM WRITER CONTENDS THERE ARE WITCHES AT WORK IN TODAY'S AMERICA

Jack Norton, a writer who lives in Salem, Massachusetts, says that on Halloween Eve he will prove there are witches at work in the U.S. today.

At midnight on Halloween at the old Salem burial ground, Jack Norton will be assisted by Dame Fiona Forsyth and six other self-proclaimed "white" — or good — witches. They will call forth the spirits of dead white witches and conduct a sacred, and benign, Halloween ceremony.

Jack Norton is a widely published magazine writer who has written over thirty-five articles on the occult.

# # #

Accompanying Photographs
    #A — Black/white line drawing of witch's "coven" in Salem, Mass., ca. 1990
    #B — Dame Fiona Forsy

The above news release is for national media only. One prepared for local media will say <u>ADVANCE,</u> and on the next line <u>FOR RELEASE OCTOBER 30, 1990</u>.

• SAMPLE NEWS RELEASE •

Letterhead Here

<u>**FOR RELEASE AT WILL**</u>
Contact: Marilyn Henry
         (713) 698-0028

WRITER ASKS, DO YOU KNOW WHY RETIREMENT LIVING ISN'T ALWAYS LIKE "THE GOLDEN GIRLS"?

If you think your "golden years" will resemble the happy-ending hi-jinks portrayed on television shows like "The Golden Girls," think again, says retirement planning expert Marilyn Henry.

Ms. Henry, who regularly writes on retirement planning for various publications, says that the popular media, especially shows such as the successful NBC TV "Golden Girls" show, are probably causing harm to Americans. "These shows make it seem like all of us can look forward to a retirement replete with interesting leisure time activity, a generous supply of money, and one marked by good health." In the same (bound to be controversial) vein, she goes on to state, "While the four women on this show are unmarried they have terrific social lives. It's just this kind of myth-making that is doing us all harm!"

Ms. Henry believes that the American media must immediately begin presenting realistic alternatives for all types of people, "rich, middle class, the poor, couples, and those on their own in their later years."

Marilyn Henry holds a joint degree in economics and sociology from the University of Nebraska at Lincoln. She lectures and writes on the subject of pre-retirement planning.

# # #

(In his initial mailings to book publishers he would not send a proposal or book outline. However, if he finds interest at any of the book publishing companies, he would be ready to create this material.)

Example #3. Here, a novelist is hoping to garner as much publicity in her local community as possible. In so doing, she hopes to achieve several goals: to attract people to her autographing party, to familiarize people with her book and thus sell copies locally, to interest a local college—where she had applied for a position teaching creative writing—to take her on, and also to possibly secure a part-time position as an arts reporter on her local weekly paper. *Note:* As this writer wants the public to attend an upcoming event—her autographing session—the release's dateline bears the word "Advance." This alerts editors to the fact the release contains news information that should be used prior to a forthcoming event.

Example #4. This writer has no actual news, so he creates an event that is timely, hence newsworthy. His objectives are multi-faceted. He wants to broaden recognition of his name to a general audience nationally. He wants magazine editors to recognize his name when he approaches them with story concepts. Using this press release along with his press kit, he will approach the national media for this colorful happening. He will also send this to local newspapers, magazines, and radio and television stations. *Note:* In this instance, as this release will be used for both local *and* national media, a slightly different release will be prepared for mailing to the local outlets. On this release, as the writer wants to alert the local media to his event (hoping they will attend and report on it), he types the word "Advance" just above the date on the release line.

Example #5. This magazine writer will use her *feature release* to interest local and national electronic media in interviewing her, since she has no specific article or book to promote. (And as her release is not a timely one, she creates this in the form of a "feature" versus a hard news release.) As she is unknown to these people, she will mail her press kit along with the release.

Sample Lead Sentences. Following, you'll find several sample lead sentences that vary the five *W's* and the *H* emphasis.

- **Who lead:** Author Jake Smith will speak at the Smithtown's Memorial Day observances.

- **What lead:** Writer Bill Brown says there are dangers in using over-the-counter medications.

- **When lead:** Tuesday, October 12th is publication day for local author Mary Jones's controversial new book, *She Killed Six Husbands.*

- **Where lead:** Blue Falls, Iowa, is site of writer Melissa Larkin's new novel, *Blue in Blue Falls.*

- **Why lead:** Writer Dan Feld says a new study—being summarized in the July issue of *American Teacher* magazine—finds that increased physical attacks on teachers are leading to fewer people willing to enter the profession.

- **How lead:** Travel writer Jane Browning points out ways to overcome jet lag in a November *Redbook* magazine article.

> **TIP:** When you're not sending your entire press kit out always include a short biography at the end of your release. (This is exemplified in Examples #2 on page 40 and #5 on page 43.)

More Tips on Creating Winning News Releases . . . .

In the May 1988 issue of *Writer's Digest* magazine, Audrey Fisher provides helpful advice on creating successful press releases. As we've discussed here, she suggests that you target your audience carefully:

> Identical press releases sent to a huge mailing list waste time and money. Editors discard press releases that are not on target. Word processing allows you to tailor several versions of the same release, each aimed at a specific audience. . . . [there are four types of releases:]
> - Very short ("sometimes two paragraphs can be too long") for sophisticated media.
> - An expanded version for less selective media.
> - A regionalized, personalized version for hometown media.
> - Technical, specific information for trade press.

The article goes on to suggest that you write for the most selective media first, then expand for others. "Never be content with a first draft. Make your goal to shrink your first effort by at least 25 percent. Usually you'll find you can reduce that much without altering the essence of your story at all. Engage the reader's attention. Good vivid writing, short simple sentences, and lively action verbs all contribute to a readable piece. Moving the verb as far forward in the sentence as possible is an old trick that forces a writer to use the active voice."

In a *Publishers Weekly* article, *Chicago Tribune* editor Dianne Donovan offered an editor's view of press releases:

> Certain stock phrases . . . bother me. "Stunning debuts" for example, on first novels. It's like giving everybody who enters the Olympics an

automatic ten. Comparisons are suspect, too. If a Southern writer isn't "the next Eudora Welty" she's "in the great tradition of William Faulkner." That kind of copywriter hype does the author a disservice.

The Importance of Follow-up . . . .

Successful salespeople know the importance of following up on a sales call. When you mail off a "pitch" it's important that you follow up to make sure that it's been received and determine if there's interest in what you're proposing.

When you undertake your phone follow-ups to your mailings, there are several things you should keep in mind:

• Write out a script — or at least the key points — for your follow-up calls. (Make certain you have the exact name of the person you had written and the date your material was mailed.)

• Wait about five to seven working days from the time you mail your pitch before you begin your follow-up phone calls.

• If the person you reach indicates they cannot speak with you, always ask when would be a more convenient time for you to call back. And, no matter how brusque the person may be, stay cool and then quickly hang up.

> TIP: **When you call back and you reach someone's assistant or secretary, immediately tell that person that you are calling back as you had been asked to do so. And, if you are returning a call, immediately say this. Doing so makes it likelier that you will be put through.**

• If the person you reach says they never received your material, say that you will call back in a few days to check whether it's arrived. If it hasn't at that point, tell them you are resending it.

Sample Phone Scripts . . . .

Professional public relations people know that they have a scant few seconds to capture the attention of the people they are calling. If you write a script out beforehand and practice what you will say, you should be able to condense your phone pitch to about fifteen to thirty seconds.

Here are some sample scripts:

Script #1

YOU — "Good day, Miss Taylor, this is Jean Jones. On July 15th I sent you two story ideas, with my background material. I hope you've had a chance to consider these concepts for use in your newspaper." (She replies that she receives so much mail you will have to "refresh her memory.")

YOU — "The story ideas are related to my work as an archaeology teacher here at the University. In one, I would write about how my students and I discovered a trove of Native American artifacts downtown in our city at Founder's Park. In the other story, I would write about the fact that when an area was recently excavated around City Hall, it was discovered the building was built on the site of an 18th century lunatic asylum!" (The editor expresses interest in the second of the two stories.)

YOU — "Shall we meet in person to discuss the details?" (If she says yes, you would then proceed to arrange an appointment.)

Script #2

YOU — "Good morning Ms. Diggs, this is Fran Miller. I sent you a proposal four months back for a book I call *My Days In Heaven,* about being one of the nation's first airline stewardesses. I know that you must receive many book proposals, but I wonder if it's been received and is under consideration?" (If you're told that the book is being evaluated, ask when you might reasonably expect some feedback.)

Script #3

YOU — "Good morning Mrs. Thomson, this is Jane Black, of 'Jane's Fix-It Shop.' I'm calling about my letter of November 1st. I asked if you would be interested in my creating a new service column for your newspaper. The column would help your readers with home maintenance and home repair problems, and would also help them find local home repair people and contractors. As I've not heard from you, I wonder if it is of interest to you?"

A writer might ask if it's necessary to follow up on a press release. That depends. If it's something sent to a specific editor and you want to make sure the material's been received, go ahead. Obviously, on a large mailing, you can't follow up on every release, though in some cases I've targeted certain publications for a follow-up phone call.

4

Protocol and Etiquette for Writers

At the risk of sounding avuncular, how you approach editors and media people is often as important as what you say. Too often, writers will be done in by not realizing the effect they create if they act inappropriately.

In his splendid book *Professional Etiquette for Writers* (Writer's Digest Basic Bookshelf Series) William Brohaugh truly tells it "like it is."

> It's not just that editors get grumpy when they encounter obnoxiousness or unreasonableness or rudeness, because *discourtesy works against the writer* on a number of deeper levels. It does more than annoy; it *signals amateurism.* It signals trouble.

Breaches of protocol (e.g., dropping in to "chat" with an editor who's facing a deadline) and gaffes (getting the editor's name or title wrong) demonstrate a lack of knowledge of the business, or simple carelessness, Brohaugh says. Such lack of professionalism can undo all your best efforts and can hurt the next writer as well. Brohaugh explains:

> So many of these publishers received one ridiculous, inappropriate sub-mission too many, and decided to close their doors to unsolicited mate-rial. None of those submissions—none of the handwritten manuscripts or the historical tomes sent to science fiction houses or the stories typed single-spaced on both sides of the paper—none of them is your doing, but the door is as closed to you as it is to those who did submit these manuscripts.

This chapter talks about working with editors on stories being developed, but the same principles apply to working with media in developing publicity. For a further discussion of dealing with radio and television people, read "The Writer's Golden Rules for Working with the Media," pages 96-97.

Meeting Editors in Person . . . .

If you will be meeting with an editor in person to present story ideas, it is import-ant that you present *yourself* in the best possible manner. This is especially the case for initial meetings.

However informal your lifestyle, when it comes to dealing with editors, just "dropping in" without having set up an appointment is definitely not a good idea. You cannot expect that just because you are free the editor(s) you would like to see will drop their work upon your arrival to spend time meeting with you. Write or (if last-minute plans will bring you to the city that the publication is based in) call ahead of time to set up appointments.

If you are unknown to the publication you contact, you are best served by first writing, and, in your initial contacts, sending along your press kit and clips. If time precludes your writing, it is all right to phone for an appointment. If so, be prepared to briefly and quickly explain what it is you are calling about.

Especially in a first contact with a publication, be ready to concisely recap your background to the editor, editorial assistant, or secretary, so you can interest them in seeing you—without first having seen your clips. If you must "sell" them on the idea of seeing you, be prepared to say who you are and what you want to meet about. (E.g., say that you are an out-of-town writer and have several story ideas you would like to present. Add that, as you'll be in their city, you hope you can meet with them personally to discuss their policies and briefly present your story concepts.) Whoever you'll be speaking with, be it secretary or editor, be concise; speak succinctly, clearly, and politely. Even if you are flatly refused an appointment, ask if you can send your background material and possibly call again at a later date.

In attempting to set up appointments, be flexible. Give several dates when you will be available. Don't be surprised if you aren't immediately given an appointment. Editors and other publishing people do not set out to be rude, but are usually super-busy people. Seeing new writers might well be at the bottom of their priority list.

Don't Act—or Sound—Like a Rank Amateur

To increase the odds of arranging an appointment you must persevere. Followup is important here again. If you hear nothing in response to your letter, wait about seven to ten days after your material would have been *received,* and call the editor's office. Again, be prepared to explain who you are. (Working from your file copy, refresh their memories. Say what you are calling about: that you had written on such and such a date, and about what, etc. Again ask for an appointment.)

If time pressure means that you are calling without having first sent your material and are told they will call you back and they don't, don't be offended. Be prepared to call them and to proceed as outlined above.

Appearances Do Count

If you do set up an appointment, be on time and dress accordingly. Flowing, unkempt hair, blue jeans, soiled running shoes, and rumpled clothing are out. While being a writer often means you are used to working at home dressed in your most comfortable clothing, when you meet with editors, dress in suitable clothing. You needn't invest in a wardrobe of uncomfortable, expensive clothing that is "not you." Do, however, realize you will be venturing into a workplace where certain standards of dress are expected of even the most creative people.

About Your "Portfolio"

When you meet with editors in person, be prepared to show (and if requested, leave) samples of your published articles and your background material. Here, too, your press kit and business cards are particularly valuable.

For in-person meetings, if you have a hefty file of clips, in addition to taking along duplicate copies of your press kit, you should have a portfolio of samples of the *original copies* of your published articles. Most stationers (or art supply stores) sell loose-leaf binders in varied sizes, with vinyl pages. You slip the original copies of your articles into the pages for presentation purposes. Do not, however, expect that busy editors have time to immediately sit down and read your original clips. What you want to do at this point is to create a favorable impression . . . garnered when they flip through your portfolio. Then if they express interest, leave your press kit and the *duplicate copies of your published articles*. It is not a good idea to leave original materials. Given the pace most editors and publications move at, your portfolio might well disappear permanently. Thus be prepared to leave behind only material that is expendable.

Make absolutely certain that your business card is easy to find in your material. (If, for example, you do not use a press kit folder with a slotted space for your card, paste your card onto the front of your folder, or set up your kit so that the stationery bearing your name, address, and phone number is the first thing seen upon opening the folder.)

Hickory Dickery Dock . . .
Don't Chase the Editor up the Clock!

Keep in mind that while your schedule might be fluid, the editor's is probably rigidly defined and the amount of time he or she can give you will be limited. Therefore, especially if it's your first meeting, be prepared to "present" yourself. If need be, rehearse ahead of time what you will say. What you want to do is verbally present your story ideas and allow the editor to respond. You will want to know, if the editor expresses any interest in your story ideas and allow the editor to respond. You will want to know, if the editor expresses any interest in your story concepts, something of the magazine's policies: rate and time of payment, whether a "kill" fee is paid (that is, what you will be paid if they assign the piece to you and then decide not to publish it). You want to ascertain as much about the magazine's policies as you can. If the editor immediately accepts your story ideas then and there, ask if you will be working directly with her or him or if you'll be assigned to another editor. If this is the case, it would be a good idea to briefly meet this person.

Fear Not the "Idea Rip-Off"

Finally, put aside any fears you have that your ideas will be ripped off. While it's not unheard of, it's rare that editors will be that unethical or foolhardy.

Editors have a reputation to uphold, and if word got 'round that they were doing business in this manner, they'd quickly find their pool of freelance talent drying up.

What If You Can't "Sell" Yourself In Person?

If your are concerned that you are not verbal and will not be able to sell your ideas for yourself, and you'd still like to try the in-person approach, honesty would be the best route to travel. Tell this to the editor immediately. Then hand the editor a brief, neatly typed outline of what you propose to write, along with your press kit. Explain that you hope all of the material is self explanatory and that while you don't expect the editor to go through your press kit then and there, you hope that your written proposals are of interest.

However shy and unassuming you are, you must somehow learn to communicate your competence and belief in your ability to deliver what you propose. (In this regard many self-effacing types find that gentle motivational tapes can be helpful. What you *don't* want is to turn into a strident, pushy, hard-sell person. Rather, you should be able to quietly present yourself in the best possible light.)

How *Not* to Approach Editors . . . .

When you reach out to magazine or book editors keep the following in mind:

• Don't boast of your expertise or knowledge. (If you must do so to buttress your "case," simply refer to your background sheet. Or, if you are the author of a book that had previously garnered good reviews, include these encomia in your press kit.) As an aside, it's the hallmark of an amateur to say that your family or friends (or if you're a teacher, your students) "love your work," nor should you include other such personal comments anywhere in your credentials.

• Don't be overly familiar addressing editors you do not know. (Unless you've attained a personal relationship, "Dear Jim" is not to be assumed; it should be "Dear Mr. Jones.")

• Don't employ what you think are "clever" salutations to start your letters. Heavy-handed clever leads (especially ones that mask anger or impatience) are never warranted. If it's near Christmas, for example, and you have been unable to reach an editor, resist the urge to address him as "Editor Scrooge." For that matter, you should never take an aggressive (or threatening) tone anywhere in your letters or calls. (i.e., "I used to think your publication was splendid. Now I plan on telling all my friends, family, and associates just how terrible you are. We'll all be cancelling our subscriptions!")

• Flattery and unctuous comments are also out! Be sincere.

• Avoid the overly cute. If you write on American history, forget approaches like: "What happened to Custer at Wounded Knee is mild compared to what my family will do to me if someone doesn't buy my work, soon!"

- Don't muddy the waters. Only raise one issue per letter.

- Do not provide a detailed list, if you're submitting a story (or book) concept, of every other place you have been turned down.

- Avoid ending your letters in a "unique" manner. Do not give in to the temptation to end with "Anxiously Yours," or "Frantically Yours," or "Hopefully Yours." A simple "Yours Truly" or "Sincerely" will suffice.

- Never place collect calls to editors to query them on story or book ideas, especially if they do not know you.

- Never use recycled business stationery in writing editors or the media. In other words, do not ever use stationery from your current (or past) place of business. Not only is it bad form, and in the case of a past employer, a little unethical, but you'll confuse recipients who might want to reach you.

- If you use a computer, never use a dot matrix printer for either your correspondence or your manuscripts. It's definitely worth the investment to buy a letter quality or near letter quality printer (that is, one that produces copy that looks like it had been prepared on a good electric typewriter). Not only will a letter quality printer present you in a better light, but you will—particularly when submitting manuscripts—be showing courtesy and understanding. Most editors say they hate to read dot matrix-printed materials. The quality of type produced is quite hard on the eyes.

Keeping in Contact with Magazine and Other Editors . . . . .

Whether you are a beginning writer who has not yet had any of your articles published, or one who has not yet broken into nationally circulated publications, or if you are someone who has been published in major publications in the field, it is important to keep yourself "alive" in editors' minds.

You can do so in many ways. Naturally, you'll be contacting editors with your story ideas. And, in doing so, it's always a good idea to "think angle."

Lead Time Factors

One good way to proceed is to start by referring to your files. If you want to write for newspapers, you should have information at hand supplying data on lead time factors.

The same applies for magazine articles: Keep in mind that most magazines have long lead times—often working six, eight months, or even further ahead of time. Therefore, try to pitch "timely" stories. This is an especially good idea in pitching general interest publications. In your cover (i.e., "pitch") letter to editors, draw special attention to the timeliness of your proposal.

Here are some examples of timely pitches:

- If you are proposing an article on how to hire a home repair contractor, realizing that most Americans undertake such repairs in the spring, key your pitch to this season.

• If you write solely about dogs, theme your letter so that any resultant article would appear to coincide with the local kennel club's annual show.

• If you are pitching an article on the early life of Mark Twain, you could take a light-hearted tack. Start your pitch letter mentioning that the annual jumping frog contest held in Calaveras County, California, takes place on [insert date here], and you feel, therefore, this would be a good time to run a piece on the man who made this contest famous.

• If you are proposing an article on stamp collecting, aim for July. This is usually the month the International Stamp Exposition takes place.

• If you write on legal matters and are interested in writing about the Supreme Court and how their decisions affect everyone, June would be a good month to propose publication of an article — marking the anniversary of the important Miranda Decision.

• If you are pursuing a career in writing for special interest publications geared to the construction industry, and have an idea for an article on changing standards in commercial construction, you might key your proposal to be published in July. The connection here would be to mark the date in 1981 when scores of people were killed and injured in the collapse of two suspended walkways in a hotel in Kansas City.

If you are totally unaware of off-beat holidays, observances, and events, there are several excellent references you can use — refer to our References section for specifics. One such book that is particularly fine is *Chase's Calendar of Events.* (Most libraries stock this book. If yours doesn't, it might be worthwhile ordering it.)

Localizing Your Submissions

If you write for local or regional publications there are equally good possibilities to pursue. Find out about special observances, festivals, and other possible tie-in dates in your area. The local Chamber of Commerce often publishes a calendar of events that can give you some ideas.

Whatever your story concept or the type of publication you will submit it to, there is always some angle you can employ that at best will enhance your chances of acceptance, and at least bring you before the eyes of editors.

By always thinking of a "hook" or angle when you propose articles, you'll *also* be creating built-in publicity hooks for yourself when and if the story appears. As evident in each of the previous examples, should the article be published, you will have an excellent publicity hook with which to approach media.

These special dates can also occasionally be used in between those times you will be writing editors with story ideas, once again, to keep your name alive in editors' minds.

You can do so by *occasionally* sending editors humorous notes or greeting cards keyed to holidays or events. For example, when you know that National Pickle Week is at hand you could send editors a "pickle" greeting letter. Just paste a picture of a pickle atop your letterhead, then type your letter beneath it. Have your letter photocopied. (Or depending upon the number of editors you'll be writing, you could also have it photo-offset.) And here you absolutely can do multiple mailing. However, do try to personalize your letters by individually typing in each person's name and address and the salutation. (Easily done if you have a computer program that permits you to mail merge.)

In the same light vein, you could send an unusual New Year's greeting card, to arrive on January 1st—which is the official beginning of National Prune Month! (It is also the beginning of the Frozen Foot Winter Rendezvouz and the day the hearty Polar Bears of Coney Island take their traditional dip into the Atlantic Ocean, all of which present you with varied reasons for sending a note of greeting.)

Remember, however, not to overreach and not to inundate editors you don't know with such greetings. You want to achieve a light touch, not to have them think you're a flake.

If humor isn't your cup of tea, then find an event that bears some connection to your type of writing. Use *it* as a reason to write.

For example, if you write about food and health, in September you could send a group of your own "heart healthful" recipes marking the American Heart Association's healthy food month. Or, if you are a poetry critic, you could send editors a brief note in June—the month of the birth of Nobel Laureate poet William Butler Yeats.

If this type of approach makes you uncomfortable, you can always take a direct route: Write editors to say that you enjoyed a recent article in their publication. If, for example, you read their piece on Dr. Salk's creation of the polio vaccine, you could mention that when you read it, it struck you that they might consider your doing a future article on life in the U.S. before the era of the polio vaccine.

A personal letter, especially if you have expertise in an area, and particularly when you are *not* pushing for a sale, is sometimes a good idea. Such thoughtful letters can be of multiple benefit. Not only does it show the editor you're reading their publication, but that you are taking time to write a letter that's not totally self serving.

Other Ways to Keep in Touch with Editors . . . .

Why not also be someone who shows thoughtfulness? When, for instance, you read of an editor's winning an award or being promoted, or if they have married, or have moved their residence, become engaged, or have become a parent, take the opportunity to not only congratulate them, *but* to do so in a way that connects to your area of expertise.

Here are some examples:

 • If you write mainly on wildlife you might congratulate an editor on her engagement by sending a card from the National Audubon Society or other organization.

 • If you write on astrological subjects, and learn of the birth of a child to an editor, you could send a personal (positive, of course) astrological chart for the newborn.

 • If you write works of fiction set in 18th century New England and you read that a New England-based editor has moved into a new home, you could write the editor a brief note on the way people lived in his community in the 18th century.

The overall idea here is to think in nontraditional ways, and to keep yourself in editors' minds. Don't just think of sending a card that "shows you care enough to send the very best"—rather, think in a fitting, sincere, and personal manner. Don't however, presume to write lengthy missives to editors you barely know. And whatever tack you take, use good judgment. Never write totally nonsensical cards or letters. And never, never become a nuisance.

5

Establishing and Enhancing Your Reputation

What if, after all we've discussed in the previous chapters, you're thinking, "I have nothing to promote! As a writer, I'm not a recognizable name. So what do I do?"

Establishing yourself as a "promotable" writer is a building process. In this chapter, we'll look at how novices can establish their names, and how experienced freelancers can enhance their reputations and even make themselves "experts" sought after by editors and others.

Building a "Clip File" . . . .

The usual way for writers to show evidence of their experience is by compiling a "clip file." (Materials published under your byline are usually referred to as "clips" or "tear sheets.") If you are new to writing for publication and need to build a file of "clips" there are various ways you can do so.

The obvious first step is to be published! The basics of getting started in writing are, of course, outside the scope of this book, but there are many useful volumes on the subject. (Refer to our Resource Section for information on some of them.)

"Try to get published any way you can, in newspapers, magazines, journals, whatever," suggests John A. Glusman, executive editor for Collier Books. "Build up a track record and experiment with different types of writing—book reviewing, interviews, articles, essays, editorials—to show your diversity as a writer."

A Little Knowledge Is a *Valuable* Thing . . . .

If you have a subject in which you are particularly knowledgeable—a business, a hobby, or some other area of interest—it's natural to build on that. Kenneth O. Gilmore, editor in chief of *Reader's Digest,* commented in *Writer's Digest* (December 1987) "It's an old saw, but a true one: Write about what you know. ..."

Besides the obvious appeal of writing in an area of particular interest, the magazine or newspaper writer who writes one, then two, then three, articles on a specific topic is doing something else: building a reputation as an "expert" on that particular subject.

How to Become a Newspaper or Magazine Columnist

Let us look at several mythical writers to see how to go about establishing credibility as a writer rather than being viewed as a dilettante. The following examples show how these writers would become visible and build a file of their by-lined published pieces.

Example #1. Jane Smith lives in a small American city and would like to build a file of articles in the field of handicrafts—in which she is interested, knowledgeable, and adept. The first thing she would do is approach the local newspaper and ask if they would like her to report periodically (say, once a month) on local handicraft activities. This is a particularly attractive idea that should appeal to the newspaper people, since Jane will be reporting on the activities of local people and on local events.

In her discussions with the newspaper's publisher or editor, she tells them that in the proposed column she would regularly provide readers with a calendar of craft shows, fairs, and meetings. While the newspaper probably wouldn't want to take Jane on to merely create a calendar of such events, which could probably be done by their staff people, she would be valuable to the paper for the other things she proposes to do with this column. Given her expertise in the field, Jane tells the newspaper's editors that she will also "cover" (i.e., personally attend) a select group of events and report on them for the paper. In her column, she would give a general report on the craft shows, as well as providing specific descriptions of craft items exhibited by local residents. She might also offer to occasionally do in-depth interviews ("profile pieces") of local craftspersons. Additionally, she might suggest she could write columns describing crafts per se. (For example, one month's column might relate the history of macrame, another month the role the patchwork quilt played in the social life of the American farm wife.)

If the newspaper expresses interest in having Jane write such a column, she must be prepared to receive little—or no!—pay for her efforts. Such arrangements are common, but it's not important that the pay is paltry (or non-existent); having a by-lined column would give Jane credibility, visibility, and a hefty file of clips. These clips would prove invaluable when Jane approaches the larger national crafts-oriented magazines.

Example #2. Mary Silvers is a financial analyst with a large multinational financial services company. She lives and works in a suburb of a fair-sized city. Mary would like one day to write on financial affairs for a national magazine, but at present has not done any writing since college days. Hence, Mary must create a file of clips.

She too would first approach her local newspaper and offer to write a financial news column. Her professional credentials would stand her in good stead in this area. And the same principles outlined above might later open doors for her in the highly competitive magazine world.

Example # 3. Frank Farmer, an expert on antique china repair, would like to become a columnist for special interest publications in his field. His goal is not only to build a clip file, but to use it as a springboard for other publishing opportunities. When he is awarded a prize for "Outstanding Achievement in Antique Restoration" by an association of antique restorers, he writes a press release announcing same. He sends the release, along with his background sheet, to the publications he has targeted as likely prospects for his column.

Regarding the so-called "special interest" publications (single-topic magazines with, generally speaking, a depth of knowledge beyond the "general interest" publications), if you are a recognized name among those involved in a hobby, sports activity, or in your profession, you have an edge. For instance, let us imagine you are a collector of artwork, photographs, and memorabilia of fire houses, fire uniforms, and equipment, and that you belong to the leading organizations for like-minded people. If you would like to write on the subject for one of the special interest publications in the field, you would most likely be given a fair hearing. (This is based on the assumption that you read these periodicals and know they don't already have a column of the type you would write.) You would, therefore, approach the publication with your credentials: your membership in the major organizations in the field, samples of photocopied pieces drawn from your collection, and proposals for the type of column you would like to contribute to the publication.

Once you have established yourself as a by-lined contributor to this special interest magazine (hence, acquiring the mantle of "expert") you can more easily approach general interest publications proposing to do stories of broader general appeal. You might, for example, buttress a proposal with your writing and other credentials, and suggest an in-depth piece on New York City's Fire Museum to the *New York Times* Sunday Travel Section or a piece on the fascinating history of San Francisco's famed Coit Tower to the *San Francisco Examiner.*

Returning to our example of the antiques expert, we see, hypothetically, how the building process continues.

When he connects by becoming a columnist, he could continue along the following lines:

• He could compile a group of his columns into book format.

• When and if a book contract results from his approaches to publishers, he would continue his self-promotion. Some opportunities might include: the publisher entering his book in any and all contests; having several copies donated to the local public television station to be used as a "giveaway" during their on-air fund-raising week; having several copies given to local charities for use during auctions.

• If subsidiary rights sales of his book ensue, he would add all resultant materials including publicity to his press kit.

All of these activities would provide widespread general publicity, which would intensify name recognition.

Becoming an Expert Who Is "Quotable" . . . .

If you are a writer who specializes in one subject area, you are already something of an "expert." As such, you can broaden the public's awareness of your name. Doing so means editors and agents will also become better acquainted with your name. If they don't, we'll tell you how to parlay your being quoted.

If, for example, you work in the field of home remodeling and have written several articles on the subject, you could gain enhanced visibility by positioning yourself as a "quotable expert." Contact editors of general interest magazines that regularly run home remodeling features and offer yourself as someone willing to talk with writers of forthcoming articles in your field. (Or articles that will touch upon your field. Do not expect, or ask, compensation for this. This is personal publicity of the best kind.)

These approaches to busy editors must be made via mail. (Do not phone and expect to get a hearing; in this case you are definitely better served putting your offer in writing.) This would be an excellent time for you to include your background sheet or your press kit. This will help you show that you are an expert in your field. Any resulting articles in which you are quoted will be particularly good additions to your press kit.

If, in the future, you want to contact these editors with your own story ideas, send the article in which you are quoted along with a brief cover letter. (Say that you don't know if they saw your contribution to the piece, but are sending it on as you were pleased to be included, or some such.)

Promoting Yourself if You Have an Article Being Published . .

When you know for certain that an article you have written will be published in a general interest magazine, there are ways you can draw wider attention to yourself using the article as a door-opener for publicity and self-promotion.

Touch base with the magazine's publicity promotion person to ascertain what, if anything, they might be planning to do to publicize your piece, then proceed. You might be told they don't want you to do anything at all, or that they will be doing some things. If they ask you not to do anything at all, explain what you have in mind.

You'll need an outline at hand of what you'd like to do, so you can readily inform the magazine's publicity person of your plans.

If your article is set to appear in a general interest magazine, you have a wide field to mine. Those of you who write special interest or scholarly articles want to alert professional groups (particularly those you belong to), and alumni and business-related publications of your forthcoming article. You can parlay publication of your general interest article into publicity in advance of its publication.

If, for example, you have written an article on the history of chocolate, write to the food editors of all the newspapers in your area about four to six weeks ahead of your article's publication. Tell them your piece will shortly appear in such-and-such a publication and that you would be pleased to speak with them about it before the magazine hits the newsstands.

You can do the same thing—again, in advance of the magazine's publication—with any locally based radio or television shows. (Start three weeks or so ahead of time.) Only approach those shows that you know cover such subjects and use guests on the air.

> **TIP:** Many radio shows do what are called "phoners," in which guests are interviewed on the telephone. If you are booked to do a phoner, you don't have to leave your home to "appear" on the show—terrific for writers who are on a deadline. For more about this, see our chapter on "Radio."

In doing this type of publicity, don't send the media an advance copy of your unpublished article. Save your best shots for your interview. If the media people specifically ask to see the piece first, explain that the magazine would not want you to do this (which is more than likely the case). You can say you will be pleased to send them your press kit. *And do it immediately.* Include a cover letter clipped to the outside front of your press kit, stating that you had spoken on such-and-such a date about [insert the subject] and are attaching the promised material. End by asking them to call you to set up the interview you had discussed.

What you want to accomplish is not to merely sell more magazines, but to secure interviews to raise awareness of your name and to gather more clips for your personal publicity file. Further, you want to be taken seriously as a person the media finds interesting and worthy of interviewing, one they will turn to again when expert comment in your field is needed for future stories. If, in contacting your local television shows, they say they are interested but do not have a show for you to appear on that originates in their studio, volunteer to speak from your home or office or to demonstrate your subject. (This might work especially well as a "soft" news feature at a local station.) If, for example, you are expert in some aspect of sports, fine arts or crafts, cookery or baking, offer to hold a demonstration of some sort at your studio or home and invite them to film it.

Speak Up! . . . .

There are other things you can do when you know you have a general interest article set to appear. If you are comfortable speaking to groups, then contact (either by mail or phone, depending on whether you know the people you'll be contacting) any local civic, fraternal, charitable, or religious group that holds meetings featuring speakers. Offer to speak to their group on the subject of your article. It's most likely they will not pay a speaker's fee. While you need not bring up the issue of money, if they immediately tell you they don't pay speaker's fees, volunteer to speak "gratis" if you are willing to do so. Here again you will be accomplishing the goal of becoming better known and probably garnering local media coverage, including clips to add to your file.

Obviously let good judgment prevail: If you have written a political article which is pro-Republican, don't volunteer to address a group that is made up of staunch Democrats!

Becoming a Syndicated Columnist . . . .

While few writers can hope to attain the superstar status enjoyed by syndicated columnists such as Ann Landers, Abigail Van Buren, Erma Bombeck, or Art Buchwald, those of you willing to invest time, money, and effort into this may succeed. We say "may succeed" because each year the highly competitive market for syndication shrinks. But if you have specific expertise, a fresh new style, or can craft unique stories, you can gain excellent exposure and prestige.

The 1990 edition of *Writer's Market* reports syndication is a very competitive and challenging field. One syndicate said that in the previous year they received seven thousand submissions and accepted four. Even though the market for syndicated general-interest newspaper columnists continues to diminish, there has been a spurt in the number of special interest syndicates that sell to trade journals, business publications, magazines, and also to newspapers.

According to the 1989 *Writer's Market,* the most popular subjects for special-ized features and columns were "how to, business, health, and finance." The 1990 edition noted that in "the past year, syndicates have launched columns with topics ranging from living with disabilities to the political views of former U.S. Attorney General Edwin Meese."

Writer's Market also provides helpful details on the entire field of syndication. They advise that most of these columns are short, from 500 to 750 words; that potential columnists should never submit imitative concepts to syndicates; and they suggest first building "proof of ability" by writing a column for a local newspaper before approaching a syndicate. *WM* carries a detailed run-down of syndicates, including their needs and pay scales. And writers interested in syndicating their own work are given specific advice.

Below is a book list to help those interested in learning more about syndica-tion and column writing. Most of these reference books may be found at the public library. (We also have information on publishers in our Resources sec-tion.)

- *The Editor and Publisher Syndicate Directory*
- *The Gale Directory of Publications*
- *How to Write & Sell a Column,* by Julie Raskin and Carolyn Males (Writer's Digest Books)
- *How to Make Money in Newspaper Syndication,* by Susan Lane.

Note: That last book might not be found in libraries, but information on it can be obtained from: Newspaper Syndication Specialists, Suite 326, Box 19654, Irvine, CA 92720.

Do You Know about the "Op Ed"? . . . .

The "Op Ed" section of a daily newspaper is an excellent place for you to submit an article that can help build name recognition.

The "Op Ed" page is usually placed just opposite the newspaper's editorial page. Here, writers can respond to a newspaper's editorial, or they can write an original article on a subject with which they are concerned. In either case, they always receive "credit line" information—that is, their name and whatever "credentials" they would like shown are printed beneath their piece. A typical credit line might read, "Jane Smith is a physician's assistant and writer." Or, "John Johns is author of *Public Housing Policy from FDR to George Bush* and Professor of Urban Planning at the University of Pennsylvania, Philadelphia."

To find out more about the policies of newspapers you are interested in writing Op Ed articles for, contact the Op Ed editor (preferably by name). Query that person on policies, such as word length, deadlines, and pay offered—if any—for such pieces. Make it clear that you are not submitting your article as a "Letter to the Editor." A long screed will immediately find a home in the editor's "round file"!

How an Op Ed Article Could Work for You

If, for example, you are a nurse and would like to carve out a second, or a new, career as a writer, you could begin in the following manner.

You submit an Op Ed article—one that is relevant or timely to one major paper in the city nearest to you. We specify only *one* newspaper per city, as exclusivity of Op Ed articles in each city you target is absolutely necessary. If the city you select has more than one major daily newspaper, start with the one with the largest circulation. If they aren't interested, move on to the next paper.

You could also submit the same article to newspapers in *other* cities. But again, keep in mind that you must always only submit to one paper in *each* city. When and if you are turned down, in a two, or multi-paper town, you may then submit to the next paper on your list.

In thinking of original articles versus those in which you're responding to an editorial, think of a timely tie-in—and make sure you have something fresh and original to say. In November, for example, America observes a "National Smoke Out Day." On this day the nation's smokers are asked to give up smoking for the day. A health professional who deals with cancer patients could write an effective column in connection with the smoke-out.

Or, if you are an auto mechanic-cum-writer, and your city is considering enacting new regulations affecting procedures and charges at auto maintenance centers, you could write a relevant, original Op Ed article. The article might offer suggestions on questions to ask at the repair shop, or could highlight several maintenance procedures car owners could take on themselves that would spare them unnecessary trips to the mechanics.

Another possibility for an auto expert is an Op Ed piece responding—pro or con—to a newspaper's editorial in support of an issue such as increasing the automobile speed limit to 65 miles per hour nationwide.

The point of writing these articles is to get your name before the public in connection with an area of specialization — that's why the credit line is important. You want the connection made between you and your subject. That way, the next time an editor is looking for an expert, he or she may think of *you.*

Whatever type of writing you do, there are always issues you can write about. Even the most esoteric of writers can find something about which they are concerned. Having these published articles in your clip file will prove very valuable. This is particularly so for those of you who have been having a difficult time obtaining any published pieces for your portfolio.

Giving "Old" Books New Life . . . .

The Op Ed article is also particularly valuable if you are the author of a book that has been out for some time (one that is on your publisher's "backlist"). For example, if you authored a serious work that explores the mindset of the airplane hijacker and there is a spate of hijackings making headlines, you have an excellent opportunity to write a timely article. Of course, your credit line would mention your book's title.

Or if you write young adult books dealing with sexual matters, you could center your submission either on St. Valentine's Day observances, or key it to any relevant story (such as a local news account of teen marriages and the subsequent high divorce rates).

If you had authored a scholarly work on the history of the Narragansett Indians for a university press, Thanksgiving might provide you with an excellent opportunity to discuss the issues concerning the "facts" about the relationship between Native Americans and the Pilgrims. Here again, your credit line would help raise awareness of your old book.

Overall, you must think carefully where you can create a niche for yourself. You will never get rich writing Op Ed pieces, but you will broaden your name recognition and build a nice clip file!

"Name Recognition" for Fiction Writers . . . .

If you have read what we suggested so far, and think that as a writer of fiction you have little to offer — think again!

Recycle Your Research

If you write novels in which you have undertaken background research, then you have an excellent opportunity to bring yourself to wide attention. Your background material will probably lend itself to shorter articles. And writing these articles can bring you to a wide audience. Keep in mind, especially, that if you have not yet been published, writing such articles is particularly valuable.

Even writers of short fiction have ways to bring themselves to the public's attention. Consider the following: A science fiction writer with a store of scientific data at hand could use that as a stimulus toward the creation of other publicity-generating opportunities. (One need only look at the multi-faceted career of an Isaac Asimov to understand just how productive this approach can be!)

Or, a person who writes romance articles set in Victorian England would probably also be able to write short nonfiction pieces about the period she is expert in for general interest publications. In doing so she would, of course, prominently mention her *fictive* work.

A writer who specializes in fictional works set in today's Soviet Union could apply her fiction writing research towards other ends. She might well offer herself as a "Soviet affairs expert" to the media when comment on contemporary affairs in the U.S.S.R. is needed.

A man who writes articles of fiction set in the American West in the 19th century could offer to talk on the topic before any group with relevant interests.

Or a writer who has done extensive research on any area of popular culture might be well positioned to comment when the media is seeking such input.

In these cases a letter to media outlets, and specific publications or shows would be warranted. The writers would draw attention to their areas of expertise and offer themselves for interviews and commentary.

Spot News?

When there are major "breaking" stories occurring, the media frequently quickly need experts to comment. This is particularly the case for radio and television shows. For example, if you write fiction for and about the problems today's young adults encounter, you are probably a good candidate for "expert comment." (If, for example, less than pleasant teenage-themed stories are making news, you would be a likely person to comment.) Or, if you write articles of fiction set in prehistoric Egypt and a major archaeological "find" is making news, you would probably be of special (read that as "timely") interest to the media.

If you write in the mystery genre, even if you've not yet had a large number of articles published, and if your research has provided you with a hefty file of current information on foreign countries that are newsworthy, you can probably parlay that knowledge in some way.

Whatever the topic of your writing, you can find ways to position yourself to gain public attention. The main thing is to keep thinking and not to limit yourself to traditional modes of thought *vis-à-vis* self-promotion.

Some Practical Examples . . . .

As a case in point, let us assume that you have written a book of historical fiction set in New York City before and during the Revolutionary War. You have done extensive research for your novel and possess a good store of information on the subject. Approach the major metropolitan daily papers in New York proposing to write articles keyed to significant Revolutionary War dates (for example, you might propose to mark the pivotal Battle of Long Island with a piece on the subject tied into the anniversary of that battle). Proposing to write timely pieces would probably enhance your chances of being published. And, of course, such a by-lined piece would carry the information that you are the author of [your book title].

Interestingly, few writers of fiction ever think of ways they can promote themselves. Yet I have found that quite a few fiction writers take the book promotion and publicity workshops and courses I teach, probably in response to the pandemic lack of attention paid to their books! Yet, most often, when we reach the session or portion of the course where we investigate the specific methods that writers can use to promote themselves, I find that the fiction writers look crestfallen.

Those honest enough to express their feelings usually plaintively say something like, "But *I* write fiction! I can't do anything to promote myself—all I can hope for are book reviews!"

To belie this belief, let's look at several "hopeless" cases.

Consider a fictive work set in a hospital during World War II. The author's main character is an Irish-American woman who is an Army nurse. The author has never been asked to fill out an author's questionnaire. (We'll cover these in a later chapter.) We ask her to do so. In reading through her completed questionnaire we discover many publicizable angles. First, we discover that the author was born—and spent her early years—in Ireland. We discover that she emigrated to America as a young woman, and that she maintains close ties with her large family in Ireland. We also find that she took her nurse's training in the United States and that she was herself an Army nurse.

We also learn from the completed questionnaire that after leaving the military she was employed as a translator, working for a large international organization. (She is fluent in several languages.) Further, we learn that when she worked as a translator she lived in several major European cities. All of this material presents her with many interesting opportunities.

Her Irish heritage presents several possibilities: Not only would American-based Irish-American organizations probably review (or at least announce publication) of her book in their newsletters or bulletins, she might also be interviewed in these publications. And she could well become a likely speaker at any of such groups' meetings.

Further, her employment experiences mean that she has an even wider net to cast if she is interested in speaking engagements. Namely, given her nurse's training (and the focus of her book), she and the book would probably be of interest to publications geared to nurses.

Her work as a translator presents equally good promotable pegs (via professional associations in her field to which she belongs).

Finally, her military background means that those publications read by present or former members of the armed forces (as well as those geared only to World War II veterans) would likely be interested in learning of her novel.

One might read the foregoing thinking, "Ah, but this gal had an interesting life. I've hardly done anything I can use!" However, let's examine just such an "ordinary" life for ways to publicize works of fiction.

The author of a collection of short stories is a man employed full time as a telephone repair person. He hasn't attended college, and has lived in several small American towns since his high school graduation. He's unmarried and has few relatives.

Each of the stories in his collection is set in a different time period and location and each has a different theme. One story, titled: "A Hoboken's More Than a Town in Jersey" details the protagonist's experiences working as a short-order cook in a roadside diner in the 1950s while trying to "make it" in the music business. (This story provides a good view of what life was like for someone so employed in this time and place. It has graphic descriptions of the "diner culture.")

Another story, set in New York City in the 1930s, is centered on the relationship — and conflicts — between two Mohawk Indians employed as construction workers on the Empire State Building. (One of them feels that his work on the structure represents a turning point . . . and a way to break with his past life.)

This writer's completed questionnaire would seem to present little to work with. His work (and the attendant overtime it usually entailed) makes it impossible for him to take time off to undertake personal appearances. Further, his reticent personality removes the idea of public speaking from his "list" of possible activities. There are, however, ways for him to seek publicity.

In this case, mailing of *focused* (targeted) news releases would be paramount. His high school's alumni association, the publications put out by his employer and by the union he belongs to, would be sent *individualized* news releases (that is, ones that emphasize relevant angles. Thus, each of these releases would stress his union membership, the type of work he does, and his place of employment. Another release would focus on where he attended high school.)

Publications interested in the subject of Native American life provide other possible avenues to pursue. And, given the restaurant business details he provides in his story of the short-order cook-cum-musician, publications serving this area of the restaurant business would also be sent a targeted news release.

To clarify just what we mean by "targeted," here are the headlines or leads for the news releases for this last work.

Targeted Release #1 (angle = High School Alumnus)
JACK IRWIN, 1958 GRADUATE OF RICE LAKE HIGH SCHOOL, WRITES COLLECTION OF SHORT STORIES: BROKEN FEATHER LOVES FAY WRAY

Targeted Release #2 (food angle)
NEW COLLECTION OF SHORT STORIES FEATURES EXCELLENT PORTRAYAL OF "DINER CULTURE" CIRCA 1954

In the lead story in his new collection of short stories titled *Broken Feather Loves Fay Wray,* writer Jack Irwin pens an insightful and factual rendering of what "diner culture" was like in America in the 1950s. The story, titled "A Hoboken's More Than a Town in Jersey," is written from the perspective of a roadside diner's short-order cook and provides a fascinating glimpse back in time.

Targeted Release #3 (angle = Native Americans)
NATIVE AMERICANS DEPICTED IN LEAD STORY IN NEW COLLECTION OF SHORT STORIES ... MOHAWK CONSTRUCTION WORKERS OF THE 30s PROTAGONISTS IN BOOK, BROKEN FEATHER LOVES FAY WRAY

Overall, keep in mind that if you have written a work of fiction that has several themes, you, too, have enhanced publicity possibilites.

One first novel that I helped publicize provided just such opportunities. (And this was the case even though the author lived in Europe and was not available for any U.S. publicity appearances.)

This book, set in the Belgian Congo when it was still a colonial nation, was centered on the work and love life of a man in the oil business. (The author was formerly an executive of a major international oil company.)

The novel presented the following publicity "opportunities":

• Given the book's historical angles and the author's career, it might lend itself to reviews or feature articles in oil industry publications;

• Or, it could be mentioned in political/historical publications geared to the time period and to the history of the region(s) discussed.

Interestingly, this author also undertook a "radio tour," one that was done while he remained at home in Europe. He "toured" via radio show phoner interviews. (Refer to page 112 for details on how this works.)

Other Promotional Venues . . . .

If you don't have extensive research to play off of, there are still ways you can get your name into print. You might, for example, offer to be a book reviewer at a local newspaper. Here too the remuneration would probably be infinitesimally small or nonexistent. However, as you would have the newspaper send a press release to the Calendar Editor of *Publishers Weekly* announcing your appointment as Book Review Editor, you would not only be bringing yourself before the publishing community, but you would also start receiving many books.

Writers of fictive works should also find they have good friends at their local public library. If you live near to any branch library that holds book readings or offers talks by writers, contact the branch for information. You may also discover that your library sponsors an annual "Book Fair" to which writers and authors are invited. Pursue any of these areas. Refer to pages 155-156, the section on librarians, for more information on the subject.

Give . . . and You May Well "Receive"

Many times radio and television stations, as well as varied cultural institutions, hold fund-raising drives or auctions. You might consider donating autographed copies of your books, with the understanding the sponsoring organization will publicize your donation.

Often religious or charitable organizations hold annual book fairs or book and author luncheons. Here, too, you could offer to participate.

In the case of a book fair or book and author luncheon, the sponsoring organization will doubtless do advance promotion. Make certain to provide them with material on your participation, or, if need be, write a news release for their use.

Parlaying Contest Participation into Free Publicity

There are scores of writing contests and competitions held annually. Whether you actually win a top prize is frequently not as important as you would think. Entering these competitions can be a superb way to gain attention. Even a secondary prize can be an excuse to send out a press release or add an impressive note to your background sheet.

Important: Most often *books* entered in competition must be submitted by the publisher. Here, as in other instances, many publishers overlook entering the competitions their authors could compete in, so it's important that you familiarize yourself with the possibilities.Thus, if need be, you can direct your book publisher's attention to suitable competitions. If you write for a magazine or newspaper, first check the company's policy before personally entering your work in competitions. More than likely these submissions will have to be handled by the publisher.

There are several fine references you can use to locate competitions. *Literary Market Place* (listed in our Resource Section) has information on competitions and contests, as do the annual editions of *Writer's Market.* For fiction writing contests and awards, there is information in the book, *Novel & Short Story Writer's Market,* while for poets, there's *Poet's Market.* (The latter three writer's market guides are published by Writer's Digest Books.)

Perusing these listings one finds scores of competitions for all types of writing open to novices and to established magazine and newspaper writers, as well as book authors.

A random reading of these listings will open your eyes to just how many contests might be open for your work. For example, if you have a first book of European history you could qualify for the award granted by the American Historical Association. Or if you write regional books or articles, fiction or nonfiction, there are scores of contests, akin to the Ohio Arts Council award given to Ohioans for all types of writing. If you are a poet there is the American Poetry Association Award which is given for unpublished work by new and as yet unrecognized poets. There are contests sponsored by many different special interest groups such as the Housewife-Writer's Forum, the American Bowling Congress, the Dog Writer's Association, the National Marine Manufacturers

Association, the Golf Course Superintendents Association, and the Herbert Hoover Presidential Library Association.

In addition, many writing groups sponsor contests or offer grants in aid.

You will also find contests sponsored by a large number of general and special interest magazines such as *Present Tense, Political Woman, Nebraska Review, Business History Review, Hadassah Magazine, Redbook,* and *Mademoiselle.*

Research the references we mention here and you will find a terrific array of contests sponsored by little- and better-known groups. It behooves all writers to acquaint themselves with such competitions.

Poets, Take Note . . . .

Do you write poetry and despair of ever being noticed? It's an odds-on bet that you have never publicized your "scores." When you have had a poem accepted for publication or awarded a prize, however esoteric the publication, have you announced it? Why not make it a practice to send out news releases when you have your work published! And, if you have any experience you feel would make you a likely interviewee—or media-valuable "expert," why not offer yourself? Of course, you do so with the proviso they publicize the fact that you are, in fact, a poet.

Many of the ideas we suggest in this book can easily be applied to those of you who write poetry. If you are creative enough to dwell in the wonderful world of poets, you are more than creative enough to devise ways to publicize your work.

6

Networking for Writers

It's possible that in years past, writers, like the proverbial *artistes* we read of, could lock themselves into a quiet garret and spend all their time entertaining the muses. Nowadays part of the writer's life should include belonging to a writer's organization and attending writing-related seminars, workshops, meetings, and courses.

Not only is it nourishing to meet our sister and brother writers, but often it is an excellent way to meet editors, agents, and others who might advance our careers. (And you might want to check with your accountant about the possibility of taking a tax deduction for attending these workshops and meetings.) There are meetings and organizations for writers of every conceivable type. A random reading of such groups' listings (you can find these in many places, which we discuss in the following pages) proves the point. There are associations for dog writers, garden writers, education writers, football writers, and even more specialized groups ranging from the Oregon Association of Christian Writers to the Sherlock Holmes-themed group—the aptly named Baker Street Irregulars!

The Dangers of "Playing Ostrich" . . . .

Being a writer today usually means establishing a presence and a reputation. It also means keeping up-to-date on developments in the field. (This last point is particularly important if you are interested in writing books and are unagented.) And whatever type of writing you do, you'll want to learn about editorial people changing jobs, since editorial staff jobs often take on the features of "musical chairs." Attending conferences is a good way to learn about other developments that could affect your writing life.

If you are turned off by crowds or are simply much too shy to attend meetings on your own, try to line up another writer who might like to attend with you. (Better yet, try to find one who would be willing to volunteer for committee work with you.)

What to Expect at a Writers Conference . . . .

In his introduction to writers conferences in the May 1988 *Writer's Digest,* writer and book editor Michael Seidman presents an excellent word picture of what you can expect if you attend a meeting. He also offers some fine suggestions:

> I once thought that writers conferences were a waste of time; if you were a writer you'd be home writing, not sitting around with other people looking for answers. ... One evening, however, I was listening to a speech and realized that I hadn't written anything since 1981. So I listened a little more closely, and recognized that the speaker was addressing me. Since that evening in 1985, I've written and sold one novella and fifteen or twenty articles. As jaded as I had become, I thought there was nothing to be gained.
>
> I was wrong.
>
> And most frightening: *I* was the speaker I was hearing that evening.
>
> As both speaker and attendee, I've found that the hours spent at a writers conference are some of most productive you will ever spend, but only if you pay attention while there — and only if you're prepared. *(Reprinted by permission of Michael Seidman)*

Seidman suggests finding out about, and attending, any informal get-togethers (cocktail parties, coffee hours, etc.) during which you can meet both the other participants and the "pros" in a relaxed atmosphere. These sessions aren't the time "to ask an editor what he or she is looking for, or to discuss your manuscript," he adds. "It is time to listen." Conferences frequently schedule opportunities for "business" meetings with editors. Seidman adds:

> Take advantage of the speakers, of the experience. Attend the conference with an open mind, not a chip-laden shoulder. Listen to the other people you are meeting and share your knowledge with them. Ask questions. Don't be ashamed of any supposed weakness in your background or your interests. And, remember that your actions may be remembered long after your project is forgotten.

Finding Writers Conferences and Workshops . . . .

If you are not certain where workshops and conferences are going to take place and which are of interest and accessible to you, there are several sources you can turn to.

Each May, *Writer's Digest* magazine provides a guide to workshops, conferences, and seminars held throughout the nation.

You can also consult *Literary Market Place's* list of writing courses. *LMP* — as it's widely called — provides details on writing workshops and courses offered all over the U.S. Another helpful book, *The Guide to Writers Conferences* (edited by Dorlene V. Shane) provides details on international seminars, writing workshops, and retreats. This paperback is issued annually (in December) and is $14.95 in bookstores or $16.95 by mail (including postage) from Shaw Associates, Box 1446985, Coral Gables FL 33114-4695.

Poets & Writers Inc. annually issues a Writers Conference list, and three times a year issues a list of free and fee-charging poetry and fiction workshops in the New York metropolitan area. See our Resources section for detailed information on ordering these.

Fear Not the Taint of "Novice" . . . .

Please don't think these courses and workshops are only for novice writers. At classes I have taught for writers at university workshops I have had students (and met others taking other sessions) who were polished professionals.

Obviously, there is no guarantee that attending a workshop will mean you'll hook up with an agent or editor, but in being where the action is you at least enhance the possibility of your being noticed.

I've seen firsthand examples of how such classes can bring together writers and agents. Elizabeth Frost Knappman, president of New England Publishing Associates and my co-speaker at a university seminar on "How to Get Your Book Published," successfully agented *two* books for a writer she met at that seminar.

I have also seen writers connect with other writers they were unaware of in their own geographic areas. These meetings made it possible for the writers to join, or to start, writer's groups.

It's well worth your time to peruse these workshop offerings. There are a slew of fine courses, seminars, and workshops offered throughout the country. There is much to be derived from attendance. At the least you will have an opportunity to meet other writers, and you will probably benefit from the collective wisdom of other writers and teachers. And often you have the bonus of being able to combine a vacation with your workshop attendance.

Workshops and Seminars Outside the University Setting . . .

In addition to writing workshops offered through colleges and universities, short-term workshops (each generally of several hours' duration) that are widely attended by book and magazine company personnel are offered by several groups, including the semiannual New York City session by the Folio Division of the Hanson Publishing Group. The Folio Show (book-oriented) and the Magazine Publishing Congress are offered jointly, generally in late spring and fall.

These workshops are taught by people with substantive publishing backgrounds and they provide inside information on a wide number of topics. A recent group of offerings that would, for example, be of interest to writers included sessions such as: "The Year in Book Buying: The Gallup Report," which gave attendees information on Americans' reading habits and on purchasing trends, changing characteristics within the book market concerning pricing, retail versus mail order, fiction versus nonfiction, hardcover books and softcover. There was also a course in trends in children's book publishing, others on desktop publishing, and a session on negotiating author's contracts—which is a workshop for agents, editors, and publishers *but* which offered insightful information to authors. For writers who want to understand more about the publishing process, "The Basics of Book Marketing" is regularly taught by veteran marketing person, Shirley Sarris. To gain an insight into the ways publishers approach varied aspects of the book business — and thus give you a better handle in discussions with your publisher — the Folio seminars on "Penetrating the Library Market," and "The Fundamentals of Mail Order Book Sales" could also be of value.

While the magazine seminar offerings are geared to staffers, I've found that freelancers are also often in attendance.

Recent workshops that would probably be of interest to magazine writers have included: "Magazine Writing: Sharpening Your Basic Skills"; and a follow-up, companion workshop that guided attendees through short writing assignments geared to putting the concepts learned earlier into practice. Other workshops included "The Craft of Interviewing," one on ways to "add life and sparkle" to magazine pieces, and a session called: "Editing and Writing for the Business Audience." Valuable handouts are usually given away at each seminar.

Refer to the Resource's section for Folio's address and write or call for their catalog. These courses bring together many interesting and influential publishing people. And the informal get-togethers, free to attendees, provide people with a good opportunity to meet one another.

In 1990 the Cahners Exposition Group, in conjunction with *Publishers Weekly,* held, in New York City, their first book publishing conference called Book PubWorld. They too offered a wide number of book-themed seminars. To find out about future PubWorld meetings contact Cahners at: 999 Summer St., P.O. Box 3839, Stamford, CT 06905-0839.

There's Strength in Numbers . . . .

Beyond making contact with other writers, there is much to be gained if you work together with other writers on the *noncreative* areas of the writing life, including the marketing. By joining forces with other writers you can realize numerous benefits.

Being a member of a writer's group can provide you with creative encouragement and support, peer advice, and sharing market information. It can also mean you will be able to join forces for more practical purposes. For example, if your group decided to assume a professional name (like, "The Writer's Block" or "Writer's Ink" or whatever you deem suitable) you might find it easier to work with companies that only do business with other business enterprises. For instance, mail order or local companies that sell office supplies, stationery, promotion items, and office furnishings may not accept orders from individuals. And you might find that local suppliers, printers, and stationers who do accept individual orders will give you larger discounts if you buy in bulk.

If you pool resources you could invest in your own set of reference tools, media directories, and even establish a library of your own. This could be particularly helpful if there is no full-service public library near you. Several group members might want to subscribe to the same publications to split costs. This can be particularly helpful if you're regularly reading book trade magazines like *Publishers Weekly, Library Journal, School Library Journal,* or those publications that service the magazine and newspaper industries, such as *Folio* and *Magazine Week.*

Another way that being a member of such a group can prove beneficial is if several of you need a place to write or work on marketing away from your homes. You could join forces and rent — or possibly even buy — space for an office or professional apartment to be used solely for these purposes. This would be the place you maintain as your office, where you would keep your files and other important items: copies of all of your correspondence and those reference books and magazines that are specific to your interest area.

Other Benefits

If the purchase of a computer is beyond the reach of your individual budget, this manner of cooperative purchase could solve that problem. You might be able to buy one or even two computers. Depending upon the type of hardware purchased, you might be able to use the same word processing software for both. (Or you might purchase a hard disc system that allows you to install several different word processing programs.) And if others in your group are using the same word processing program, you'll have the added benefit of being able to help each other should you run into problems. Any writer who has ever gotten stuck using a computer can tell you the benefits of having another person to turn to who understands the intricacies of the hardware and the software and how to extricate oneself from a frozen screen!

The same benefits apply to group purchase of a computer modem, allowing you to access all types of databanks, or to buying a fax machine or a photcopy machine. If your home phone is usually too busy to take business phone calls, you could consider group purchase of an answering machine or answering service. Or, budget and mutual interests permitting, you could set up a toll-free 800 phone number so editors and others can quickly reach you — and at no cost to them.

If computers do not interest you and your writing colleagues, you might want to group purchase new typewriters. Whatever your needs and interests, you can probably strike a better deal with a supplier if you buy as a business entity or collectively.

If you will be setting up this type of special workplace and more than two or three people are involved, it's vital that you all agree on the days and times each will have access to the space, especially if the rented space is itself small. Obviously, if several of you need to use the group's computer you will have to work out a schedule.

You will probably find, if the other writers are congenial and reasonable, that having a place where you can work in peace and quiet is a terrific way to enhance the creative and (of special interest to us here) the business areas of your life.

Setting up this type of writer's group might also mean, if you have sufficient numbers of people involved, that you can look into creating your own group medical/hospitalization plan and similar benefits.

Join Forces to Sell Your Talents

Another way to capitalize on your group would be to create a joint publicity effort. Not only would this defray the costs of printing, mailing, and getting the publicity out, but you could also offer the media a much richer field to mine.

Begin by sending an inexpensive mailing out to introduce yourselves to the media. (You can photo-offset your material onto your group's letterhead or onto plain white paper that you assemble into a group press kit. Or, if just a few sheets are to be included, you can collate and paper clip them.)

Sending this material out serves several purposes. It brings your group to the attention of the media, positioning each of you as an "expert" available for comment. And, when contacting print media that you know hires freelance writers, you could also offer yourselves for writing assignments when articles are needed in your fields. (This could be sent to local, regional, or if relevant, national print and electronic media outlets.) It could take the form of a cover letter and fact sheet that might read along the lines of those on the next pages.

• SAMPLE LETTER •

Your Group's Letterhead

The Writer's Group

- Barbara Cohen
- Karen Kettering
- Marylou Zucker
- Martin Howard
- Franklyn Peters

Dear Media Person:

We hope if you need an expert comment for any upcoming features you will keep the enclosed information on file and turn to us. We would be pleased to speak with you and your reporters and writers.

We can offer a wide range of interesting and intelligent comment that ranges from expertise in computer sciences to zoology.

And if you need articles (or background data) *written* in any of these fields, please contact us. As you see, we each have wide-ranging publishing and professional credits.

We have enclosed information on our areas of expertise, on topics we can speak on, as well as on our backgrounds and how to contact each of us.

We look forward to working with you.

Sincerely,

[*your name signed here*]

For: The Writer's Group

• SAMPLE BIOGRAPHY SHEET FOR WRITER'S GROUP MAILING •

Group's Letterhead

The Writer's Group

• Barbara Cohen	• Karen Kettering	• Marylou Zucker
• Martin Howard	• Franklyn Peters	

Barbara Cohen

Subject areas: using a personal computer—for small businesses and home use

Background: Lecturer in computer sciences at Smith College, Holyoke, Massachusetts. Leads workshops in Wordstar and Wordperfect at the University of Massachusetts, Amherst—Division of Continuing Education.
Contributing editor to: *Your Personal Computer.* Published 45 articles on the subject (in *PC Daily, Your PC, PC Family Magazine, Today's Personal Computer*).

Can discuss: personal computer applications for the average personal and small business user.

Contact at: 114 Elm St., Northampton, MA 01234. Call 413/789-0123.

Martin Howard

Subject areas: Local Northampton/Amherst history, ca. 1700-1800

Background: Published novel (*Unsung Heroines*, Valley Publishing, 1987, set in Revolutionary Massachusetts); published 12 nonfiction articles on regional history (in *Massachusetts This Month; Boston Magazine; Valley News Sunday Travel Supplement; Boston Herald*—Travel Section).

Can discuss: New England history circa 18th and 19th centuries, specializing in local areas.

Contact: 58 Maple Lane, Northampton, MA 01011. Call: 413/887-0965.

(Dr.) Karen Kettering

Subject areas: Education topics (primary schools through secondary)

Background: Ph.D. in Education. President of "Valley Parents for Better Education"; contributor to: *The Valley News Weekly.*
　　Associate Professor of Education at the University of Massachusetts, Amherst. Author of *Values Clarification for Today's Public School Teacher* (Foreman Education Books, Inc.).

Can discuss: public education issues, general topics in education.

Franklyn Peters

Subject areas: Contemporary American music

Background: Author of *Hot Licks* (Dwight House Publishing, 1978) and *Cool Sounds* (Freeway Press, 1990).
　　Contributor to *Jazz Today, Today's Guitarist*, and *Sounds* magazines.

Can discuss: today's American music, the history of American music, and jazz topics.

Marylou Zucker

Subject areas: Zoology, home pet care

Background: Curator of West Valley Zoo. Author of *Your House Pet* (Truman House Publishing, 1988). Published 10 articles on New England wildlife, house pet care, and teaching children about animals.

Can discuss: home care for pets, endangered species, New England's wildlife.

Contact: % West Valley Zoo, Park Center, W. Valley, MA 01900. Call: Monday-Friday 10 A.M.-6 P.M. 413/555-0000, ext. 6. Other times 413/890-6432.

7

Taking Your Show on the Road

To this point, we've given you some basic principles on promoting yourself and your talents. We've discussed working with editors and other writers to further enhance your writing career. Now it's time to begin putting things together and do some face-to-face promotion. It's time to meet your public!

Speaking Your Way to Success . . . .

Public speaking is an excellent way to build your reputation. (This is said on the assumption that you are comfortable speaking before a group. If not, consider joining a club that helps people master these skills. The Toastmasters International is one very popular organization that you should have no difficulty finding, as they have almost 6,000 clubs throughout the world.)

There are many ways that writers and authors can create or arrange speaking engagements for themselves. Some will be strict publicity venues; others will afford you the opportunity to garner publicity, *and* if you have written a book, of selling it directly to the public as a source of added income. We'll talk more about this later.

If your topic lends itself to speaking engagements, you can try for many different types of sponsors and places. No matter the subject of your writing — whether you specialize or write on topics that interest large numbers of people, or if you write in a narrowly focused business or professional area — you can enhance your reputation by addressing groups of interested individuals.

Public speaking brings you multiple opportunities for self-promotion. Not only will you be appearing before your public, but it's also likely you will be given some type of publicity coverage.

Whatever Type of Writing You Do
. . . There's a Place to Speak . . . .

If you are a writer who specializes in linguistics, you can address those groups involved in this field. Or, if you write on militaria, further confining your writing to the subject of ordnance, you can probably find special interest groups interested in hearing what you have to say.

If you are a chemist/writer, specializing in pharmaceutical research, and have been working on new and interesting procedures in your field, there are probably like-minded professionals who would be interested in learning of your work.

To learn more about potential places you can speak, you should be familiar with the *Encyclopedia of Associations,* a directory from Gale Research (see Resource Section) that is available at most libraries.

This Encyclopedia is a rich trove of information, one that most writers — especially those who write special interest or scholarly works — should find particularly valuable. In it you will find listings for a staggering number — and type — of organizations and special interest groups, along with detailed information on their activities, and where and when they meet. What's particularly valuable for you if you wish to pursue the idea of speaking engagements is the information on annual and semiannual meetings and the names of contact people, helpful for targeting organizations and groups that are relevant to your writing. Given the fact that the Encyclopedia lists information well ahead of time, you can contact organizations relevant to your work and try to set up speaking engagements. (Be aware that national associations work at least one year ahead of time on conventions and annual meetings, so you will have to do likewise.

Speakers Bureaus . . . .

If the prospect of approaching groups and selling yourself as a public speaker is intimidating, investigate the possibilities of being represented by a speakers bureau. *Literary Market Place* has a section that lists speakers bureaus that represent writers. Before you do so, honestly ask yourself these questions: Do I have something unique to say? Can I say something new about a familiar subject, or present a different approach to it? (Evaluate whether you can do so in an engaging and lively manner.) If I am signed on by the lecture bureau, do I have the time to undertake trips to address groups in far-off locations?

Have Your Sponsor Publicize Your Talk . . . .

One of the benefits of appearing before an organization or club is that you can usually expect the sponsoring organization to publicize the event. (And if it's not offered, ask. Remember, most of them are looking for free publicity too.)

It would be best if the sponsoring organization sends the media some type of advance notice of your talk. (See sample of a Tip Sheet and Advance Notice in Appendix 2, Sample Publicity Forms.) The sponsor should also prepare a news release about your talk. (This can be sent to media who will not be attending, hence covering, your talk.)

If your sponsor is unfamiliar with how to do this, you should be able to help, based on what you will have learned after reading this book. And, if your sponsor cannot or will not undertake this publicity, it is important that you do so. Depending on who your sponsoring organization is, and the media that would have to be contacted, you might find you have to circulate your information far ahead of time. (If, for example, you'll be speaking at an annual meeting of a professional association and you know that publications in your field are only published semiannually, you will have to see that your press releases are sent to the professional publications early on to meet their deadlines.) If your sponsor will not be sending out a news release after your speech to media who didn't attend, you should do so. Here you provide details on what you said, and who attended.

Speaking About Books: Direct Selling . . . .

A common complaint among authors is that their books get short shrift in the publicity department (we'll discuss more about that in Chapter Ten, Especially for Authors) or that their books are not readily available in bookstores. Some authors have taken matters into their own hands, combining public speaking engagements with the chance to sell their books directly to the public. It's not uncommon to hear stories of how now-famous authors once loaded boxes of books into the trunks of their cars and set out on national speaking tours. And how at the end of each talk, they would sell autographed copies of their books.

> TIP: Before you consider doing anything of this sort, clear all such activities with the publicity or promotion people at your publisher's office.

In *How to Become a Bestselling Author,* Stanley Corwin describes how one writer combines speaking and sales opportunities.

> . . . Robert G. Allen has parlayed his master salesmanship techniques into two long-running Simon & Schuster best-sellers, *Nothing Down* and *Creating Wealth.* Both books tell how to make a lot of money through real estate and other financial ventures.
>
> The primary reason for the extraordinary success of the books is probably the author himself. "Robert Allen is a masterful promoter," said the business-book buyer at B. Dalton. "He goes into an area, sets up a seminar, A Free Evening with Robert Allen, and gets people excited about his ideas. He never fails to sell books."

While your book may not lend itself to a seminar arrangement, there are many other avenues to explore. We'll discuss traditional bookstore autographing parties later in this chapter, but it's important to think beyond the bookstore in looking for places to promote your book.

If you have written a nonfiction book, there are many places to appear, limited only by your imagination: An energetic cookbook author I worked with approached her local butcher, who agreed to have her at his store autographing and selling her cookbook. In her small town it was a big event to have a local person "make it," to have a book published. And, as her ethnic cookbook emphasized meat recipes, the butcher was delighted to help her promote her book.

Another author whose marketing I handled had written a guide for parents planning the Jewish child's Bar or Bat Mitzvah. She became actively involved in her publicity and promotion and helped line up various places to appear. In her locality she spoke at a number of synagogues, and also addressed meetings of local, regional, and national Jewish organizations.

Ways to Meet Your Public and Sell Your Book

If you have written a nonfiction book there are probably many places you can appear. (Again, this applies to both new books and to those that are backlist.) If your publisher will not, or cannot, help, this is an area you can undertake. As one who is knowledgeable in your field, you will, in any case, probably be better equipped to know who to approach.

Before you begin scheduling appearances, however, it is vital that you clarify with your publisher what they are willing to do. Mainly, what you want is for them to agree to ship books on consignment to stores (other than bookstores) that agree to have you appear to autograph and sell your books. "On consignment" means that stores only pay for those books actually sold, and that they must return all unsold copies of your books to the publisher in clean and salable condition. Some publishers are reluctant to do this, so tread lightly.

If you obtain your publisher's agreement to ship books on consignment, it is important that you make certain that store personnel understand the nature of the arrangement. If you are unable to get your publisher to ship books on a consignment basis, but you still believe it could be a worthwhile undertaking, you might want to exercise your contractual option and buy your books using your author's discount. (See the Especially for Authors, Chapter Ten, for information on this.)

If your publisher refuses to consider shipping books on consignment to non-bookstores, and if you are not going to purchase books yourself, you can always try to convince your local bookstore that this would be a good time to stock up on your book. This works especially well where the local bookshop has either not purchased your book at all, or has purchased only a handful of copies.

Examples of How Authors Can Direct Sell

Bookkeeping aside, let's examine various ideas authors can use to direct sell nonfiction books. In all of the following examples, it is implicit that each author (or the organization he or she will be working with) undertake a pre-event publicity campaign. This entails mailing press releases publicizing the event and the fact that the author will be on hand to autograph and sell books. In all the following examples, speaking engagements include having the author or the sponsor selling the book. This would be done with the agreement of the sponsor—ahead of time and in writing. If you plan to sell your books at your speaking engagement it must be an agreed-to condition of your appearance. In instances such as this, you should not expect to be offered a speaker's fee.

Book #1. *Buying Your First House*

This author could approach many different types of organizations: civic and charitable organizations and church-affiliated groups. He would offer to speak on one or two aspects of his topic. In the commercial sphere, he could also approach the owners of furniture and appliance stores. Here he would suggest his willingness to appear at the store at a mutually convenient time to either deliver a set talk or take customers' questions. Again, he would inform the store owners he would do so with the understanding he would autograph and they could sell the book. In a case such as this, he might have to split the profits with the store owners.

Book #2. *Cooking for One*

This author would have a particularly rich field to mine. With the large numbers of single people of all ages interested in cooking single portion meals for themselves, she would have many ways to attempt direct sales. For example, she could approach the local Senior Citizens Center (not a resident facility where all meals are provided to residents, but rather a day program that offers older people daily activities). She would offfer to demonstrate several recipes and to autograph and sell books. Any number of groups, especially those catering to large numbers of single people of all ages, could be approached.

Book #3. *The Parents' Basic Medicine Chest*

This book geared to the needs of parents, providing information and advice from a pharamacist-cum-author, has equally widespread potential. Local PTAs could be targeted, as could any group where large numbers of parents attend meetings. Any charitable or religiously affiliated organization would probably be interested in hearing what this author suggests.

Book #4. *Tracing Your Irish Heritage*

This book, for amateur genealogists, could be promoted by talks to Irish-American organizations.

Book #5. *How Safe Is Your Home?*

This policeman-author—an expert on home security—would also probably be of interest to large numbers of diverse peoples. He could speak almost anywhere, offering advice and tips to lecture attendees. And, obviously, areas experiencing higher burglary rates would be especially receptive.

In each of the previous examples, the motif is using the talk as a fulcrum, to elicit audience interest in the book. And sometimes the "talk" does not have to be one in the conventional sense.

A student in one of my courses wrote on the occult. She wanted to specifically publicize her books on ghosts. As she was already conducting bus tours to buildings in her area where ghosts were known to "hang out," I pointed out that she had a built-in audience. Further, if local bookstores were not willing to stock her book to coincide with the bus tours to their town, she should consider purchasing and then selling her books on the bus.

How to Create Bookstore Sales Tied into Other Store Appearances . . . .

To enlist the support of local bookstores when you have set up non-bookstore appearances, inform bookstores near where you *are* appearing of your upcoming appearance. Tell them that you will be referring customers to them to purchase your book. Get permission from the place you're appearing to place a copy of your book—along with your announcement or invitational poster—in their window with a card saying something like: "Books Available at:" inserting name of bookstore(s) you've contacted.

If there are no local bookstores that stock your book, or one cannot be convinced to do so to tie into your talk, and your publisher refuses to ship books to the non-bookstore on consignment, you would then have to purchase a quantity of your book to sell on your own. If this is the case, financial arrangements—as to who would take what percentage of book sales—could be worked out between you and the owner of the store at which you're appearing.

Nontraditional Book Selling

Here are several examples of nontraditional ways that authors could promote and sell their books outside of the normal bookstore channels.

Example #1. For a book on fishing, the author approaches a store in his community that sells fishing gear and offers to autograph and sell books at this store. He would create window posters—announcing his visit and inviting the public to stop in. These posters would be displayed in the store window for several days in advance of this appearance to draw attention to his upcoming visit. (For details on how to create inexpensive and easy-to-make posters, refer to page 94.)

In this case, as the store regularly runs local newpaper and radio ads, they might decide to announce this event in their ads. The author knows that his publisher—as is the case in most such instances—would not underwrite the costs of local advertisements. He would be prepared, therefore, working in conjuction with the store personnel, to create his own publicity, mainly in the form of a news release announcing his appearance. This would be sent to all local media.

Example #2. This is a fairly expensive, heavily illustrated, backlist book (one that had been out for some time) whose subject is antique military uniforms. Knowing of an antique shop in a town near to his that often sells this type of antique garment, the author approaches the shop's owner and suggests their doing an in-store event themed around the book. Hypothetically, this store owner likes the idea so much that he includes an announcement of it in his mailing to customers. Again, advance publicity—in the form of a news release—announcing this appearance would be sent to all local media.

Example #3. An author of a book on graphology queries her local stationery store on the idea of a handwriting analysis session tied into a book autographing. Where better to discuss handwriting than at an establishment that sells writing instruments? Here again, advance publicity — in the form of window posters and news releases to local media — would be important.

Example #4. For a book on the lore and legends of gemstones, this author queries the owners of a local jewelry store and asks if they would like her to give a brief talk to their customers. The store owners balk at the idea, concerned that the author will disrupt sales activity, so she suggests holding this session after their store hours.

Important Reminder

If you are interested in undertaking this type of promotional activity for a forthcoming (or just published) book, it is vital not to begin approaching businesses until you know for certain your publisher will have books ready to be shipped to stores that will offer it for sale. You only want to approach a store when you are certain bound books will be available for shipment.

For new books, make initial contact with the store several months ahead of time, but don't set a firm date for your appearance until you are 100 percent certain books will be ready for shipment.

Magazine Writers and the Public Appearance . . . .

If you write for periodicals, you're not concerned with using public speaking engagements to sell a book, but you, too, can use public speaking engagements to enhance your reputation. And realize that you never know who is in your audience!

Here are some examples of how writers could create in-person appearances:

• If you write travel articles, you can approach a local travel agent and suggest the agency sponsor a talk on a geographic area you're familiar with that is a popular travel destination.

• If you write on cookery you can contact a local housewares store (or housewares department at a major store — in the latter case you will probably have to speak to the Promotion or Special Projects Director) and offer to participate in any forthcoming promotional events they are planning. Tailor your talk — speak about a topic that relates to their theme and to your area of expertise. For example, stores will often center such promotions on timely or thematic subjects.

Large stores are likely to hold events such as:

- **Hawaii Week**
- **Bride's Month**
- **Revisiting the 1950s**
- **American Design**

- **Town Heritage Month**
- **Back to School Week**

Or you might learn about shorter (possibly one-day) promotions such as:

- **Creating Chocolate Desserts**
- **Designing with Bed Sheets**
- **Vegetarian Thanksgiving Recipes**
- **Antique Doll Collecting**

All of these events present *splendid* possibilities for writers' participation. We suggest that you use these concepts as stimuli for public appearances. And if stores (or departments in stores) in your area aren't presently holding this type of thematic promotion, why don't *you* suggest they do so! Develop a theme and prepare a brief written plan for the store outlining the type of event(s) — and participants. And, of course, include yourself!

The Thematic Promotion . . . .

Some time ago I created a well-received promotion for a major housewares store that I represented. I named the event Heart Smart Week, to tie into the annual — and very well publicized — American Heart Association observance of Heart Month. Primarily, we planned to promote the sale of no-stick cooking and baking pots and pans, assorted cooking implements, and other tabletop items. But to attract customers, in addition to having demonstrations and food tastings by manufacturers' representatives from the cookware and bakeware companies, I also lined up other people for personal appearances. We had men and women from local chapters of national weight control groups, from the local chapter of the American Heart Association, and other organizations. Talks and demonstrations ranged from Heart Smart Recipes to New Ways to Cook Without Fat and Picture Yourself Thin. (For this last one, we arranged the loan of a weight control club's "magic mirror" which presents viewers with a slimmer image.)

Our schedule was crowded with speakers, demonstrations, and events, and publicity was good in both the trade and consumer press. If time had permitted we would have had even more speakers, including writers who had expertise in the diet cookery field.

How You Might Proceed

If you have written articles on weather-proofing homes to maximize heating and cooling efficiency, why not contact your local utility company and offer to speak on the topic? The utility company could offer a free seminar at which you would be the guest speaker. In my area, one of the major utility companies regularly holds these free seminars, which are very well attended. Holding such seminars, as you might mention to your utility company, reflects well on the company. And it offers writer/speakers a terrific opportunity to meet people.

Whatever type of article writing you do, there is bound to be someone interested in hearing what you have to say! If you write articles on local history you might well be a likely speaker before any number of local organizations. But don't confine yourself to only historical associations. Be imaginative when seeking public speaking engagements. Even if you write what are sometimes called "think pieces"—that is, observations on the passing scene or such—you too can find an audience. People are often fascinated hearing how writers approach their craft and what the writing life is actually like.

Press Conferences . . . .

While you may think that you have news to impart that the media shouldn't miss and you decide to hold a press conference, let's look at some realities:

In major urban areas, press conferences are prolific. Media people are hard pressed to keep up with true newsmaking events, not to mention attending what, in many cases, are viewed by them as "non-events."

If you're considering holding a conference in a major urban area, you had better be absolutely certain you have a real story. Meaning that merely holding conferences in cities such as New York, Chicago, or Los Angeles to announce the publication of your article or your book is a waste of your time and money. So is holding a conference to merely rehash what you discuss in your article or book. Unless you have a real story to tell, the major market media simply won't turn out. In smaller cities and towns you might fare better. But even here, this might be a hard sell.

Here are some suggestions on how to hold a successful press conference:

• It's always best to first check on what other events or conferences you will be competing with. For example, if you know that the mayor of your town will be holding an important ceremony at the time you are considering for your conference, shift your time or date.

• Avoid weekend conferences, and schedule for the period of Tuesday through Thursday when media people are generally less pressured. (Some press conference planners favor Sundays, which is generally a slow news day.)

• Schedule your conference for early in the day to allow media people sufficient time to write, edit, and prepare their coverage of your conference.

• It's important that you select a convenient location. Or, choose a place where you know there are bound to be reporters at work. (If you've written an article calling for changes in the political process, and there is an election taking place, hold your conference at a major polling place where you know you are likely to encounter media people who are already "on assignment." Or, if you've written a newspaper series somehow related to income tax time, have your event at your area's largest post office on April 15th to capitalize on the many people who will be "covered" rushing into the post office to mail their tax returns.

• Write a media Tip Sheet and send it to media representatives a week before your conference. Always follow up with a phone call to see if they will, in fact, cover your conference. (We have provided samples of some of these in the Appendix.

• At your event, always have extra copies of your press kit with a specific news release — one that recaps your conference and provides information on what was discussed. Keep extra sets for use afterwards.

• If at all possible, have visuals at your conference so TV people have something interesting to film.

• Be prepared to take questions. If you provide snappy answers, you could be used as one of the attending radio or TV shows' "news bites." (A news bite is a brief extract used to entice people to tune in to a show.)

• At your conference — particularly if you anticipate a low media turn-out — do the following:

1. Use a *round* table seating arrangement.

2. Bring you own tape recorder — don't trust your memory. You want to have a good record of what transpires.

3. To keep a high level of activity, line someone up to take photographs and have freelance writers attend.

4. Don't forget to invite all cable TV people.

5. Finally, invite *all* local media, including the weekly newspapers.

• If you are determined to hold a conference and you know your topic may be a weak one for the media, refocus it. For example, if you have written a groundbreaking study on a health issue, rather than expect the general media to immediately see its value, tie it into a situation currently making news in your area. Or, if you have written about the destruction caused by drunk drivers, use local news stories to buttress your subject.

• If you are an expert on something — say, home repair rip offs — and you will address this subject, consider taking a controversial tack.

Your news release might start off:

WRITER JANE SHANE SAYS AMERICA'S HOMEOWNERS ARE BEING RIPPED OFF.

Then, have charts at your conference that will show how much money Americans spend annually to contract work out, *versus* what they could save undertaking do-it-yourself projects. And be ready to demonstrate easy, seasonally timely projects that homeowners can do.

Or, if your writing centers on how people can undertake simple legal transactions without an attorney, create a press release that addresses people's concerns.

You could head it:

WHY AMERICANS AVOID LAWYERS
and use the subhead:
WRITER BOB JONSON OUTLINES WAYS FOR AVERAGE PEOPLE TO BE THEIR OWN LAWYERS

Then make this the basis for a conference in which you discuss the facts of how increasing numbers of people are avoiding legal counsel today, and the consequences of their doing so. You could also cite instances of local people who eschewed lawyers in undertaking simple processes such as divorces or the creation of wills.

Whatever your subject, you must find a way to convince the media it's worth their time to cover your conference.

TIP: Always make certain to send local, or nearby, branch offices of the two major wire services, UPI (United Press International) and AP (Associated Press) copies of your press release. Address your release to the Day Book Editor. If they deem it sufficiently interesting it might be added to their Day Book, which lists events that will take place on a given day, transmitted early each morning to their subscribers (newspapers, some magazines, and radio and TV shows).

If you do this early in the morning on the day of your conference always follow up to verify receipt of your press release. Either call the wire service offices or one of your local media outlets (such as your local television station's newsroom — ask for the Assignment Desk Editor or Producer). As this is a courtesy on their part, politely ask if they could please check to see *if* your conference has been included in the Day Book. Doing so will give you a better idea of the type of press coverage you might anticipate at your conference. Once you know what type of advance coverage your event has been given, you can then move into action. If need be, you can quickly contact your area media to see if they will, in fact, be covering your event.

If you have a poor turnout, after the event be ready to immediately contact the media to impart what took place. If you have what you honestly feel is "hard news" then it's acceptable to *call* the local media. ("Hard news" might, for instance, be that you've written a major political expose in a local paper, or an announcement that your book was nominated for a Pulitzer Prize.) Conversely, if you have other, less pressing news to share, then do use your extra press kits.

In this instance you might also want to add a special — and very succinct — cover letter, highlighting what took place at your event.

The Bookstore Autographing Party — Truth and Consequences . . . .

This section will bring you down to earth once again, this time on the subject of autographing parties.

While gratifying to the ego, the truth is, in most cases the time and effort you'll expend to set up this type of promotional event might better be spent on other types of publicity activities described in this book. Realizing, though, that a book signing is considered one of the "perks" of the writing life, we'll simply point out some of the drawbacks, and follow with some hints to making an autograph session as profitable as you can.

Chain Store or Independent?

Today many of America's bookstores are branches of large chains, with decisions for most promotional activities emanating from headquarters far removed from each outlet, so it is usually quite difficult to set up bookstore autographing sessions. It's not crass monetary considerations alone that make this the case, for not only are these events generally not profitable — often they are merely customer distractions! The truth is that, in many instances, it's not worth the publishers' and the bookstore personnel's effort, nor is it probably worth much of your energy, to attempt to set up this type of appearance.

While you might fare better with owner-operators of local bookshops, it is the rare shop owner willing, or able, to effectively undertake these events. (In many cases the independent store owners might prefer to work with proven "winners" — that is, established writers who have a large and dependable following.)

Fern Edison and Jane Heller suggest in "How to Conduct a Successful Authograph Session" (*Fiction Writers Magazine,* Spring 1988) that to choose a site you look for a local bookstore that stocks your books and has a regular, dependable clientele. (Authors in larger cities, they suggest, may want to drive to a suburban bookstore that has a "local flavor and where you'd be given more attention.")

When should you approach stores regarding an autograph session? According to Edison and Heller:

> If you're a veteran author who has written several books, the best time to approach a bookstore is just before the publication of your latest title. Interest in you will be at its peak then. If you're a first-time author, you'll most likely have to approach a store where you've been known as a customer. Just inform the store manager . . . that you'd like to help them sell copies of your book.

TIP: Make sure the store has ordered copies of your book *well in advance.*

A successful autograph session is more than simply plunking yourself down at a table of books, Edison and Heller caution. It takes careful preparation and advance promotion.

You should do the following:

• Alert all local media a couple of weeks prior to the event. Send newspapers and radio/TV people your press kit with a separate cover letter explaining you'll be at _____ on _____. Emphasize that you expect a good turnout and that it should be a local event they'll want to cover. Follow up with a phone call.

• Ask the store to remind their customers during the weeks prior to the autographing of the exact date and time.

• Ask (gently) if the store will run an ad or two in the local newspaper announcing the autographing. If it's not in the store's budget, find out the cost and consider running the ads yourself.

• Have copies of your publicity kit on hand. Not only will the store's clientele enjoy learning more about you—but some . . . customer may turn out to be a TV producer checking (you) out for a possible guest spot!

The authors also suggest that you propose a mall promotion featuring your book. Many promotions are centered around the holidays. They suggest contacting the mall's promotion director or special events coordinator about these events well in advance, and finding a tie-in to the mall store featuring your book.

An article in the American Bookseller Association's *Bookseller* magazine reported on the successful book signings run by Ladds' Book Shop in Raleigh, North Carolina. The shop's owners reportedly spend many hours making these sessions successful, primarily by creating a well-organized plan and frequently working closely with publishing company personnel.

The owner's way of handling the physical aspects of the sessions are particularly instructive:

• He seats authors two-thirds of the way back in the store.

• Book displays are rearranged to ensure that traffic flows smoothly and that customers waiting in line have the opportunity to see display copies of all of the author's books.

• At autograph sessions where a large turnout is expected and occurs, several staff members "work the crowds," talking with customers and managing traffic in an inobtrusive manner.

An Unusual Bookstore Effort

An unusual effort made by a bookseller was described in a *Publishers Weekly* article (August 21, 1987) entitled: "Wedding Fair at Bookworks." This Albuquerque, New Mexico, bookstore took part in an unusual event. Along with other retailers and over twenty local entrepreneurs, Nancy Rutland of Book-works, staged a wedding fair featuring Martha Stewart, author of *Weddings*. (Ms. Stewart is well known, but this concept, if as well planned and executed, could work equally well for other authors.) The bookstore was located in a strip shopping center with a florist, a printer, and a store that sold the author's cookware. Caterers, musicians, interior designers, seamstresses, and other wedding specialists displayed their goods and services during the two-day event, but the highlight of the event was Ms. Stewart's appearance. And Ms. Rutland noted that even though the time the author had available to come to their city for the fair was not the best (it was on a Sunday and Monday) they proceeded.

Heavy advance publicity helped. An invitation describing all events was sent out, including a mailing to 500 people whose names were compiled from local newspaper engagement announcements and from wedding lists provided by the other participating specialists. The bookstore did a mailing to 3,000 people on the store's own list. This mailing included a reply form for those customers who wouldn't be able to come by but who wanted autographed copies of Ms. Stewart's book. Crown, the publisher, helped—handling the publicity, contacting newspapers and radio and TV stations. They sent press kits to their own contacts and to those the bookstore suggested.

The store owner personally contacted the food, fashion, and entertainment section editors of the major newspapers in her town. She sent her own press releases out, and to increase the chances of her material being used, she included a reproducible book jacket and photos of author Stewart. Her hard work paid off. Both Albuquerque newspapers ran her story. Ms. Stewart was interviewed on radio. (TV presented scheduling problems and, therefore, wasn't possible.) Other promotional efforts ensued and Ms. Rutland reports that people were lined up from the counter to the front door long before the author arrived. They estimated selling up to 150 copies of *Weddings* and a total of 75 of the author's other books.

Exceptions to the "Rule"?

Outside of celebrities, one exception to the autograph session might be the genre author, someone who writes romance, science fiction, Westerns, or other category fiction. If you're a genre author you will probably find Janelle Taylor's experiences interesting. Taylor is the author of seventeen books, one of which was a *New York Times* best-seller. She is also the winner of several awards in the romance field.

In an article titled: "How To Have A Successful and Exhilarating Autograph Party" in the *Romance Writers' Report*, she shares the secrets of her success on the autograph circuit:

> If you go to the time and trouble to do autographings—they will be time consuming and troublesome, especially when a deadline looms—go to the time, trouble, and *expense* [Ms. Taylor's emphasis, not ours] to make

them successful and fun, especially, for your readers and the book-stores. . . .

Ms. Taylor suggests contacting local writers groups; given the focus of her writing, she specifically suggests Romance Writers of America members. She also points to the importance of sending press kits and announcements to all the local media. And she mentions how you should—if your signing will be in your hometown—also use your high school reunion list to send out invitations to old friends, classmates, and teachers.

Micki Perry suggests that genre writers can have fun with their autograph sessions:

> Make your inscriptions special, memorable—find out something about the person and put it in the inscription. You'll have a friend for life!
>
> Always look and act like a professional (Mystery writers might wear a trench coat, etc. for an added touch of pizzazz—look what pink feathers did for Barbara Cartland!) Your readers have an idea of what you're like, so don't let them down!

The Best-Laid Plans . . .

Don't be disappointed, though, if, even with advance planning, your autograph session doesn't "draw" as you'd hoped.

At one signing in what promised to be a very good bookstore—heavily trafficked and in an excellent urban location—even with the personal planning attention of the author and the store's owner/operator, the event turned out a fiasco. The author sat in embarrassed silence and isolation for many hours. The only time anyone approached her was when a customer asked if the store had a public restroom!

My personal experiences on the autograph "circuit" were uneven. As the author of a favorably reviewed cookbook, *Going Bananas,* I appeared for a signing at a chain bookstore in a busy mall. Yet even with intense advance publicity, sales didn't meet our expectations. Although I was recognized and greeted, sales weren't huge—I am not a major celebrity. Several people did call the store. They had seen me earlier in the day on a top-rated local television show, and said that they wanted to ask me "important questions." (These were either nonsensical or bore no relationship to my bookstore appearance. One man called to say how upset he was that his local market sold bananas that were too green or almost rotten. He wanted me to somehow intercede!

I quickly learned that even though all augured well, and my bookstore session looked promising, it was no guarantee of selling books. Mine had received salutary, widespread, national consumer review coverage. And other authors of worthy books have experienced uneven results. Why?

In days gone by, before the era of mass communications, actually meeting a writer of any kind was a big event in most people's lives. Then, the bookstore autographing was an excellent way to sell books. Today, with the proliferation of radio and television talk shows and the large number of celebrities out on tour meeting the public, the average midlist author stands little chance of attracting much attention. Or, more to the point, of selling large numbers of books.

While meeting our public feeds our egos, if you're going the book signing route you had better have a tough hide.

Offbeat Approaches for Magazine Writers

While bookstore people (and the general public) are familiar with the concept of author autographing parties, if you live in a small town or city, you might consider approaching the owner of the largest newspaper and magazine store about a similar promotion for your articles.

If you go in person, however, make certain you visit at an appropriate time. In other words, do not hope to discuss your idea when you see the storekeeper is busy taking in stock or when it is crowded with customers.

When you speak to the store owner, explain that while autographing parties are not ordinarily done for magazine writers, you thought it might generate a lot of trafffic and interest if you were to autograph copies of the magazine containing your article. If the store owner has the space for you to do so, offer to conduct a question and answer session on the subject of your article. Explaining your expertise in the field may encourage the store owner's interest. To make your idea even more attractive, say you would be willing to do the advance publicity. Tell the store owner that you would provide them with a poster for their window announcing the event if this is something they cannot (or do not want to) do. You can, of course, turn to a professional sign maker, or a graphic artist to create a sign or poster for you. If, however, you don't wish to incur this expense, you can create your own professional quality sign or poster at modest cost—even if you're not artistically inclined. Art supply stores sell packages of what is known as "press-on type" that you can use to create attractive posters.

> TIP: **At the art supply store, buy brightly colored, sturdy poster board. Paste the magazine's name, cut from the cover of a recent issue, onto your poster. Then using the press on type, add all the information about your appearance.**

Your announcement might read something like this:

Come Meet Jane Jones Here At UBC Magazine/Newstore, on Saturday, January 28th from 11 A.M. to 2 P.M., when she'll discuss her February *Woman's World* magazine article, "Our Love Affair With Chocolate: A Sweet History." Ms. Jones will take your questions. **FREE** samples of chocolates will be given out.

Once you have set up this appearance, create a news release about the event— see if the store will provide you with its own letterhead for this release. Send this release out two weeks or, at the very least, ten working days ahead of time to all the local media in your area. (You will, of course, have already researched who to contact at each place.) To encourage coverage of the event, send this news release to each Assignment Desk Editor of local TV stations. And send it to the appropriate person at any radio show in your area that you know assigns reporters to cover this type of local event. If there are no radio shows in your area that do live coverage of this kind, send your release to the producer of the morning and evening "drive time" shows or to any show that seems a likely bet. Also send the news release to the City Desk Editors at newspapers in larger cities, or Managing Editors of newspapers in smaller towns.

If you were the writer of this chocolate-themed article, and the newsstand/ magazine dealer you approach turned you down, try approaching a local candy shop offering to speak in connection with the publication of your article. Here you would not autograph magazines (although you would definitely have several on display), but you would talk about your subject and take customers' questions. If they would want, the store personnel could give out free samples or they could demonstrate how they dip chocolates.

You would do the same type of publicity as outlined previously for the maga- zine dealer. If there are no candy shops for you to try, you could approach a local bakery. Try to interest them in not only having you as a guest speaker but in holding a Chocolate Day the day of your appearance. (That is, ask if they'd be willing to feature several different chocolate items for sale on that day.)

The candy shop or bakery might want to advertise this event, which is even better for you. All the advertising will support and broaden the impact of your publicity program.

8

Working with TV and Radio

Chapter Four, on Protocol and Etiquette, stressed the importance of a polite and professional manner in all your dealings with editors. It's perhaps even more crucial in dealing with the electronic media, since competition for air time is fierce.

A *Publishers Weekly* article entitled "Author Tours: The Bloom is Off the Rose," quoted a producer of a major market morning talk show who estimated that the show receives at least one hundred mailings per day, all offering guests for the program. A segment producer for "Live at Five," a WNBC television news show in New York, once told a publicist that hers was the 1,845th call of the day!

For the novice, dealing with the electronic media can be a frustrating experience. There are times when you may think these people are incredibly rude. But please understand how beleaguered most television and radio people are. Knowing how *not* to work with them is critical.

Writer's Golden Rules . . . .

I'll list here what I call my Writer's Golden Rules of Working with the Media. They're good to follow in working with print media as well.

Golden Rule #1. Thou shalt never appear uninvited, sans *appointment, at a media person's office.*

In other words, no matter how anxious you are to arrange an interview, never, ever just drop in, hoping to see a contact person. If, for example, you are in a city far removed from your hometown, it is a bad idea to arrive at a radio or TV station's offices hoping to see someone. While occasionally you might gain entry and actually get to see the person you hoped to meet, more often than not, even such "luck" can boomerang. You don't want to be remembered as unprofessional, or a pushy, overly aggressive writer!

(In very small towns this "rule" might not apply. And media people may not be put off by your appearing in person.)

Golden Rule #2. If you are new to publicity, thou shalt never attempt to sell yourself to media — particularly major national media — via phone, without first having sent written material.

While it is definitely all right to use the phone to *follow up* what you had previously sent, do not attempt to interest media in interviewing you by calling and "cold selling." The art of the cold call and sell is a finely honed skill that professional public relations practitioners spend years perfecting. Again, while this type of outreach might be acceptable in small towns, in cities of any size it is not a good idea to descend on people via phone and expect a fair hearing.

Golden Rule #3. Thou shalt never ask to be included after *you have read, heard on radio, or seen on television a* completed *story or series on a similar or related subject.*

It's useless to try to convince media people who have *finished* a particular story or series to broaden their coverage to include your work. You can, if you're not certain if the subject coverage or a series is on-going, contact the medium and query them. But, we repeat, it is absolutely a waste of time to try to obtain media coverage as part of the story being reported *after* a broadcast, an article, or a series has appeared.

We'll be getting into a lot of specifics for TV and radio in the pages that follow, but there are a few more hints to be given here that will make your experience go smoothly and have the greatest impact.

• Unless the show you're targeting airs only on the weekend, try to schedule your media appearances for midweek. Weekends are usually the least desirable times for media interviews.

• Always confirm the details of your interview in writing (see Confirmation Slip, Appendix 2) and keep a photocopy.

• Always take along extra copies of your press kit and all relevant materials, including a copy of the books or articles you will be discussing.

After Your Appearance

While sending an interviewer a gift as a "thank you" is generally frowned upon, there is absolutely no reason that you shouldn't send a personal thank-you note. It will go a long way in making an impression. Too few people take the time to do this, and, if you are working on your own, this is a courteous gesture you shouldn't overlook.

Understanding the World of Television . . . .

Many writers may feel they haven't hit the big time unless they've been on television. But understand that merely appearing on television is no guarantee of success. One man, who has written several books and edited others, has had four appearances on a major, nationally broadcast morning talk show. Yet he reports these appearances have had little effect on the sales of any of his books. His area of expertise is in the health field and, by and large, such topics don't produce the sales that other books have when their authors are interviewed on major shows. (This writer's subjects were on serious health concerns. TV appearances usually improve sales of diet books or "breakthrough"-type books on health, diet or fitness.)

Television isn't for everyone, and it's erroneous to think you can't have an effective publicity effort without it. But it's an enormously powerful and exciting medium. Armed with the knowledge in the pages that follow, even a novice shouldn't be afraid to try it.

Setting Up Television Interviews

If you are working on your own, without a personal publicist or a magazine or book company's publicity person, ask yourself these questions before you consider approaching television shows:

• Do I have a story to tell, one that is *(a)* of general interest and *(b)* one that can be enhanced with visual materials? If so, do I have, or can I obtain, these visual aids? (You cannot expect television shows to provide such material.)

• Do I have a serious subject to discuss that lends itself to special-interest talk shows?

• If you answered yes to the previous question, ask yourself: Can I prove to the show's contact person that I am an expert in my field?

• Are there local news or other television shows in my locality that feature author interviews? (Or, are you able to travel to appear on such shows in other cities?)

• Is my subject timely? (Or controversial?)

• Can I discuss my subject in a lively and interesting manner?

• Am I able to present my subject succinctly? (Unlike radio, where you'll sometimes be given a good deal of time to speak, on television you should be prepared to complete your reply to the interviewer's questions in ten to thirty seconds.)

• Do I need any props, and if so, can I bring them to the show? (For example, if your subject is archery, don't expect the show to supply your equipment. Later in this chapter we'll discuss a prototypical list of visuals, props, and suggested demonstrations that prospective guests should send with their television pitch.)

• If I have previously appeared on another television show do I have a good quality tape of that appearance? (Ask if the person you are speaking with would like to screen it prior to committing to booking you. Refer to it as your "demo tape." Naturally, you will only want the tape viewed if it shows you in your best possible light.)

• Have I left adequate time to secure bookings? (For major [nationally broadcast] shows, eight to ten weeks ahead of time is not too early. For other shows, such as locally broadcast ones, allow at least four weeks lead time.)

How to Secure Television Appearances and Work with Television People — An Expert Speaks

Some excellent rules of thumb on working with television shows are provided by Emily Boxer, Booking Editor for NBC-TV's "TODAY" Show. Her points will generally work well when approaching all television shows.

Writing good pitch letters can help you gain the "booker's" attention, Ms. Boxer points out. But writing one *without* quickly getting to the issues or subjects you would be prepared to talk about during an appearance is counterproductive. Ms. Boxer says that authors who expect that every book received will be read and evaluated individually are foolhardy. (Most media, especially the major television shows, receive thousands and thousands of books, letters, and press kits every month.) She counsels would-be guests to first watch the show and then, if their book lends itself to the show's format, to write a brief, well-thought-out pitch letter *exactly* outlining the topics they would be prepared to discuss should they be booked on the show.

In other words, a vague letter stating you have written a "controversial" book *without* stating what you say in your book is inadvisable. If you believe that this type of "teaser" letter will make the television people anxious to read your "exciting" book, you are dead wrong! You must be able to concisely present the issues you feel you could discuss if you were booked onto the show.

Ms. Boxer has some thoughts for those who write magazine articles and would like to appear on "TODAY" concurrent with a particular article. (Here again, what applies to the "TODAY" Show probably does so for most other television shows.) Given the short "shelf life" of monthly magazines, she points out, you must work far ahead of time. Just as soon as you know that your article is scheduled for a particular month's issue is not too soon to try to set an appearance to *coincide* with the magazine's newsstand availability. Obviously, any article that will be discussed should be readily available to the public. (For nationally aired shows, the magazine should be sold throughout the U.S.) Unlike books which (optimistically) last a bit longer, magazine articles must be discussed just when they are on the newsstands.

Even More Questions

If your pitch is successful (or if your publisher has arranged for you to appear on a television show, or a television show contacts you directly after reading about you or hearing or seeing you on another show), there are things you will want to know, so be prepared to raise issues either with your publisher's publicist who has set up your appearance, or with the show's contact person.

Ask some or all of the following questions:

- How long will my appearance last?

- What is the show's format? (Will it be a one-on-one interview or will I be appearing as part of a panel? Will my segment be a straight interview or will I be expected to do a demonstration of some kind?)

- Will someone be available to do my makeup? (More about this later.)

- Should I bring visual materials? (Be prepared to discuss the type of material you have in mind. You should know ahead of time what you will be able to bring to television interviews. Don't offer anything you cannot actually produce.)

- Will the segment be taped for later use or aired live, and will the broadcast originate from the studio or another location?

About Visuals . . . .

The type of "visuals" you bring might be similar to the following examples:

- If you have written an article or book on Native American life on the American Plains in the late 19th century, you could offer to bring large color reproductions of paintings that depict that time and place.

- To enhance your discussion of a magazine article about an international surfboarding competition in Hawaii, you would offer to provide 35mm transparencies of earlier years' events. (Most often, television shows can use 35mm color transparencies, but always check first.)

- If yours is a novel that concentrates heavily on your geographic region, you could offer to bring line drawings (in full-color) showing your region at varied time periods.

- For a book discussing a major golfer's career, bring a videotape — in VHS format — of this person in tournament play.

> **TIP:** **VHS, not Beta, is the tape format generally preferred on most television shows.**

All in all, it is important that when you think of doing television, you remember it's a visual medium. Unless your topic absolutely doesn't lend itself to *any* graphic representations, or the show you are pitching never uses such visuals, you almost certainly won't be asked to appear if you aren't prepared to offer this material. In television parlance, "talking heads" (one or two or more persons sitting and talking) is definitely not good television. However, do realize that there are some shows that prefer serious discussions and do not require, or want, any visual aids. It's best to know the format of the shows you are speaking with.

> **TIP:** **If you are booked for an appearance that involves visuals, call the contact person one week before your appearance to discuss them. This will help them plan your appearance. Use a Visuals Sheet (examples on page 101 and 102) to make clear what you will be bringing.**

If you're doing a demonstration, ask if you should bring your own props. If, for instance, you've written a cookbook, or a book about a handicraft, and will want to demonstrate a recipe or a craft, verify what *you* should bring versus what

• **SHEET LISTING YOUR VISUALS-PROPS & DEMONSTRATIONS, #1** •

THE TRAVELER'S BEST FRIEND, by Joan Cheney

Partial List: Visuals/Props/Demonstrations.

(*Note:* These can be combined depending upon your focus or the type of segment.)

PROPS to be supplied by the guest:

• Varied sizes/types of luggage (carry-on bags, totes, hard- and/or soft-sided valises),

• Items of men's, women's, children's clothing (also toiletries and notions),

• Offbeat and helpful items to pack for a trip.

PROPS (to be supplied by the show, please have the following available):

• A large table on which to place luggage,

• A garment rack to hold items of clothing,

• A table to hold other items to be packed.

DEMONSTRATIONS:

• How *not* to pack for a trip. (Guest will open an incorrectly packed bag and explain how to overcome these problems.)

• Point by point information/demonstration on packing for trips by plane, car, bus, or train.

• Packing special items such as bulky clothing or "change of climate" outfits. Also, children's packing needs.

• How to minimize the load and underpack for a trip (showing women how to color-coordinate outfits for maximum use).

• SHEET LISTING YOUR VISUALS-PROPS & DEMONSTRATIONS, #2 •

SAN FRANCISCO'S BEST RESTAURANTS, by John Martin
Partial List: Visuals/Props/Demonstration possibilities

(*Note:* These can be combined depending upon your focus or the type of segment. Please note that seasonal recipes can be demonstrated only at a relevant time of the year.)

VISUAL to be supplied by John Martin:

• 35mm color transparencies and/or 8 × 10 inch color photos (black matte board mounted) of the interiors of five to eight Bay area restaurants included in the book.

• 35mm color transparencies and/or 8 × 10 inch color photos (black matte board mounted) of four to eight items from menus of restaurants in the Bay area included in book.

DEMONSTRATION possibilities to be arranged by John Martin:

Chefs and/or representatives from those restaurants mentioned in book will be available to do as follows:

• Bring finished recipes drawn from their menu items,

• Create, on-air, recipes drawn from their menu items,

• Create, on-air, the most popular mixed (alcoholic) beverages served at their place,

• Create seasonal dishes drawn from their special (holiday) menus (chef from Ernie's will demonstrate Christmas foods and drinks; owner of Chinatown's "Jade Dragon" will demonstrate how to re-create their Chinese New Year "Dim Sum").

SUGGESTED LEAD-IN TAPE (to be supplied by your show):
• Footage shot at restaurants that we will discuss—interior/exterior shots,

• Footage showing restaurant's kitchen (and chefs, sous chefs, cooks, preparing items; bar; dining rooms; finished dishes drawn from menu offerings).

the station can provide. (Usually, except for the major national shows, you should be prepared to bring all your own materials. In some cases this even means, for instance, you should be prepared to bring your own foodstuffs and a means of cooking or heating your recipes.)

If the show is one you do not receive in your area, or if you will be traveling to appear on a show with which you are totally unfamiliar, ask the show's contact person about the show's format and what will be expected of you. In other words, will you be asked to sit with your interviewer(s) to discuss your topic, or will you be expected to do some activity that relates to your subject? If you've written an article or a book on gardening, will you be asked to stand at a table and demonstrate how to pot indoor plants for transfer to one's garden? Or, if you are being presented as the writer-expert on packing a suitcase for international travel, will you be asked to demonstrate this skill?

Determine if the contact person wants to conduct your interview at a location removed from their studios. Sometimes, especially on interview segments of news shows, or in discusssing topics that lend themselves to what are called "remotes" (that is, off site), television shows will conduct interviews or discussions outside of their studios. These are either taped or broadcast live.

If a remote is planned to be aired from your home or office, you'll want to be prepared for it.

If You're Part of a Panel . . . .

A writer who is asked to do a panel or multi-guest appearance can often encounter problems. Blanche Brann, former publicity director of the Henry Holt Company, addressing the Center for Communication on the subject of book publicity and promotion, provided a graphic example of just such a problem:

> I convinced "Good Morning America" to do a segment on a new young novelist. I pitched [her], which is not just one phone call to the programmer and a personal rave for an enchanting new novel. It is a lot of phone calls back and forth. They finally booked [her]. A few days later they called and said that they could get Tama Janowitz as well. They wanted to air Tama Janowitz and [our novelist] together. We hemmed and we hawed, we pleaded and we begged and, finally, I got the distinct impression that we were going to lose the segment to Tama Janowitz. She had a rock-and-roll book video and we didn't. Instead of giving up the segment, we agreed to do them together. Tama Janowitz and [our author] who is warm, intelligent, and lovely. The effect was not one that I had hoped for. I was extremely embarrassed for [our author.] She and Tama were asked the same provocative question: Why do you write books? Tama responded in a trendy, bubbly way, talking about sales. [Our author's] answer was that she hoped to create something that would last, not necessarily on a book shelf but in the memory of a reader.

However meritorious the unnamed Holt novelist's work was, overshadowed by the high-power personality of author Janowitz, she fared poorly.

As with "solo" appearances, if you're going to appear with one or more guests, it helps if you rehearse in advance questions your host may ask. If someone in the group monopolizes the conversation, try what I call "appropriate assertiveness." Politely interject, if need be, to capture your share of air time. All's fair in love and television!

Special Tips for Book Authors . . . .

If you will be appearing on television promoting a book, it is an excellent idea to not only bring along several copies, but to do the following: Purchase a sturdy, matte (dull) finish blackboard, sized at least 8 × 10 inches and paste (only) the front cover of your book on this board. Tell the show's contact person ahead of time that you will be bringing this so if they need to use it before or during your appearance, the camera can move to it and shoot it for broadcast. If you will be bringing artwork from your book that can be shown on the program, advise the contact person you have this and have it ready for their on-camera use. (As noted above, this should be pasted onto matte finish blackboard.)

Bring several 3 × 5 inch cards to give to your interviewer and to also leave with the show's producer and/or contact person and also with whoever takes viewers' calls. Many times viewers catch the end or only a piece of an interview and want to track down a book. Providing this information card makes it much simpler and more likely that viewers will be given this information.

If you will be promoting a book, try to find out from your publisher where in the program's viewing area your books are for sale. As this is often difficult for a publisher to determine (books are sold to book wholesalers and distributors, meaning the publisher often has little idea which bookstore has purchased what book), try to find out if your publisher has sold your book to a company that handles *consumer's* book orders, such as Book Call or DBS Express (both mentioned in Chapter Ten).

Once you know where people can find your book, you can announce it. A good way to do this, without alienating any retailer who might stock your book unbeknownst to you, would be to say, "My book is available at bookstores nationally, and also through [giving the name and phone number of any phone-in book ordering service that stocks it.]"

Just a postscript regarding TV appearances and your publisher: The author who arranges TV appearances and neglects to advise his or her publisher well in advance is undercutting this exposure. It's vital to inform your publisher if you are to be on TV. And four to eight weeks ahead of time isn't too soon. (The publisher needs the time to inform their sales reps and wholesalers, jobbers, and retailers.)

Appearances Count . . . .

Unlike doing radio show interviews, on which one's physical appearance does not count, on television you can sometimes quite literally be done in by your looks. If, for example, you write on diet and weight control but you've not yet conquered your personal Battle of the Bulge, avoid television. Or if you write on contemporary men's fashions, but refuse to wear anything but sweatshirts, cut-off jeans, and old running shoes, don't try for a guest appearance as an arbiter of men's fashions.

There are a few tricks to appearing relaxed and confident in front of the camera. You'll master them with a little practice.

Dress for (TV) Success

The camera does tend to add weight, so pay attention to the clothing that you wear. If you are overweight, dress to hide as much avoirdupois as you can. These days, women can find all types of outfits that will accomplish this. For men, a well-cut outfit will help.

Dress "real" and dress down! That doesn't mean you should be attired like a hobo. What we do suggest is that, unless you are a recognized "glamour girl" or guy, or a celebrity, wear traditional street clothing.

Unique or special outfits are fine if they tie into your avocation. If you're a soldier of fortune-cum-writer and always wear military clothing, that's okay, or if you're a writer and auto mechanic and will be doing on-air demonstrations of your work, your coveralls will be fine. But extreme outfits are out.

Women should eschew plunging necklines, overdone evening wear, extreme hair styles *a la Cher,* or loads of clanking jewelry (which itself presents sound problems). Vivid colors should also be avoided. Red on television tends to "bleed" (i.e., blur at the edges). Choose soft tones and solids instead of overly bold, printed, or plaid materials. (If you're confused about this, tune into the morning news shows and see what the female anchor women favor.)

Men take note: A white shirt will not do. Choose a shirt in a soft tone. (Light blue is always a safe bet.) As to your suit color—if you'll be wearing a suit— bypass overly dark colors and opt for a medium-toned suit (tans, medium blues, and medium browns are good). If you'll be dressing in a sports jacket and slacks, realize that on television, bold, large plaids tend to make the wearer look heavier. It's always best to wear a plain suit or sports jacket and slacks duo and neat shirt and subdued print tie. Wear a long-sleeve shirt, allowing about an inch or so of your shirt cuff to extend out of the jacket sleeve. Your socks should be knee length. If you'll be seated, keep your jacket buttoned.

Finally, fellas, silly as it sounds, make certain your shoes have a nice shine. And, even if you must shave twice in one day, do it. The stubbly, unshaven look might have been fashionable on television stars for a time, but for the average guy, it's definitely out. And if you are as bald as the proverbial billiard ball, if you don't already own and can comfortably wear a good toupee, don't immediately rush out and invest in whatever you can get. Better to be natural than to sit nervously aware of what looks like an alien outgrowth atop your head.

A word to women about skirt lengths: If you know you'll be seated, remember to wear a skirt of a comfortable length. You definitely don't want to be seen constantly fidgeting to modestly keep your skirt down!

About the "laid back" look—even if you subscribe to Thoreau's dictum to beware of all enterprises that require new clothes—if all you own are message-imprinted T-shirts and faded jeans, unless your subject area makes it necessary for you to be so attired, and you have cleared it with the show's contact person beforehand, dress as we suggest. If you arrive for your appearance wearing a message-bearing T-shirt—especially one that is somehow "political"—you may likely be "uninvited" to appear.

> **TIP:** If you will be on tour, or traveling to appear on a TV show, it's always a good idea to carry along an all-purpose outfit that will not show wrinkles or creases. If you're flying, this outfit should be tucked into your *carry-on* baggage (to guard against lost luggage). Women should also always stow extra sets of simple costume jewelry in their carry-on bag, along with their makeup. Gentlemen should take along an extra shirt or two and an extra tie in their carry-on luggage.

Makeup

This is of particular interest to women, as television makeup is distinctly different from street makeup. For smaller market TV appearances, even if you are told there is someone to do your makeup, you might want to investigate having a professional teach you how to apply it if you are especially concerned about your appearance.

If you do your own, avoid frosted eyeshadow, or screamingly bright red or orange lipsticks for television. And unless professionally applied, lip gloss can present problems for the camera.

A word to men who tend to perspire: If the show won't be doing any makeup for you, a tiny amount of neutral facial talcum powder should absorb any moisture that beads up on your face. (This is common on the bridge of the nose, the forehead, cheekbones, and over the eyes.)

Speaking of eyes, if you wear glasses, this is not the time to rush out and invest in contact lenses. You *do,* however, want to invest in a good dental cleaning before your appearance. (We are presupposing that your smile doesn't show gaping spaces due to missing teeth.) In fact, before you launch any campaign that includes personal appearances, you really must consider the state of your teeth.

What to Expect at a TV Station . . . .

When they turn up for a television interview, writers are sometimes startled by the activities they encounter. (At small stations you might not experience what we describe here, but the adage about being forewarned makes sense in this context.)

There is usually a television crew at work on every show and you will probably find producers, directors, technicians of all kinds, lighting experts, sound people, writers, and others—all of whom might well show as much interest in *you* as in hearing the political views of the losing entrant at the state fair's hog calling contest. While you are probably terrifically excited by your appearance, often the show's crew can be nonchalant to the point of rude indifference. You simply must not take any of this personally. To crew members, you are just one of thousands of people they will encounter in their careers. In some cases, to lighten the pressure of their hectic jobs, you might even become the butt of their jokes. Again, you cannot take it personally. Also, do not be at all surprised if your interviewer hasn't the slightest idea who you are or why you are there! And, if you are appearing to promote your book, don't expect that the person conducting the interview will have read it. Though there are exceptions to this, quite often they simply don't have the time, or inclination, to take more than a cursory look at the book's jacket or cover a minute before you turn up on the set!

Keeping Your Cool

Besides knowing what to expect, you'll appear more relaxed if you follow a few simple suggestions before and during your appearance:

• Get to the station at least fifteen minutes ahead of the time you've been asked. Obvious as it sounds, always visit the restroom beforehand to comb your hair and attend to all other details.

• Ask if you could have a glass of tepid water at hand during your appearance to soothe your throat and calm you down.

• If you'll be seated during the interview—be you a man or woman—it's best to sit with knees together, feet on the floor. (Men sometimes find that crossing their legs also works well. But, only cross legs *at the knee,* not at the thigh or ankle.) Hands should be folded one over the other—never clasped—and placed in one's lap.

• Don't fret if you use gestures to emphasize your point. Should you be seated in a chair with armrests, it's okay to rest your elbows on them. However, *never* become so comfortable that you forget your image. You want to convey confidence and ease.

• Don't keep shifting and changing position when you are on camera or, for that matter, on the set. You never know when the camera will move to you. And while Johnny Carson can get away with pencil tapping, under no condition should you do anything of this kind. Foot tapping or jiggling is definitely out! If you know that you have a tendency to exhibit nervous mannerisms, rehearse relaxing ahead of time. Find a way to use body language to control these tendencies.

The Eyes Have It

As has been written, the eyes are indeed the window to the soul—and can be especially so on TV. Therefore, you do want to sit in front of a mirror and rehearse eye contact ahead of time. Or practice with someone who can tell you what you are conveying with your eyes. As anyone who has seen "60 Minutes" or other confrontational shows can attest, a shifty-eyed guest conveys a distinctly poor impression. And you don't want to be televised with perpetually downcast eyes either. For interviews in which you'll be seated speaking with the show's hostess or host, you always want to look directly at your interviewer. Playing to the camera is definitely out! *Always* look at your host, even if he or she is busy looking elsewhere—at copy or other papers, for instance.

Smile—You're Really on TV!

While it's perfectly natural and nice to smile in greeting, if you are sincerely amused, or at the end of your segment, to sit with a fixed smile on your face throughout your appearance might convince viewers that they've time-warped back to the "Howdy Doody Show"! In other words, don't bend over backwards to be "nice." Just relax and be yourself. In the same vein, don't waste precious air time with fulsome thank-yous. If your interviewer or host thanks you for being there, *briefly* respond with something like, "Thanks for asking me."

Later we'll discuss in depth what to say—and not to say—while being interviewed. The radio interview is, obviously, one place where your actions don't speak louder than words!

Working with Radio Shows . . . .

If the very mention of television appearances makes you break out in a cold sweat—take heart. There is still a place for you to try to publicize yourself. Radio shows of all kinds can provide writers with a terrrific opportunity to reach large numbers of people. (It's estimated that there are between 8,000 and 10,000 radio stations—AM, FM, commercial, and noncommercial outlets—in the U.S., compared to about 600 commercial television stations.)

Many magazine writers and authors have found that doing radio interviews has not only proven to be rewarding but has cured them of their fear of the electronic media.

Starting at the Beginning— How to Work With Radio People

First, if your story is one that will be viewed as "soft" (a feature story concept that's not of timely importance, hence not "hard news") then you must allow at least three to four weeks lead time to book yourself onto local shows. (You want to allow significantly more time to try for major market shows and the nationally aired radio shows. For these, five to eight weeks in advance is a safe bet.) While writers are sometimes called to "fill in" at the last minute when another guest backs out of a scheduled appearance, it is vital that you allow sufficient time to set up your appearance. After you are booked, the show or station's people have much work to do. Often—for a major segment—they have to conduct research, devise a format for your coverage, and integrate it with the show's other segments. Further, they have to arrange for studio time and the myriad details connected to your portion of the show.

Second, you must determine which radio shows that conduct interviews are possibilities for you. Initially, this is a simple task. You can tune into the shows listed in your local newspaper that indicate they do guest interviews. Or, if your newspaper doesn't carry that type of information, call the stations yourself to check if they have such shows. Barring that, you can approach your locally produced news shows.

We stress "locally produced" for the following reasons:

• If you have never done any radio interviews this would be the best place for you to start.

• If you begin with local shows you can easily build a tape library of your interviews which could be used as door openers at other radio (and possibly television) shows.

• There are generally more opportunities on local radio for writers than on the few — and highly competitive — nationally aired radio shows. (Don't forget the "local guy or girl" angle.)

• Doing local interviews means that — even if you do interest the producers of the national radio shows — you won't have to travel to New York, Los Angeles, or the like. (Although you might not have to anyway — see information on "phoners," page 112.)

If you cannot find any radio talk shows in your area, then you can always try the locally broadcast news shows or, if they exist, the local morning and/or evening "drive time" shows. The "drive time" show is one that will have a specific name (e.g., "Good Morning: Cincinnati" or "Bob White's Akron in the Afternoon Show.") These radio shows are referred to as "drive-time shows" because they are broadcast to coincide with the time people are driving to and from work. The drive time show is equivalent to television's prime time viewing hours.

In most markets, drive time or prime radio time is from approximately 6 A.M. to 9 A.M. and 3 P.M. to 7 P.M.

Don't Forget: When you are pitching local radio stations, hit on the local person angle. If you live or work in the area, be sure to stress that in your approach.

Breaking In in the Big City

If you who live in a large metropolitan area (known as a "major market"), you will probably find quite a few shows that do interviews, both live and taped. To help you focus on where you stand the best chance of securing a booking, again, try to listen to the shows. Or, read the newspaper listings that provide information on the type of guests each show interviews. If you find six or ten shows on your list of possibilities, you can mail your pitch to the top three or four shows. If your follow-up calls to these shows don't produce any nibbles, then send out another batch of letters.

TIP: **If you live in a large city and are readily available for last-minute bookings, add this to your pitch letters. Shows sometimes need guests who are available on short notice to fill in if a scheduled guest cancels.**

If you live in a city with several radio stations, and you aren't certain which would be the best station(s) to approach, your public library's reference shelf should have books to help you. Refer to either the directory called *National Radio Publicity Outlets* or the "Radio/TV" volume of *Working Press of the Nation*. (See our Resource Section for details on publishers.)

What you want to determine is the power—that is the "reach"—the radio station has. The "reach" of AM stations, for example, can range from as little as 100 watts to the huge 50,000 watt stations in the major cities. If you live in what is known as a "medium market," you'll probably find your radio stations put out between 1,000 and 5,000 watts.

FM Versus AM Stations

In many areas you will find that, by and large, FM stations are mainly devoted to music shows, save for an occasional government mandated public affairs show. The AM stations will most likely offer you more opportunities. If there are several AM stations for you to choose from, look for those with the most "power"—again, the widest geographic reach.

Be Precise in Your Pitching . . . .

The fastest way to determine who you should contact about securing a local radio booking is to call the station and ask the switchboard operator. If he or she doesn't know, then ask to speak with the various shows' producers. No matter how difficult it is to reach the producers, never call when shows are just about to go on the air—or when they are on the air.

You may find, especially at smaller stations, that the program you are interested in doesn't have a producer and that the show's hosts do their own production. In this case, ask the operator to verify the spelling of the hosts' names and to also verify if they receive their mail at the station or at another address. If the latter is the case, ask if the operator can give you this address. If you will be writing the station, this is a good time to ask the operator to confirm that you have the correct address.

It's possible you will immediately be put through to the show and will be asked what you are calling about. Simply ask the person answering the phone who you should contact about a booking. If you are pressed further about the nature of your call, unless you are comfortable in pitching yourself over the phone, at this point just introduce yourself and say that you will be mailing them material. You can politely explain that you wanted to know for future reference, as you'll be writing them with a specific interview suggestion. Or, if you have a current book and article or another angle you want to use, briefly state this.

What to Send Your Contact Person

When you have determined who you should contact, send your contact person a letter proposing yourself as an interviewee. In writing this letter, remember the "KISS" formula and keep it simple.

Immediately state the topic(s) you are proposing to discuss. And in your letter, refer to your "attached list of suggested topics." (On a separate sheet of paper, stapled to your letter, provide a list of suggested topics and questions that could be posed during an interview. We provide samples of such in this book.)

To buttress your case—proving you are a good interview prospect—send along your personal press kit.

Example of a Radio "Pitch" Letter

Here is a brief letter of the type we have just discussed. Remember to keep such letters as short as you can, no more than six to twelve sentences in all.

Dear _____:

Crash! Bang! Crunch! Two-year-old Baby Jones has just toddled into the room with the Christmas tree and is wreaking havoc!

In my syndicated *Parents Today* column I regularly offer a "tip sheet" on "baby proofing" a home.

I'd be happy to offer your listeners *specific* advice for doing just this for the upcoming holidays. Some of the things I'd include:
[Here the writer would go on with short, specific "samples" and also information on when, where, how the author can be reached.]

No Shows in Your Area?

If the station you have targeted for your pitch is in a small town, there are no radio talk shows, and you cannot find any local shows that do guest interviews, you can still try to secure radio appearances. What you want to do is to find out who is a pivotal person at the radio station, the person who is in a position to make a decision to set up an interview. Depending on your subject and your ability to sell it, and the fact that you are a local person, you might become the exception to the rule!

In small or medium-sized towns and cities, the station's receptionist will probably be able to fill you in. You might have to contact the person with the title of Radio Program Director or the like. In larger towns—and even here there are cases where talk shows or interview shows do not exist—you might have to contact the station's Public Affairs Director.

There are times, and places, where it seems that there are absolutely no radio shows for you to appear on. But, government regulations do mandate that every radio station allow a brief period of time each week for public affairs programming. Therefore, if you choose a station that you know has a good listenership and one that has public affairs shows on interesting issues, there might be a way to create an appearance. You can request free time to respond to an issue or issues raised on the station's public affairs show. But only if you have something worthwhile to say on the issue.

Another way to gain air time is via the on-air response to a station's editorial. Here again, you request free air time to respond to the station's stated position. The FCC requires that all stations airing editorials also include a statement along the following lines, "This station welcomes opposing views."

Let's suppose that a local station airs an editorial in support of the construction of a new road that will route traffic through the one remaining open "green" area in your community. And, let's assume you have either written a book on the history of your community, or that you write a real estate column for your local paper. If you are opposed to this road, this presents you with an excellent opportunity to request air time to "oppose" the station's support of the proposed road. When you secure such air time you will provide the station with your credentials. Ask that they introduce you using these. Give them a very brief written line or two. An introductory credential would read something like this:

"Jane White is the author of *The Greening of Our Town—A History of Our Town, U.S.A.*"

Or:

"Bob Smyth is the real estate columnist for the *Our Town Weekly Newspaper.*"

Phone-in Interviews . . . .

In contacting radio shows and stations you might learn that live, on-air interviews are never done, but that "phoners" (which is radio-speak for interviews conducted via the telephone) are possible. If this is the case, it makes life even simpler for you! Doing a phoner means you never have to leave the comfort of your home or office. Once you and the show's contact person have set up a time for your interview, all you need do is to stay near a phone. Generally, you will be called five or ten minutes before the interview to set up last-minute details for the live phoner.

Some shows prefer to do pre-taped phoners—which is even nicer for you. If you commit a verbal *faux pas,* this can usually be edited out of the tape prior to the show's airing.

Preparing for Radio Interviews . . . .

When you have set up a radio interview it is usually a good idea that shortly ahead of time, you *again* provide your contact person with the list of topics or questions that can be used during the interview. Doing this is especially important if you have written a book and you know that the person doing the interview has not read it prior to your interview—which is most often the case. (*Authors take note:* sometimes publisher's warehouses are painfully slow in sending out free "review copies" to the media—even when a booking has been secured.)

Tinker, Tailor

It might well be that, depending on the nature of the show, you have to tailor your topics accordingly. A public affairs show obviously uses different material from one that is broadcast as a segment of an all rock-and-roll music show.

This information must be put in writing by you. Don't expect your contact person has the time — or will take the time — to jot down information you call in to them.

Here are samples of the types of material you should give to your contact person.

- If you have a hard to pronounce name, you will want to provide phonetic pronunciation.

- If you will be discussing a book, provide its complete title, price, publisher's name, and where and how to get it. (If the title or subtitle of your book doesn't indicate the subject of your book, give a one-line description.)

- If you will be discussing an article you have written that has been published, or is about to be published, provide the name of the article and the name of the publication it will appear in, and the date of its newsstand availability.

Examples of Interview Materials

Here are some examples of the type of material writers might provide for radio interviews.

Example #1. For a book that is just about to be published:
Name: Joan Micylewski (*pronounced Mick Lew Ski*)
Author of: Bed & Breakfast Vacations in the St. Augustine Area, published by Jones & Jones, a $22.95 hardcover book, which is being published on March 15, 1991.

Suggested topics:

- Definition of the term "B&B."

- Why increasing numbers of travelers today are choosing to stay at B&Bs instead of at hotels or motels.

- The ten top St. Augustine area B&Bs.

- Discussion of the growth of the B&B industry throughout the U.S.

- Ten tips for listeners on selecting a B&B that suits their needs. This includes tips for people traveling with pets, those who seek a romantic weekend getaway, those who want to be near to public tennis courts or golf courses, etc.

Suggested questions:

- Why are people giving up the "guaranteed" comforts of a chain motel or hotel for the uncertainties they might encounter at a B&B?

• Do you personally visit and stay at all the places you list in your book? If so, how much of the time are you on the road?

• Do you pay to stay in each place?

• Do the B&B owners know you are a writer? Or, do they think you are just another guest?

Example #2. For a show set to air several days before the appearance of this writer's newspaper article:

Background: Bob Benson has written a newspaper article for a forthcoming issue of the "At Home" section of the *Durham Sunday Bulletin,* "Maintaining Rattan and Wicker Furniture."

Topics Mr. Benson can discuss:

• The growing interest in this "old time" type of furniture, which was popular years back and is again today. It's been estimated that today 70 percent of all outdoor furniture sold is made of wicker or rattan.

• The difference between porch furniture of yesterday and today.

• How today's busy person who buys wicker or rattan furniture can easily maintain it.

Suggested questions:

• What is the appeal of rattan or wicker furniture?

• Isn't this type of furniture very difficult to maintain?

• Is it a fact that antique pieces of this style of furniture have appreciated in value? Wasn't there a recent auction in our city of this type of furniture that produced record sales?

• How is today's rattan and wicker different from Grandma's porch furniture?

• Are more and more people using this type of furniture indoors?

Next, are some outlines for writers who have lined up an interview but who have no specific "news" to impart.

Example #3. For a writer who hopes to spread recognition of his name and to possibly interest an agent or a book publisher in his book in progress.

Background: Jim Taylor is a Galveston-based writer who has a multifaceted career—he is a part-time writer of general interest articles and is employed as a real estate salesperson at G&D Realty in Galveston.

Mr. Taylor is presently writing a historical novel set in ante bellum Galveston.

Jim Taylor has done extensive research on the architecture of Galveston. He has learned a great deal about the area, and about the legends surrounding some of the city's oldest homes.

Suggested questions:

• What is the legend of the "Good Gray Lady"—the friendly ghost who has been seen at the Silversmith Homestead?

• Is there any truth to the frightening tale of the headless horseman of Galveston Gulch?

• Where would we find the oldest continually occupied home in the city?

• Is it true that pirates once lived in an area home?

• Why is the mayor's residence of special interest to psychic researchers?

Example #4. For a "backlist," i.e., in-print book.
Background: Professor Irene Loomis teaches African-American History at Macon Junior College and has contributed articles to the magazine *African America*. She's written a book, *How Hollywood Portrayed African Americans: 1929-1969,* published by Macon University Press, $11.95 in paperback, available in bookstores.

Suggested topics:

• The stereotypical portrayal of African Americans by Hollywood in the so-called "Golden Years" of film making.

• The unknown stars of African-American Hollywood.

• Where are these people today? What happened to "name" African-American performers who worked in films in the period covered in her book?

• What lessons can we learn from these portrayals?

• What impact has the portrayal of African Americans had on the consciousness of all Americans?

How to Be a Good Radio Interviewee . . . .

Once you have set up a radio interview, take a cue from the Boy Scouts—*be prepared.*

Before you set off for your interview, do the following:

• If you will be discussing a specific book or a magazine article that you have written, take several copies along with you and be prepared—especially if it's a book of general interest or a novel—to be asked to leave it with the show's producer or host.

• Always arrive at least fifteen minutes ahead of air time.

• If your appearance is to publicize a specific book, also bring along at least three copies of a 3 × 5 inch card with clearly typed or printed information of the following kind: your book's complete title, your name, the name of your publisher, and your book's price and binding (hardcover or paperback).

At the bottom of your cards, indicate the show you are appearing on and the date of your appearance. (If you will be appearing in conjunction with a specific magazine article, do the same thing.)

As soon as you arrive at the station, if you don't personally see the receptionist at the front desk, ask the show's producer (or anyone who would know) if you may leave one of the cards with the phone operator. (Realize that at very small stations you might have to leave this with the show's interviewer, who wears many "hats.") You are providing this information to help answer any of the questions that listeners may have if they call in during or after your appearance. *Note to authors:* If your book is not being sold in bookstores and listeners can order the book by mail or via an 800 phone number, add this information to the 3 × 5 inch card.

It is important that *you* always keep the second card at hand so you can refer to it when you are being interviewed. The third copy is for the show's host or hostess. Give it to them along with your other material to facilitate the interview.

Unless you are a performer with many hours of professional experience, always rehearse ahead of time.

When you secure your booking ask your contact person how long a time period, generally speaking, you should prepare for. Once you know how long you'll be given, use your set of possible questions and rehearse your answers.

To do this, ask someone to read your prepared questions, and to also throw several in that *aren't* on your list. Ask that they also wander far from your topic and pose questions that are *totally* irrelevant so you can practice shifting back to your subject.

TIP: **In your rehearsal — and, if need be, at your actual interview — be prepared to reply to offbeat and hostile queries. In case you are asked odd questions, or are treated poorly, you should be ready to respond. You can always say something like, "That's interesting, but in my *Outdoor Sports* article I don't get into that area. It's not one I'm familiar with, as I am with . . ." and then segue into your topic. The idea is to comfortably buy time.**

Tape your mock (rehearsed) interview, so you can hear how you sound, and then, if need be, polish your act. Remember you want to keep your answers and comments crisp and succinct.

If you are unable to enlist the aid of anyone to act as your rehearsal partner, take both roles yourself.

Doing this will be time well spent. I have seen the results of being unprepared versus that of being ready for any type of situation. One nationally famous radio show host seems to delight in embarrassing his guests. I experienced this person-ally when he interviewed me along with the editor of a new magazine. He was unconcerned that he'd not read anything I had sent to him, nor had he the slightest idea who the other guest was, or why she was on his show. He arrived moments before we were to begin, wearing thick stage makeup and dramatic clothing. He spent the better part of the show posturing and poking fun at the title of my book and at the name of the editor's magazine. We subtly tried "capturing" the show back from his forced frivolity, frivolity which was at our expense. Being ready for such treatment, I was able to turn what could have been an embarrassing event into productive exposure.

Quiet: We're on the Air!

When you are actually on air, or taping for broadcast, here are some ground rules:

• Be prepared to have a sound engineer set your voice level to match the level of your interviewer's.

• Sit still; do not keep shifting in your seat.

• Speak in a normal, well-modulated tone of voice. Do not continually lower or raise your voice during the interview.

• Do not lean into the microphone or pull away from it.

• No matter how heated the discussion, never emphasize your state-ments by banging on the table.

• Keep your answers brief and to the point; do not ramble. If possible, strive for responses of twenty to forty seconds' duration. (If you're being taped, this is especially good. You'll decrease the likelihood of being edited.) If you say something particularly salient, your short comment might turn up as one of the station's "news bites" (short "takes" used to promote upcoming shows).

• If you are doing the show to promote a book, do not attempt to inject your book's name into *every* sentence! You can guarantee that attempting such blatant "commercials" means you will become *persona non grata* and never be asked back!

• No matter how well rehearsed you may be, your interviewer may ask you questions that are far afield. Hopefully, you will have prepared for this eventuality, and can gently and politely shift back into your topic. You might use your host's name to draw him or her back to the subject. ("Well, Bob, as you know, the latest University of Minnesota survey in the field indicates . . ." and so on.) Doing so serves several purposes: You include your interviewer in your discussion, and you imply that you know he or she is up to date on what's develop-ing in your field. At this point you should then immediately be able to return to talking about your subject.

How Not to Self-Destruct . . . .

One travel book author I worked with started a major New York City radio show interview off on a bad note. (In spite of the fact we had worked with her, preparing her for her appearance.) Even more surprising was that she herself was a broadcaster turned writer. As the first question of her interview she was asked by the show's hostess what had brought her to the city. Instead of a reply related to her book, as we had rehearsed ahead of time, she artlessly replied, "Oh, I was going to come here to shop anyway . . ." and her voice trailed off. Her reply, of course, should have been something as we had rehearsed—that is, "I'm here to appear at [name of bookstore] tomorrow at 2 P.M. and to talk about [name of book]."

In this instance it would indeed have been appropriate to mention her book and appearance in her reply, other authors too frequently sabotage themselves by *repeatedly* mentioning their book. And, too often, neophyte interviewees refuse to answer their interviewer's questions except to say, "I cover that topic in my book," or they sit clutching their book and (on TV) hold it up at every opportunity. This is something that media interviewers find highly objectionable. They know that they are expected to mention the book's title occasionally. But to have a guest continually plug a book is anathema.

In doing any interviews, don't—*and we repeat, do not*—repeatedly refer to your book or answer questions by suggesting that your interviewer "read the book." This type of oversell is overkill and will act against you.

How to Handle Difficult Situations . . . .

Another suggestion: Never evade difficult questions. Even if you are trapped into an area that you find impossible to discuss, don't stonewall or, worse, flare up in anger. Never just sit in stony silence and refuse to reply. Use the time for your reply to turn the topic back to one you *are* comfortable with. No matter whether you are doing radio/TV, or print interviews, you can always do what canny politicians do: Smile or, at least, don't grimace or stammer as you collect your thoughts!

There are times when your interviewer, or people who call into talk shows, become downright hostile. *However provoked you feel, never, ever respond in kind.* First, overcome the inclination to immediately say something. Then, sit in silence for a second. This may defuse the situation. If it doesn't, try this: Take fifteen seconds or so (*not much more!*) to respond, but then make a five second "bridging" statement, one that shifts the focus into a more positive framework. And then take only about another fifteen seconds to state *your* positive conclusion. Doing so keeps your response within a forty to forty-five second time frame which is best for broadcast purposes.

If your interviewer continually interrupts you, and doesn't let you complete your thought or statement, try either of the following tactics. Sit quietly for a moment and then pick up the thread saying, "As I was just saying. . . ." Or, completely ignore the interruption and say, "Well, Bill, you wanted to ask me something else. Please tell me again what it is."

If your interviewer simply doesn't allow you a moment, take a long, silent pause—count to five. That should allow you to regain control of the interview. If not, repeat your silence—which is truly anathema to broadcasters—and your interviewer should be sufficiently squelched to back off. If your interviewer twists your words to cast you in a poor light, stay calm and restate what you said. But again—no matter how bizarre or unkind your interviewer (or caller) is, do not take up the gauntlet!

As a "worst case" scenario, if you are confronted with a host who acts truly deranged, you can always hang on until there's a commercial break, and then claim another appointment, politely excuse yourself and leave!

If you're stuck, though, keep your cool. Realize that it's often an interviewer's style to skewer guests. Even if you think your questioner is rude, uninformed, or downright demented, *don't say so*. This way you will always emerge from the fray with your dignity intact.

Creating a Radio News Release . . . .

There are times when you can submit a news release—in the form of a special script—to a radio station for on-air use.

In doing so, you should be aware of the following:

• When typing your release, use no more than a sixty-space line (i.e., set your margins at fifteen and seventy-five).

• Indicate a release date and contact person's name (see example here).

• Type in an "attention line" indicating the job title of the person who will most likely find your radio release useful (see following example).

• A radio release is to be read aloud, so never divide words between lines.

• KISS applies here! Keep your radio release very brief. If, for example, you aim for one that can be read in ninety seconds, keep it to about 200-225 words.

• If your radio release is keyed to be read at a special hour, it should state the time. Or if not specifically time-dated, this line should read: **FOR BROADCAST AT WILL.**

• If there are more than one or two stations in your area, you can create different radio release scripts for each station. If so, use a slug line (all caps and underlined) **EXCLUSIVE TO YOU IN YOUR CITY.**

• Any proper names and foreign words with difficult pronunciation should be typed phonetically and placed in parentheses just after their first

• SAMPLE RADIO NEWS RELEASE TO BE READ ALOUD •

(Letterhead)

Release date: March 25, 1990
Contact person: Betty Gregory
Phone: (xxx)xxx-xxxx

**ATTENTION NEWS DIRECTOR FOR BROADCAST AT WILL
EXCLUSIVE TO YOU IN YOUR CITY**

**GARBAGE RECYCLING CAN BE EASY FOR ANYONE, SAYS
LOCAL EXPERT JOHN MILES**

John Miles, a resident of Smithtown and author of the book *You Can Save Our Earth*, has practical tips on quick and easy garbage recycling.

Mr. Miles says that the average person usually finds garbage recycling messy and time consuming. He says that with Smithtown's mandatory recycling law — and the infrequent pickup of certain items — it's a good idea for homeowners to set space aside for a neat and sanitary recycling area. Mr. Miles says that, space permitting, a corner of a back porch, a basement, or a garage would be a good place for this type of holding area. He suggests that people use several large, labeled, *covered* garbage cans, plus a rack or a box as an old magazine and newspaper holder.

Jack Miles suggests labeling one garbage can for rinsed glass bottles, another for plastic containers, another for rinsed metal cans, and using a plastic-lined garbage can for daily wet food refuse. Mr. Miles says that keeping a large ball of twine on hand to tie stacks of newspapers and magazines is another way to prevent mess. In his book he lists mail-order companies that sell all types of special items for the home recycler.

John Miles is a resident of Smithtown and is employed as a sanitation engineer for the municipality. His paperback book, *You Can Save Our Earth*, was published by Ryan Press at $7.95, and is sold in local stores, including Books & Stuff on Elm Street.

use in the release—such as Micylewski (Mick-LEW-ski). Separate syllables with hypens and type accented syllables in all caps.

Now "Ear" This

In his fine book, *Getting Your Message Out: How to Get, Use, and Survive Radio & Television Air Time,* (a Prentice Hall, Spectrum book, paperback $12, hardcover $20), Michael M. Klepper sagely suggests that you "write for the ear." He points out that "Broadcast style is conversational, not stiff or stilted. It's the language of friend talking to friend across the kitchen table." And he offers specific advice under headings that include Short, Simple Sentences, Keep Numbers and Statistics to a Minimum, Use Quotations with Caution, and Read Your Writing Aloud.

Book Plugs on Radio. . . . .

If you have written a nonfiction work of general interest but are unable to travel, will not be undertaking radio show interviews, and do not have a large quantity of books to send out *gratis,* there still is a way to get word of your book out.

One such tactic was employed in a campaign I created for a quiz book. The following cover letter (below) and question sheet (page 122) was photo-offset on publisher's stationery and sent to a group of radio shows to coincide with the presidential election.

Dear Friend:

The following intriguing questions—which you are free to use on the air—are drawn from our new paperback *Presidential Quiz Book,* which contains 1,500 plus questions and answers about all things presidential.

We felt, given the timely subject matter and the interesting (and informative) questions contained in this book, you would find this the basis for a lively segment on your show.

We would kindly ask, however, that if you use this material you mention that it is derived from:
Presidential Quiz Book
published by HIPPOCRENE BOOKS,
New York City, as a $7.95 paperback.

For additional information, please contact us at the number shown above.

Thank you for your interest.

Sincerely,

Elane Feldman

Note: As the author was not offered for interview here and as he'd asked we

HIPPOCRENE BOOKS, INC.

171 MADISON AVENUE/NEW YORK/N.Y. 10016
Tel: 212-685-4371

Q - Which First Lady bought 300 pairs of gloves in four months?

A - Mary Todd Lincoln

Q - What First Lady wore hats which were described as having the look of having been found under the bed?

A - Eleanor Roosevelt

Q - Identify the presidential author of the following statement: "I wake early because I sleep well. I sleep well because I never write anything which can get me into the slightest trouble."

A - George Washington

Q - What President kept such detailed records of his scores when playing "Canfield" (Solitaire) that thousands of them are preserved in the Library of Congress?

A - Woodrow Wilson

Q - What President netted more than $100,000 for the auction of wool?

A - Woodrow Wilson

Q - What (future) President was punished for wild dancing at West Point?

A - Eisenhower

Q - What president's family owned a pony named Algonguin that was once taken up in the White House elevator and into a bedroom?

A - Theodore Roosevelt.

not use his name in this campaign, you'll notice this omission. But you would, of course, want to include your name.

Sweeten the Pie

If your subject lends itself to this, and especially if you're an author who has maintained mail order sales rights on your book, you might want to create something to offer as a "freebie" to listeners. For instance, if you have written a diet book, you could offer to send listeners a free copy of one of your diet regimens for a SASE; or if you wrote a book on interior design, you could offer to send a guide to "shopping for carpeting" or anything along these lines. The reason to do so is twofold: to excite listener interest in your book, and more important, to build a list of possible mail order buyers. When you send out your "freebie" always have an order form sent along with the material to encourage replies.

Examples of Material for Broadcast

The following exemplify the type of material that could be used on-air. Each begins with what's called a "soft" lead (one that *doesn't* try to pack all the information into the lead sentence).

Example #1. Anytown home prices are plummeting due to "unreal" expectations, states local writer-realtor, Frank Alan. But Alan has ideas on preventing further erosion in the local real estate market. Writing in his weekly column, "Anytown Real Estate," in the *Anytown Weekly* he suggests the following:
[such tips would then be listed.]

Example #2. Are you a fashion "victim"? asks *Smart Dressing* magazine columnist, Jane Brown. Ms. Brown will be at CHIC STUFF CLOTHING, Thursday, December 6 from noon to 2 P.M. advising shoppers how not to fall into "the fashion trap." She'll give advice based on her January column in the magazine, now on newsstands, which tells readers how to bypass faddish clothing and still dress fashionably.

Before "Sign Off" — Some Final Thoughts on Radio/TV . . . .

Get a Tape of Your Appearance

A tape of your appearance on a radio or TV show is an invaluable addition to your press kit. You will find these tapes helpful when trying to sell yourself to other — especially major market — shows.

When you've been booked for a radio or TV appearance, it doesn't hurt to ask ahead of time if the show can provide you with a copy of your segment.

If they can't, there are many companies that provide professionally done audio or videotapes. One such service that works nationally is Radio and TV Reports, 41 E. 42nd St., New York City 10017; (212)309-1400. At present, the firm charges $98 for a videotape of five minutes or less, $40 for a TV or radio audiotape of that length, and $35 for a radio transcript. Again, be sure to give them advance notice and be aware that prices do change. Contact them regarding their current rates.

For a firm in your city that provides such service, consult the Yellow Pages under "Clipping Service" or "Videotape Duplication," or call a local TV or radio station that can probably steer you to a similar company.

For a less expensive version, of course, you can always have a friend or family member make a copy. Just make sure it's of high quality and that there is nothing else on the tape.

Pre-tour Tips

If you will be touring (that is, traveling to make appearances in varied cities) without the help of a publicist, there are some important things you should do:

• Delegate someone to take your calls in your absence and make it a practice to speak to this person daily, or have them call you when and if they have to update you. *Note:* If you have a phone answering machine that has a remote pickup capability (that is, one that allows you to retrieve your recorded messages when you are away) your announcement should ask your callers to indicate the date and time they have called and you should, naturally, say you will call them back. Make it a habit to always check your messages, and promptly return calls. (Some of us check them several times a day.)

• Look into having someone act as your escort person in the cities you'll be visiting. You can find these escort services listed in *Literary Market Place*. Generally, these people will pick you up at the airport and arrange for your transportation to shows and to interviews. In an unfamiliar city, this can prevent numerous headaches.

• Make absolutely certain you allow sufficient time to get to each place. Even professional publicists sometimes foul up here. One TV show host tells an anecdote of how an author was booked by a publishing company publicist to do a morning TV show in Nashville, Tennessee—and three-quarters of an hour later to do his show in Atlanta, Georgia! He mused that the publicist obviously had no knowledge of geography.

Advertising for Bookings. . . . .

Those of you who have neither the time nor the inclination to mount a major publicity campaign—or who have been totally unable to set up any radio or TV bookings—might want to investigate advertising yourself in one of the publications that are provided to print and electronics journalists and people charged with booking guests onto talk shows.

One such publication is *Radio-TV Interview Report,* compiled by Bradley Communications Corporation, 101 W. Baltimore Ave., Lansdowne, PA 19050; phone (215)259-1070. The company says that ". . . publicists regularly list their authors in [the] *Report,* a monthly newsletter sent to over 4,700 [as of this writing] talk show producers and journalists." As of this writing, their ad rates ranged from $215 for a one-time, one-half page insertion to $629 for a quarter page ad to run six times.

Another similar resource is *The Directory of Experts, Authorities and Spokespersons,* put out by Broadcast Interview Source, 2233 Wisconsin Ave., Washington, DC 20007-4104; phone (202)333-4904. This company says they also have wide and broad-ranging circulation to print and electronic media people — totaling over 7,000 recipients. Their insertion costs range, at this writing, from approximately $195 for an individual taking a "Reference Section Listing" to $1,100 for a two-page display ad. They print these ads in each of their two annual editions and allow advertisers to change their ad contents and listing between editions at no extra cost.

If you consider placing an ad in this type of publication, first ask to see a sample copy of several pages from a *back issue* (where writers listed themselves). Then personally contact several advertised authors to verify if, in fact, the ad resulted in any bookings.

Broadcast Interview Source also publishes Alan Caruba's *Power Media "Selects."* It contains some "2,000 names [of those] who make the decisions at the nation's newswires and syndicates; top fifty daily newspapers; top TV and radio talk shows; most influential business and financial publications; top circulation magazines; syndicated columnists; entertainment, travel, medical, and political "influentials," and others, including service vendors.

This company also puts out *Talk Show "Selects"* which contains information on approximately 650 of "the most influential talk show hosts, producers and programming executives active in the talk show industry . . . organized both by state and by major market."

Both *"Selects"* are presently available in four formats: bound printed report, Rolodex cards, mailing list with press-on labels, and on computer floppy disks. *Note:* Talk isn't cheap! At the time of this writing, the *Talk Show "Selects"* in bound format was $185, press-on labels $175. The *Power Media "Selects"* bound version sold for $166.50 and the press-on lables for $145. Contact the company for all current prices.

The Author "Tour" . . . .

Once you have familiarized yourself with the reference books, (including *Broadcasting & Cable Yearbook* and *National Radio Outlets*) and also understand the criteria for judging which shows and stations are likely possibilities for you, you can — time, energy, and budget permitting — set up a media tour for yourself. When we say "time and energy, and budget permitting," please take heed. In your research, for example, you will likely find scores of radio shows that do both in-person and phoner interviews. You'll have to send out many pitch letters and press kits and likely make many phone calls to follow up your mailings, so you had best be prepared to spend not only a fair amount of time on this type of activity but also to invest a goodly sum for your campaign.

At times, I've found it simply more effective to hire outside companies that specialize in arranging media placements. Using such a company, one that devotes a great amount of their time to setting up radio interviews for writers, is often more productive than undertaking this laborious work yourself. (However you proceed, realize that securing radio bookings, especially in major markets, can be a difficult chore for the uninitiated.)

There are certain firms which can arrange TV/radio placements for you — an expensive service, but one which I've found to be most cost-effective in certain cases. Note here, though: A number of PR agencies say they will do TV/radio placements for you, but the type of firm I'm referring to here *specializes* in this service.

I won't endorse a specific firm by mentioning one at this point, but if you're interested in locating a service of this type, write to me at the address listed at the end of this book, and I'll provide you with information.

9

Understanding Publishing Realities

Agent Russell Galen of the Scott Meredith Literary Agency offered some good insights into the book publishing world in the December 1987 issue of *Writer's Digest* magazine.

He answered the often heard complaint, "It's harder than ever to get published without connections":

> It's true that more people are writing than ever before, with no corresponding rise in the number of manuscripts being bought. ... but in conversations with editors, I've found that the hunger to discover new writers is very much on the upswing. One has to be more clever and knowledgeable than ever before to beat out the sheer mass of competition for editors' attention.

The competition, at least in part, is due to the dwindling numbers of major commercial publishing houses. The *New York Times* reported in April of 1987 that "Already, many of the legendary publishing names are divisions of bigger units ... Many industry analysts say that in the next decade a half a dozen worldwide corporations will come to dominate the entire United States [publishing] business."

Despite this, John Baker, editor in chief of the book industry's major publication, *Publishers Weekly* told me that book authors should not despair. Increasingly, there are smaller, specialized, and regionally oriented publishing companies throughout the U.S. taking up where some of the larger houses have left off. He says, "I don't really think that getting a good book published is more difficult than it used to be as there are [these] houses all over the country."

Of course, having a book accepted by a publisher and having the finished product receive (what the author would consider) adequate publicity and promotion are two very different things! First-time authors, especially, are frequently discouraged that their offerings seem to be getting short shrift in the publicity department.

The reasons for this are multi-faceted. Publishing houses' publicity departments are generally understaffed and overworked. Therefore, other than routinely sending review copies to the major book trade media for review consideration, and if one is lucky, to a group of publications in your field, do not expect much marketing to be done on your book. The author who assumes his or her publishing company will spring into a massive promotion effort for a book is bound to be sadly disappointed.

Further adding to the problem are the growing numbers of what are called "orphan authors." A word of explanation for those who haven't suffered this fate. Orphan authors are those who have had their original editor leave the publishing house. Frequently, the consequences are that the orphaned authors are not given much attention by the new editor who has inherited them. Many editors prefer to develop their own stable of writers.

Often book publishers will heavily invest in promoting (and advertising) a book, but they do so with an eye towards subsidiary rights sales versus sales of books! "Sub rights" sales are a lucrative way for publishers to recoup their expenditures. These are sales made to paperback publishing houses who reprint, to book clubs, to Hollywood for film adaptations, to those who do production of television "properties." These sales are also made to foreign publishers and to magazines and newspapers for purposes of serialization.

And yes, it's true — often the fate of a book is cast early in the decision-making process. One publishing industry marketing person (speaking off the record) explained the way publishing companies decide which books will be given primary publicity attention:

> In the beginning of the season [at the time of the sales conference], I have already decided [after consulting with people such as the publisher and editor in chief] exactly what we are going to do — how much money we will spend, how much money we need to make . . . You look at books from a cost analysis point of view. I've already met with the authors that I know we will promote to see if they can talk. We also have to look at sales, how many books are out there, what the reorder pattern is. You look at a variety of data that is at your disposal and you make a quick decision. If you have limited staff, this is factored in. Each book is, in fact, a political campaign. It is a judgment call that depends on who the author is, who the agent is, and so on.

In *Broadway Danny Rose,* Woody Allen called it "The Emmis," — Yiddish for "the truth." Being realistic, facing the truth about the publicity and promotion potential of your book is vital. Many writers believe that having an agent will win them better treatment at the hands of a publisher, but we warned early in this book that many agents cannot — or will not — take on the duties of personal press agent. If you are represented by a literary agent, discuss with the agent early on in your relationship what they will do and what they feel you can, and should, do in the marketing area.

Armed with the truth about publishing world realities, suggestions for some proven — and a few unusual — approaches to book promotion, and advice from those who have "made it happen," you can keep your book from dying an early and silent death. And possibly even nudge it toward best-sellerdom!

Book Meetings . . . .

In the Networking section, we talked about the importance of attending workshops and writers group meetings, and otherwise keeping abreast of developments in the writing field. It's also helpful for book authors to know about the important book industry meetings that are held each year. While they are geared to book publishing company personnel, or to retail and wholesale book buyers, you should understand what transpires at these events.

The meetings we speak of in this context are the annual American Booksellers Association conclave, often referred to simply as ABA, and any of the regional or annual national meetings of the American Library Association.

Looking at the sheer numbers of people attending the ABA's annual meeting indicates its importance. In 1989, for example, *Publishers Weekly* reports that the numbers of people who preregistered for the annual convention were phenomenal. The numbers included 12,321 people listed as exhibitors, 5,177 as booksellers, 315 as members of the press, and 2,522 as "trade visitors." The first full day of the meeting drew some 23,575 people!

What's a writer to gain from attending these meetings? It's a great way to get a feel for what the book industry is about, and also to take the pulse of the marketplace—to see what's selling, to see what the buyers are buying.

> **TIP:** As the public cannot gain admission to the ABA, if you're the author of a forthcoming book being published by an exhibiting house, inquire about their sponsoring your attendance. Also ask about briefly appearing at their booth. It's worth a try.

Generally at these meetings, publishers buy exhibit space to show their newest offerings to book buyers (owners of independent bookstores, chain stores, wholesalers, distributor jobbers, and libraries.) In the main, the people who staff publishers' booths are marketing and sales people, not editorial personnel.

In that regard, while book industry meetings might be a valuable place to meet people and to pick up ideas, they are not—repeat, *not*—the places to try and sell your book idea.

You should not consider attending these conclaves hoping to buttonhole publishing people to interest them in your book concept. It is quite depressing to see would-be authors trudging the aisles of industry-oriented meetings toting bulging bags stuffed with their manuscripts. Or sadder still, to see them being turned away from publishers' booths with their manuscripts in hand.

Staying Tuned In to the Publishing Universe . . . .

The next best thing to attending the trade shows—and an absolute must for the self-promoter, is to regularly read one or more of the industry's trade journals to keep up with developments in the book field. *Publishers Weekly,* or *PW,* is the best all-around book trade review, and news-oriented professional publication of its kind. It is read widely by bookstore personnel, publishers, librarians, writers, and many others.

The official publication of the American Booksellers Association is the service magazine, *Bookseller.* While they do not review books, the magazine frequently runs book roundups for their readers who are mainly bookstore owners, managers, and store personnel. *Bookseller* is also read by publisher-members of the Association. Those publicizing books should, therefore, be acquainted with the magazine.

Book people realize that many librarians depend on *PW* reviews as a buying guide. A good *PW* review, especially when equally good ones appear in the other library-oriented magazines, can produce sizable sales.

As to what the other important trade publications do, their *names* generally tell what they are about, except for the very important *Kirkus Reviews* which is held to be one of the most important book buying aids.

With this information, you may have gained a little insight into the inner workings of publishing, but your studies aren't yet complete. In the next section, we'll discuss what you should know before and after signing your book contract.

Be a Good "Scout" . . . .

Rather than taking what can be labeled the "eager puppy" approach to being published, the wise author asks questions prior to (and sometimes immediately upon) signing a book contract—questions such as in what year and season their book will be published, and if the house will be doing any major works that season. It is helpful knowing this, at least to make you aware of your chances of getting attention and a share of their promotional dollars.

You also want to know whether your book will appear as a hard or softcover work, and the price the company projects for it. (This is important, especially if it's a specialized work and you know who the likely buyers will be and what they are used to spending on books such as yours.) However, and this is a *large* however, it's imperative that in all your dealings with publishing house personnel you do not alienate staff people. It's sadly commonplace in publishing circles to hear stories of "problem authors." (And, that's describing them in the gentlest of terms!) Too often one hears of writers who make staffers' lives miserable by their unrealistic expectations and demands. You will fare better by being reasonable, being one who understands how your book fits into the larger picture. It is not necessary that you become a sycophantic, super-understanding person forgiving of all abuses, but rather that you know what is doable and what you can expect of your publisher.

A suggestion: After you have signed your book contract—especially if you have never worked with the publisher before—inquire, pleasantly but directly, about setting up in-person meetings with key personnel at your publisher's office. (This could prove particularly helpful if you are unagented.)

A good time to have an in-person meeting is when you deliver your finished manuscript. If, however, this is not possible, a bit later on, possibly some time *before* the company's sales conference at which your book will be presented, is a good time for these meetings.

If it's completely impossible for you to set up in-person meetings, then at least open telephone communications with the key players at your publisher's office. If geographical or other factors totally prevent this, you should introduce yourself in writing.

Beyond your editor, you want to get to know those who will have an impact upon your book's production, artwork, and possibly even its copyediting. Also, of course, you want to get to know *all* the marketing people. These could include the marketing director or manager, the publicity and promotion directors, the advertising people, and, if your book is one of special market interest, you'll want to know the person responsible for special sales. If your book lends itself to this (and the company has such a person) you'll possibly also want to get to know the Premium Sales Director. If your book is one that will interest schools and libraries, you'll want to meet the people working on sales to these markets.

If possible, also introduce yourself to the heads of the sales and order fulfillment departments. And it's a good idea to get to know the folks who work in the company's mail room and the people who answer their phones. (Needless to say, if you become more than just a "name" to everyone, you might be remembered and given special attention.)

A special word of advice: Always follow up in-person meetings with a brief memo recapping anything important that transpires, and keep dated copies! In communicating on important topics it's imperative you do so in writing. It's the foolhardy author who merely makes spontaneous calls to various staff people and expects them to drop what they're doing to attend to his requests.

The Best Marketing Device You Have is Free! . . . .

The second thing you should do on signing your contract is to make certain to completely fill out an author's questionnaire. If your editor tells you that the company doesn't have one, replicate the prototype (pages 135-136) and fill it in completely. Send it on to your editor and ask that it be copied and passed on to the publicity person and all other people who will find it valuable.

Daisy Maryles, exececutive editor of *Publishers Weekly,* stresses that authors should always cooperate in filling out these questionnaires and any other information materials the publishers request. Maryles pointed out that authors are the best ones to know where there are local and regional publicity and promotion opportunities for their books, and it's in this area they can have a positive impact.

The author's questionnaire is the single best device you can use to help clarify just what your book will be about. As you will see in the following pages, it can be used by many departments. Your completed questionnaire can help promotion people create the company's catalog copy and write the jacket or flap copy of your book; your editor prepare materials for presentation at sales conferences; publicity people in a variety of ways (which we'll explain in detail in the following pages); and those staffers who work on subsidiary right sales. As you can see from the prototype, the amount and type of information that you provide in the questionnaire can be invaluable. And, who knows better than you exactly what your book is about and who its potential readers are?

How an Author's Questionnaire Might Be Used

The publicist/promotion person reads an author's questionnaire seeking information and possible "hooks," "angles," or "news pegs."

If we go through the questionnaire point by point, we'll be able to explore the possibilities it presents for promotion:

• Your legal name, if different from your pen name, might be a good peg, especially in doing local publicity. The same applies to one's residence. "Local person makes good" stories are used by all types of media.

• If you are a part-time writer, your job provides varied possibilities. If for example, you are a novelist part time, and you work full time as a lab technician, publicity opportunities are presented in the specialized trade media of your full-time profession. A publicist might, therefore, notify publications that reach laboratory technicians that one of their colleagues is being published.

• Wherever you have worked, and also the cities you lived and worked in, present possible places to publicize your book.

• Your place of birth—especially if other than in the U.S.—also presents publicity opportunities. There are a variety of ethnic publications that accept news announcements about people of their nationality. Hence, someone born in Finland who writes a book might be of interest to the editors of publications concerned with Scandinavian topics.

Information on whether or not you are a naturalized citizen is helpful when submitting books for award or prize consideration, but also it serves as a natural peg for publicity geared toward foreign interest publications.

• The same applies to listing one's religion, particularly if you have written a book with a religious theme. For instance, a nonfiction work on Martin Luther's early life would probably be of special interest to Lutheran publications.

• Your marital status can also provide "pegs." For example, a female doctor who is married to a pharmacist and writes a novel set in a hospital presents her publisher with varied news pegs. (Her mate's profession is important here, as the publicist can approach publications read by pharmacists as well as physicians.) The same type of information about one's children can present varied hooks.

• If you have served in the military there are publicity possibilities as well.

• SAMPLE AUTHOR QUESTIONNAIRE •

Date

The purpose of this questionnaire is to supply the Publicity Department with accurate information about you and your book. It will be kept in that Department's files to help answer questions about you that might arrive from the media and the public. It will also be used in preparing promotional materials.

We would appreciate your returning this questionnaire along with a black-and-white glossy photo of yourself — and if necessary, the photographer's written permission for its use. Please return this all to your editor as soon as you can.

If you have already filled out a questionnaire for an earlier book that we have published, kindly use this copy to update that material. *If you attach any separate sheets, please make certain to put your name, your book title, and date on these.*

Name: (If your name is often mispronounced please give correct phonetic pronunciation)

Legal name: (If different from pen name indicate if you want us to keep this confidential)

Residence: (Street City State Zip)

Home phone with area code: (Indicate the best time to reach you during the business day)

Occupation: (If other than full-time writer)

Company name:

Office address: (Street City State Zip)

Office phone with area code: (Indicate best time to reach you during the business day)

Date of birth:

Place of birth:

Citizen of: (*Note:* If you are a naturalized citizen, kindly state when you became a U.S. citizen. This information is needed for prize and award forms.)

Marital status: (Include name of spouse if married)

Children: (Please give names, ages and, if relevant, their occupations)

Schools and colleges(s) attended: (Please include dates of degrees)

Bibliography: (Please include all titles, publication dates, and publishers of earlier books)

FICTION   NONFICTION

Periodicals in which you have been published: (Please give names of all periodicals and titles of articles. Use separate sheet(s) if necessary.)

SUGGESTED REVIEW COPY RECIPIENTS

Please provide typed list—here or on separate sheets—with all names, titles, names of publications and/or electronic media, and complete addresses and zip codes. *Note:* Our publicity department can discuss with you your providing this material typed onto plain white gummed labels.)

Local reviewers: (Your hometown newspapers)

Contacts in book's subject area: (Use this section, or attach separate sheet. Indicate names, titles, and complete addresses of all parties. Include chairpersons of committees, or presidents of alumni bulletins, special interest organizations, editors of newsletters, bulletins, or magazines. *Note:* Here, too, we can discuss your providing same on plain white gummed labels)

Media contacts: (Your personal media contacts, other than those who would obviously be on our review lists)

Media interviews and personal appearances: (While some authors prefer not to undertake personal or media appearances, we do have to know if you are willing to do so should they arise. Please indicate your willingness below)

                                                    YES   NO

Press Interviews:

Radio Interviews in person:

Radio Interviews via phone:

Television Interviews:

Book and Author Speeches:

Department Store Talks: (which may include demonstrations and autographing)

Bookstore Appearances:

Library Lectures and Convention Appearances:

TRAVEL PLANS

If you—or your outside publicist—arrange your own interviews and/
or appearances, it is imperative that you notify the Publicity Department in writing at least four weeks in advance of same. If you will be
traveling for purposes other than book promotion, publicity tie-ins
possibly may be arranged—but please notify the publicity department
as far ahead of time as you can (four weeks minimum).

WHEN YOU TRAVEL AND WILL BE SPEAKING

Please provide our Publicity Department with written data on your complete itinerary: dates, places you will be speaking, topics, names of hotels or other places you will be staying, with phone numbers.

In the case of a lecture schedule, please provide written information on the sponsoring organization/person to contact in the event that your book can be sold where you appear.

PHOTOGRAPHS

It is important that if you send us a black-and-white photo it be a glossy photo of professional quality, no smaller than 5×7. If necessary, obtain and provide us with a copy of your photographer's written permission to use this photo. *Note:* If your book lends itself to such representation, a good line drawing or caricature, rather than a photo, is acceptable.

RESUME

We need a brief biographical resume. Please include *on separate sheet(s)* any anecdotes that relate to this book and your writing of same, or any childhood, educational, or personal or professional anecdotes that will enliven our materials.

BOOK DESCRIPTION

If we have occasion to announce your book before we have had an opportunity to read galleys, it would be most helpful if you would provide a 200-word description of your book below or on a separate sheet.

Where you went to school and college provide added publicity opportunities, via alumni newsletters and magazines.

• Any organization or association you belong to (or have belonged to) are yet other places to promote your new book. This is especially the case if you have held an organizational office.

• Leisure time pursuits are also publicity possibilities. If, for instance, you wrote a novel in which baseball plays a large part, and you also collect baseball cards, readers of sports magazines and publications geared to card collectores are publicity possibilities.

• Your "literary history" presents many interesting possibilities. Information on your earlier books and magazine articles can ease the job of a publicist and a sub rights person. This information is evidence that the author is a seasoned "pro," one whose newest work is worthy of the media's consideration.

• If you contribute articles or columns to any publication that, too, is valuable information. The place you contribute to should certainly take note of your forthcoming book, especially if it is on a related topic.

• The segment of the questionnaire asking that you provide names of review copy recipients is self-explanatory. They can be a gold mine! The same applies to the local reviewers' portion as well as to "organizations," and to your personal media contacts.

• The section asking that you indicate your interest in media and personal appearances is self-explanatory.

• Your travel plans can often be tied in to publicity opportunities. The rest of the questionnaire information is discussed in detail elsewhere in this book.

• Finally, if you're worried about privacy, know that, publishers generally keep information on an author's residence and phone number confidential. The last section of the questionnaire, which asks for your permission to release this information to the media, can be very helpful. Often there are last minute PR possibilities that the publicist will want you to handle directly. Or, a media person will want to speak directly to you prior to setting up an appearance and time is of the essence.

At the very least, when you've provided your publisher with personal information, you might have some unexpected pleasant results. Author Barbara Buckmore, of Portland, Oregon, told *Publishers Weekly* about how she received a phone call from six readers of her book, *East of the Sun,* asking for her mailing address. The six had banded together to find her, wanting to write to say how very much they liked her book! As she learned, they tracked her down from information on her book's jacket which mentioned her place of residence.

Is It Too Early to Do Publicity? . . . .

Writers often ask me when is *not* too early to begin doing publicity and promotion if they have a book forthcoming. While you won't want to prime the pump far ahead of the time your book will be in bookstores and available for sale (we set out a timetable for this in your Book Publicity Action Plan in the Appendix), sometimes you can (and should) do advance publicity.

One instance where this worked well was told to us by one of my students. When she took my class she was just putting the finishing touches on her nonfiction book manuscript. Her topic was one that was of general interest, and it was based on her university research. Following my suggestions, she sent a news release to national print media outlining the preliminary findings of her research study and indicating her credentials and the fact that she was writing a book on the subject. When this news release was picked up by one of the leading national news magazines, a major commercial publishing house approached her and quickly signed her to a book contract.

There are other ways to gain public attention and spread the word about a book in progress. When I was working on a nonfiction book project that needed input from people across the country, I created a trivia quiz centered on my subject. I sent this in the form of a press release to major national print media and to nationally aired radio shows and commentators. This campaign produced great results. Both wire services — UPI and AP — used my quiz, producing hundreds of "pick-ups" in newspapers throughout the country. Radio shows aired my quiz and asked listeners to contribute their experiences. As a result, not only did I receive hundreds of valuable letters from people, many were interested in knowing when the finished book would be published.

In another instance, a writer at work on a special interest nonfiction book already contracted for, sold an article on the topic to a special interest journal. The credit line carried information to the effect that he was writing a book due for publication in spring 1988 and the name of the book and the publisher. This produced early interest and even advance book orders.

Another time, when I wanted certain people to contribute their experiences to be used in an article I had been assigned by a magazine, I sent a press release out to all those publications that I knew would likely be read by these people. Here, too, I received useful replies and heightened interest in the article prior to its publication.

Although advance publicity can be valuable, if you have a book due to be published you should never do too much too far in advance. If you want to include information about your forthcoming work in your biographical data and use it as credit line information for an article, that's fine. But, for the purposes of stimulating sales — never set up radio, TV, or print media interviews until books are available for sale.

The Publication Party . . . .

Those writers who anticipate that their publishers will fete them upon publication of their books are usually bound to be disappointed. The "publication party" (also known as the "pub party"), held at the publisher's offices or other quarters is, for the most part, mainly a great salve for an author's ego. Little is accomplished at such events. Few publishers, therefore, are willing to undertake the effort.

Unless the author in question is a "name," more than likely, should the publisher be pressed into holding a publication party for the average midlist book, the author should expect to experience the type of situation that was portrayed in a humorous ad the publisher Salem House ran some time back. This is excerpted from their book, *The English in Love:*

> A big and splashy launch is like some enormous dating introduction service . . . the only person there who knows no one is the author, who can frequently be spotted alone and wretched in a corner while the party roars merrily along around him, and although only three people — author, editor, and publicist — will actually have read the book, every single copy will have disappeared by the end of the evening, often like the guests, two at a time.

Humor aside, let's be realistic about pub parties. You may expect your book's publication merits your publisher flying you to their headquarter's city, especially if they are in New York City, but don't be insulted when this doesn't occur. It's simply not usually done. Here again, unless you're a writer of interest to the media, you're bound to be sorely disappointed at the lack of response. In the major cities, these parties proliferate, and demands on people's time is intense. So do not expect that your book's publication will mean you'll be thrown a lavish party and have a chance to meet and chat with media people, notables, and celebrities.

10

Especially for Authors

If you will not be hiring a publicity representative and will be doing your own book publicity and promotion, you will need to know how to proceed.

Backlist Authors . . . .

About publishing industry parlance: Understand that once your book is officially published — that is, when your publication date has passed — your book is usually referred to as a "backlist" title by your publisher. Until you have been published you are part of the publisher's "frontlist" or "forthcoming" group of books. However, most of the ideas we discuss in the following paragraphs work equally well for new books as well as for those that are backlist.

Publicity Programs . . . .

Because you're reading this book, you already have some ideas on publicity and promotion. But you must, and this is usually an absolute must, work closely with whomever will be doing the PR and promotion at the company publishing your book. It is vital that you keep all lines of communication open, and that you be polite and businesslike, not pushy.

If you are being published by a small publishing house, you might be told that you can do anything you please in terms of self-promotion. Or, if your publisher only uses outside publicity consultants, you may be asked to occasionally touch base with this person. But realize that when your publisher says "occasionally," they mean just that. Too often over-eager authors beleaguer outside company publicists and consultants to the point that the authors are told they are henceforth barred from any contact with the publicists.

Generally speaking, most companies want to know what their authors are up to and do not want them to undertake any independent publicity action unless they are either involved or have first approved it. Following these suggestions should make everyone's life easier:

Early on in your book's life (unless your editor advises strongly against this) write the publicity and promotion people to find out what the early marketing plans are for your book. A good time for you to do this is often after the sales conference at which your book has been presented to the company's sales representatives. (These "presentations" are rapid-fire — i.e., two- or three-minute presentations are not uncommon. "Genre" titles are often omitted.) Your editor can tell you at which conference your book will be presented.

Most frequently, publishers' conferences are held twice a year, in late fall and late spring. Generally speaking, by this point publicity and promotion personnel will have given thought to the outlines of their seasonal campaigns. Ask the PR/promotion people to get back to you in writing. And also ask if you can call them (collect, if need be) to discuss their letter and do so only if it is necessary.

In your initial letter, specifically query the marketing people (or whoever is in charge of this area) on what they plan to do in the area of publicity and promotion. Do not be surprised if you are told, "It's too early to discuss the marketing on your book. We have to wait and see how the book *advances.*" The word "advances" in this context means how well the company sales representatives do selling your book.

Further, you might be told that the company "has to see what the early trade reviews look like." What they mean is what, if anything, the important book trade media, including *Publishers Weekly, Library Journal, Kirkus Reviews,* and the ALA *Booklist,* say about your book. (This is presuming they'll be sending galleys out to these media. If they say they'll not be sending out galleys — in any form — you should encourage them to do so.)

The Importance of Galleys . . . .

A particularly good way to attract major media attention for your book is to use advance galleys of some kind, either unbound long galley sheets or bound galleys (which we discuss in the following pages). As Mark Feeney, speaking as the book editor of the *Boston Globe* in a *Publishers Weekly* article put it, "If you wait until your title's arrived at a newspaper book editor's desk to worry about the review, by then you've pretty much lost the game. I can't emphasize how rarely the decision waits for the arrival of a bound book."

Few publishers will commit themselves to any marketing program, beyond the basics, until they see what interest, if any, a book creates in the marketplace and in the trade book review media.

What you want to verify — and you should explain that you are *not* asking them to tell you where the company plans to *advertise* your book (which is always a sore point with publishers) — is the nature of the *publicity* program they plan. Explain that you "want to help in whatever way" you can, but unless you know what they plan to do you don't know how you can be of help.

What You Might Be Told

You should be informed, and this is the bare minimum a publisher should do for you, that advance review copies will be sent (if yours is a general interest work of fiction or nonfiction) to appropriate book trade journals for review consideration. This means they will send it to book review editors at *Publishers*

Weekly, Library Journal, the American Library Association's *Booklist, Kirkus Reviews,* and, when *bound books* are ready (which is the only form in which this important publication accepts books), to *Choice: Books for College Libraries,* and to any other advance book review media.

There's no mystery to the excerpts from reviews in respected book trade and consumer publications that appear on some book jackets, no chance that the salutary comments from experts that bolster a book's promotional copy have been pulled from thin air. Such valuable promotional tools are, in most cases, the result of sending bound galleys out in advance of finished books.

The people who'll receive these "advance review copies" fall into a number of categories. First, of course, are the editors of major book trade publications (except, as we've mentioned, *Choice: Books for College Libraries,* which only accepts bound books.) Favorable reviews (even mixed reviews) can stimulate orders from trade bookstores, wholesalers, and, sometimes, library and school orders. Many media people read the "trades," leading to the potential for interviews and feature stories. Review quotes can be used as "lead lines" in advertising or catalog copy, in direct mail brochures and elsewhere.

Subsidiary rights departments frequently send galleys to a targeted group of magazines for possible serialization. Many publishers also like to send these advance copies to buyers at the major book chains and wholesale customers, and to editors at the chains' and wholesalers' own book review departments.

Publishers also like to keep advance copies at their convention booths (for example, at the ABA convention) and at professional/trade association meetings to give out to buyers, editors, and others.

"Gilt" by Association

All puns aside, if you can get people who are well known in your field to lend their name to your work in some way, definitely do it, in advance of publication. Whatever form this takes—be it a quotable endorsement, an introduction, or a foreword to your book—it is a valuable, and salable, addition.

If you are not yet a household name and have written a nonfiction book, and you can arrange for a well-known person to write a brief introduction or foreword to your book, it would be especially helpful. But this must be done early in your book's life: When you begin writing is not too early. Discuss with your editor the publishing company's policy on paying an honorarium for the people you line up. Usually one approaches only those who have some connection with the subject, are experts in the field, or have some base from which they can support their assertions of the book's merit. No matter what the work, there's always someone qualified to comment. Some companies will pay a small honorarium; others won't. Finally, if you cannot think of who to approach, your editor may have ideas for you.

Obtaining Blurbs

To the *uninitiated,* the "blurb" might sound like a creature from outer space. But the blurb and its many uses represents an excellent way to build up an author's reputation. Simply put, the blurb (also called an encomium) is the comment that influential or well-known people make for publication about your book. Blurbs are sought so they can be used in publicity, promotion, and advertising. (The most valuable of these comments are collected in advance of the book's publication.)

These quotes are superb marketing aids with a myriad of uses. The first and foremost use—hence the need for getting these into your publisher's hands as early as possible—is their appearance on your book's jacket or cover. And this is where you as author can play a significant role.

When you fill in your author's questionnaire you will want to indicate the names and, if you have them, the complete addresses for people you know personally or indirectly who might be willing to read your book and comment on it. Remember: It is usually a waste of everyone's time and energy to approach world famous literary figures, film or television stars, major celebrities, and other well-known people who do not know you. Notables such as these, who are constantly sought after, will usually flatly refuse to become involved. Please let reality reign.

It is vital that as early as possible your publisher have names of any people you realistically believe would be willing to read your book and comment on it. They must of course, let these people know their comments will be used in future promotion activities.

Just as soon as the publisher has galleys, bound galleys, or advance copies of bound books, the people you indicate, along with any people they know of, can be asked for their comments. If your publisher will not be sending out *any* galleys, ask them to send photocopies of your *edited* manuscript out to this group of people.

And even with a "worst case scenario," if all the people contacted are so late in commenting that their blurbs cannot be used on your book's jacket or cover, all is not lost. Blurbs can be used in advertising and in publicity and promotion, such as catalog copy and news releases. Blurbs are also valuable in helping your publisher sell subsidiary rights. (Discussed on page 128.)

Be warned: If you will be creating your own publicity and promotional materials, you must never take a quote out of context. You simply cannot turn a wishy-washy (or worse, a negative) comment into a glowing remark. One hair-raising story of the results of doing this was told by one of my students, who decided to "edit" the blurb he was given. In so doing he dramatically altered the quote.

He reported that the person who was quoted—and he had quoted him in an advertisement in a widely read and influential publication—took great exception to having his comments changed. The writer was threatened with a one million dollar lawsuit! *Never* tamper with a quote to make it more positive. Far better not to use it at all.

The Book Review . . . .

Publishers Weekly reviews some 600 to 700 books monthly, roughly 5,500 books yearly. Since about ten times that number of books are published in the U.S.

annually, it's apparent that the competition for a review in *PW* is keen.

Daisy Maryles, *PW*'s executive editor noted that *PW* editors are bombarded with requests for coverage from publishing houses, and that it's impossible to accommodate them all. Compounding the problem are the number of authors who entirely bypass their publishers and directly contact *PW*. Ms. Maryles remarks that most often their doing so is counterproductive and usually raises many questions. Editors wonder *why* the authors are not working either through their publishers' publicity people or with a professional publicist. She remarks also that it often creates doubt in the editor's mind — if the author is approaching *PW* it might be because their publishers have completely refused to deal with them, as they are "nuisances." Thus Ms. Marlyes feels that unless there is some good reason for authors to directly contact *PW* they'd be better off "leaving this in the hands of the professionals."

Newspaper book editors, too, face severe space limitations. Robert Wyatt, book editor of the *Nashville Tennessean,* chronicled the "Book Page Editor Blues" for *PW* (September 21, 1984). The book page editor on most papers is not full time, but frequently has other duties, Wyatt pointed out. He undertook a survey that elicited responses from more than 65 percent of newspapers with circulations above 100,000. Some of the survey's findings are very telling:

- Most book editors seem quite dissatisfied with what they receive from New York publishers. They rank only about a third of all review copies clearly appropriate for review, find four-fifths of press releases useless in selecting books, and judge only about a fourth of the author interviews they are offered worthwhile. . . . The editors rate another fifth of their review copies marginally appropriate for review.

- In general, as circulation increases the number of releases, review copies and author interviews offered also increase. However, the percentage of these judged worthwhile drops. . . . *Publishers often ignore important local ties in sending review copies.* (Italics mine.) Ann Merriman, book editor and associate editor of the *Richmond News Leader,* says, "It amazes me how a publisher can overlook sending a tagged review copy of a great local or regional interest to a book editor in that area."

Understanding Book Review Editors . . . .

Far too often authors feel that if their book isn't reviewed in *Publishers Weekly* or on the book page of a newspaper, they have missed the boat. In "So Many Books, So Little Space" (*PW,* April 10, 1987), writer Howard Eisenberg quotes book review editors from all over the nation on the book selection process. Ruth Coughlin of the *Detroit News,* said:

I arrive at my office on Monday morning and find 200 books in unopened mailing envelopes stacked outside my door. My office is eight feet square, with minimal shelving. There is a narrow footpath from the door to my desk, carved through a mountain of books three to five feet high—I do a book giveaway every three weeks. I begin opening envelopes, grimly aware that out of all of this week's bounty, I can select 10 titles to send out for review.

Eisenberg notes that:

Some book genres are consigned to such automatically disdainful oblivion that authors who specialize in them can expect neither mercy nor review space. Says [*Cleveland Plain Dealer* book editor Walter] Berkov, "I immediately drop self-help and how-to books, Regency romances, books about the occult, books I know are slanted in one way or another and books published by vanity presses." [While Mark Feeny of the *Boston Globe* skips,] ". . . gothics, bodice-rippers and westerns." [The *Washington Post's*] Alice Digilio reported skipping "how-tos and psychobabble."

It's not that the book editors are heartless, but rather severely constrained. Because of this, many of them see that books are sometimes directly routed to a more likely editor.

"I like to think mine is the literary page," explained Shirley Williams, "so I send business-related books to the business section, cookbooks to the food editor." Alice Digilio concurred, adding, "I get reviews in other sections of the paper if I possibly can, to leave more room on my page. Some books are nice pegs for other sections to hang stories on by interviewing the authors. I see that as a responsiblity we have to the newspaper to pass them along. . . ."

In an informative section entitled "The Local Angle" Eisenberg's article explained:

While it will come as no surprise to house publicists that many book editors toss out press releases, a local angle may delay that fate. Dianne Donovan (of the *Chicago Tribune*) said that while she realized that releases are "prepared by people pushing a product, they can offer some very good information—frequently something as basic as the fact the author lives in Illinois. We can't cover them all, but that's an added fillip; newspapers like to cover native sons and daughters."

But that's less so in areas overrun with writers. Clarus Backes feels an "obligation to review locals, but there are more than 400 professional authors living in the Denver area. If each published one book every two years, there's no way we can review them all."

Local audience dictate reviews as much as local authors *and the clever press kit crafter bears that in mind.* In Washington, for example, political books tower over other candidates. . . . A release emphasizing timeliness and topicality can also result in a review. . . .

Authors who are published by small houses may have to take special care not to be lost in the shuffle. Joseph Barbato, writing in *Publishers Weekly,* April 14, 1989, said, "I know the small presses are understaffed, but they would probably get more reviews if they followed up more."

Don Obriant, book editor at the *Atlanta Journal Constitution,* suggested that small publishers "should alert us to a book of interest; the big publishers do it all the time. Small press books fall through the cracks because they're not being hyped enough."

"Bounce Back" Postcards for Reviewers

To encourage busy book reviewers to review a book, it is a good idea to make it simple for them to request a review copy. Therefore, publishers often include a self-addressed postcard (next page) showing a book's title, author's name, publication date, and other information when they send out a book news release.

How to Move Off the Book Page

Understanding the problems book review editors face, depending on your book's subject, you might want to approach other editors. For example, if you have written a book on the history of the Bull Moose Party, you could address your material to newspaper and magazine political writers. Or, if you wrote a book on the clothing made and worn by Native Americans, you could address fashion writers and reporters.

To find these people you can consult *Bacon's Newspaper Directory,* which has their names.

Recycling Your Reviews. . . . .

Once you've landed those good reviews, you should definitely "recycle" them. It's standard practice for publishers to send copies of all reviews, *bad and good,* to their authors. If, however, your publisher doesn't do so, make sure to ask about this. Many publishers hire clipping services to provide them with articles and reviews, and you can find out about this. If your publisher doesn't use a clipping service—which is *not* an inexpensive undertaking—you might want to check *Literary Market Place* and see about hiring one to watch for mentions of your book.

If you decide to personally hire a clipping service, be very specific in what you want them to clip. Some years back a publishing company publicist found that a clipping service hired to clip mentions of a book whose title contained the word "Israel" sent virtually every single mention of the word "Israel" they found! Thus, hefty sacks of clips were erroneously sent to the publicist! If you work with such a company, give them complete information on precisely what they should look for!

It's especially important that you see copies of any and all mentions of your

book in the important advance book trade media, such as *Publishers Weekly, Booklist, Kirkus Reviews, Library Journal,* and *Choice.* Besides reviews you'll also want to have copies of any trade industry magazine mentions on you and/or your book. Use these comments in doing pitch letters or news releases; quote from these reviews. Don't forget—you must use quotes in context, and you cannot change a poor review into a positive one. If, however, you can find anything positive worth quoting, definitely do so. If you are unsure just how to do this, check with your publisher or read advertisements for other books and see how quotes are extracted.

Daisy Maryles of *PW* cautions that when extracting from reviews, not only is it important to quote accurately, *but* it's also important that in inserting ellipsis— indicating deleted passages—that you keep quotes totally within context! Juggling words and sentences is definitely out!

News Release Examples

Here are some examples of how review quotes on imaginary books can be correctly recycled and used in the headlines and lead sentences of news releases.

Example #1. Headline: **"JOHN LARSEN'S FIRST NOVEL IS A NO PUNCHES PULLED WINNER"**—*Library Journal*

Library Journal, the presitigious book trade journal, has hailed John Larsen's first novel, *Confessions of a Street Cop* as a "winner." . . . (Headline quote repeated here.)

Example #2. Headline: **"CHARLESTON AUTHOR WRITES EXCELLENT CITY HISTORY"** — *Publishers Weekly*

Nancy Jenkins, of Charleston, has written *Charleston Yesterday* which has been hailed by *Publishers Weekly* for its excellence. The book, being published by the University of South Carolina Press. . . .

Example #3. Headline: **A WINNING ENTRY** — *Choice*
AN ENGROSSING NEW BOOK — *Publishers Weekly*
A History of Harness Racing in the U.S.A.
Being Published by Racing Press

The first trade reviews for *A History of Harness Racing in the U.S.A.* (Jake Lorin, Racing Press, $19.95 hardcover) cite the book for its excellence and ease of readability.

Pitch Letters

Both of these examples represent a fairly complete, brief pitch letter.
Here's how to work review excerpts into your pitch letters.

Example #1.

Dear Editor:

"Jan Lukas's book, *Matisse — Modern Master* is a masterwork," is how the prestigious journal, *Art News World* greeted this new book. Rather than our extolling its virtues, we invite you to examine the book yourself. We have attached offprints of just some of the reviews for your perusal. Won't you let us know if you would like to see a review copy? To facilitate your reply, we have attached a stamped postcard.

Example #2.

Dear Children's Book Editor:

My new book, *Hello City Cat, Hello City Dog* has been receiving wonderful press coverage. *School Library Journal* says of it:

"A wonderful way to introduce urban-dwelling small children to the world of animals."

New Reading for Children said "This is a grand new picture book for pre-kindergartners."

I thought you might like to examine a copy and have, therefore, enclosed one for your review consideration.

Imaginative Recycling

Don't limit the use of good reviews to news releases and pitch letters. You're sure to find unusual, creative approaches that are worth a try. Joseph Barbato reports in *PW* how one small publisher, William Brinton of San Francisco's Mercury House, parlays his good *local* reviews. He reprints them in a newsletter that is sent to over 5,000 people, including bookstore personnel and other media book reviewers.

Keeping Sellers Informed . . . .

The book chains and some national and regional wholesalers and distributors provide their stores with descriptive material on new books – and news of publicity on same. But obviously they *only* do so on the books they have purchased. Make sure your publisher has alerted the editors of these organization's publications to your book. If the publisher hasn't done this, you might ask that they alert the appropriate people. (Some of these stores' PR and promotion notifications are done by these companies via computer or on microfiche.)

Announcing Publicity Successes to Bookstores. . . . .

In the same context, but one that can bear direct results by promoting *sales* of your book, see to it that your publicity appearances, (particularly radio and TV appearances) are announced to retail bookstore personnel. The best way to accomplish this rapidly is by having your publisher take an inexpensive listing advertisement in the American Bookseller Association's weekly *ABA Newswire,* under the section headed "Author Tours." At this writing, the basic cost is $64 for a five-line listing. Each additional line costs $3.40 each. (The book's title, author's name, and such information do not count as part of the paid lineage.) Ads that arrive on Wednesday before 2 P.M. (New York time) can be inserted into the next weekly issue.

Note: Given the low cost of these ads, authors frequently offer to reimburse their publishers for them. But only consider doing so *if* your publisher is reluctant to take this on. (And, in many cases it's not the *cost* that's the deterrent, but rather that the publisher is simply too busy to take on such important details. If this is the case, offer to place the ad yourself.)

The *Newswire,* which is available by subscription to ABA members and non-members is available by writing 137 W. 25th St., New York, New York 10010, phone: (212)463-8450; fax (212)463-9353. (Publishers are increasingly using fax machines to transmit late-breaking news of author publicity to the ABA.)

Newswire ads are a particularly good way to alert people to your publicity "scores." And in so doing, you'll be addressing those in a position to promote, and buy, your book for resale! I've also found that often media people themselves read the *Newswire* and seeing that an author is coming into their area, will call and ask about setting up an interview for their show or publication.

Several sample *Newswire* listings follow. The first lists specific shows, while the second indicates the cities the author will visit where no shows or interviews have yet been set; the third listing shows a combination of national and local publicity placements.

#1. Ken Loomis, *Joy to the World: Christmas Celebrations in America, from Colonial Times to the Present,* Dunham Press, $14.95, pub date 10/15/90.

• **PHILADELPHIA: 11/9-10**

Philadelphia in the A.M.	KYW-TV (NBC, live 11/9)
Morning from the Square	WCAU-AM (live, 11/10)

• **WASHINGTON, D.C.: 11/11-12**

In the District Today	WTTG-TV (CH 5)
D.C. Morning News Hour	WDCA-TV (CH 20)

#2. Les Parker, *Super Bowl Murders,* Smith & Jones, $18.95, pub date 8/90.

• **New York City 9/8**
• **Boston 9/12**
• **Washington, D.C. 9/14**
• **Philadelphia 9/16**
• **Atlanta 9/18**
• **Houston 9/21**
• **San Francisco 9/24**
• **Los Angeles 9/27**

#3. Robert Kraus, Ph.D. & Mary James, Ph.D., *Star Athletes,* Filbert House, $6.95, pub date 5/7/90.

• **NATIONAL**

Larry King	syndicated radio
Osgood File	CBS Radio
All Night America	WNT Radio
UPI Audio	interview
UPI Newspaper	interview
John Barkham Reviews	syndicated column
Today Show	ABC TV

• **NEW YORK CITY: 5/7-10**

Good Morning America	ABC TV (5/7)
Live at Five	WNBC-TV (5/7)

Barry Gray Show	WMCA Radio (5/7)
Sportsline	Cable News Network (live, 5/7)
Your Sports Show	WFAN Radio (5/8)
UPI Audio	(5/9)
New York News Names Make Sports News	interview
Times Sports	interview

Should you be asked to appear on the major morning talk shows, the *Newswire* also runs a special boxed section each week highlighting what they call, "Early Rising Authors." If you are booked onto any of these shows, always check with your publisher to make certain they have alerted the *Newswire* editors. Generally, the ABA is in touch with the shows, but to double-check make sure you or your publisher also alerts the *Newswire* staff of such bookings. This is important since bookstores should be well prepared for such appearances—which frequently create keen consumer interest.

"Midlist Authors"—Take Heed . . . .

Publishers, of course, usually save their heaviest promotional efforts for their "big name" or well-established authors. The rest of us who aren't Norman Mailer or Erica Jong are generally known as "midlist authors."

Do be aware that most publishers, as we've explained, are not equipped, especially on their midlist books, to go beyond routinely sending books to a handful of the advance book trade media. Some houses do not have a full-time publicist, nor do they hire outside talent. Some publishers do not maintain their own lists of major media, nor will they purchase lists from outside specialized media list companies. What this means for you is that the only thing they will do on their midlist titles is the most basic PR, hoping to garner advance book trade media reviews.

You might be told by your publisher that they do have house lists of appropriate publications in your field and they will be sending review copies to these publications. (Most often this group receives bound books, as opposed to advance bound or unbound galleys.) And, if your book is one of wide general interest, you might also be told the publisher will send it to varied general interest print media.

Radio and Television Appearances?

As for your publisher trying to arrange radio and television appearances for you, unless you are a well-known personage, a writer with a "track record," or are one whose book is important or controversial and expected to rise to the top of their list, it is not likely your publisher will attempt to place you for radio or TV interviews. It is not that publishers are bad business people, or that they are uncaring, but rather that they have learned this type of publicity is extremely labor intensive. Undertaking radio and television placements requires countless hours of work, and few publishers are equipped to undertake such intense campaigns. If you are being published by a major commercial publisher, you will notice that save for blockbuster books and their best-selling authors, or books written by celebrities, few of the house's authors turn up on the major talk shows.

How You Can Help "Make It Happen"

Some publishers, however, are willing to try to place authors on radio and TV shows in their localities. And this is where *you* can help. If you send your publisher the names of these shows' contact people, their titles, and mailing addresses—and especially if you do so on plain white adhesive labels—you'll narrow the odds in your favor!

Bookstore Autographings and Other Events and Parties . . . .

For special promotions (such as in-store appearances and bookstore autographing parties) the midlist author should not expect the publisher to do much. Here again, these activities take a lot of time, personnel, and effort, and most houses simply aren't equipped to provide this.

How to Proceed on Your Own

After you learn the extent of their plans, take some time to create your own *written* publicity plan.

Four to six months ahead of when your bound book will be shipped to book distributors and bookstore owners and managers (assuming that your publisher has said *they* won't be doing this), you might want to send an attractive and informative flyer on your book to these important people. (For helpful information on finding these outlets, refer to *The American Book Trade Directory*. See our listing in the References section which describes this important reference book.)

Micki Perry, a skilled and successful romance writer whom we met in Chapter Two, the Tools of the Trade chapter, has written a number of informative articles on self-promotion. In "Selling Your Book after It's Sold," written for *Fiction Writers* magazine, she says:

There are three NEVERS when it comes to promoting yourself:

  1. NEVER pass up the chance to get your name in print.

  2. NEVER forget how vital the bookseller's good will is to your success.

  3. and NEVER, I mean NEVER, discount the value of a single personal contact with the people who buy your books. . . Nothing can replace handshaking *and* eye-to-eye contact between two people.

I'd recommend visiting wholesalers, sales reps, and bookstores when-ever you're in a new city. But, since that isn't possible for the most part, I use the next best thing: the U.S. mail.

I send two main mailouts for each of my books. The first goes to about 1,000 sales reps, distributors, wholesalers, jobbers, and bookstores around the country—and a few in Canada and Puerto Rico.

Since your publisher's print run is determined by the advance orders for the book, it only makes sense to me to try and up those orders by making buyers aware of me and my work. To do this I find out from a local distributor or sales rep when the book will be ordered for the month of my release. Then I time the mailout of a flyer and letter to coincide with the order time.

By the way, I can't stress enough the importance of finding out who the sales rep is in your area. There will probably be two you deal with. One who sells directly to the bookstore and some jobbers, and another who sells directly to the independent distributors' (the wholesalers) and he might work directly for the publisher or for a national distributor and sell for several lines. This is the person WHO CAN MAKE CERTAIN your book isn't overlooked by his accounts (who may order two hundred to several thousand of single title at a time).

While Perry stresses the importance of working with publisher's sales represen-tatives, most houses flatly refuse to allow authors to do this. However, there is no harm in asking about this. Perry continues:

My second mailout goes to individuals and is mailed out much closer to the actual release date. These are people I've met at conferences, autograph parties, through fan letters, in classes I've taught, store clerks, bank tellers, parents of my children's friends, old high school pals, and on and on. Everyone who has ever expressed an interest in my books.

This is a very valuable list too, even though the people on this list are only buying one book at a time. But when you get down to it, that's how best-sellers are created—one book at a time.

About Bookmarks

Some authors, particularly novelists, use bookmarks to promote their works. If you (or your publisher) have decided to produce bookmarks, one month before your book is due out, send quantities of your bookmarks to retail bookstore managers and/or owners for giveaways to their customers.

These should be printed on a heavyweight colored paper and provide infor-mation on your book—its title, your name, your publisher's name, the book's price, and its publication date. If the book jacket (or cover) art is good-looking and you can reporduce it, that's even better.

Media Alerts

If you'll be mounting a full-scale *media* campaign, about two months prior to availability of bound books, send a Media Alert to all media that you have planned to approach. (See Appendix 2 for a sample Media Alert.)

A Common Lament and How to Deal with It . . . .

It is the wise author who understands that the process of getting books placed for sale in consumer-oriented bookstores is a chancy proposition. Given the huge numbers of books published annually and the difficulties book publishers' salespeople have in convincing booksellers to stock each and every book they are selling, it is often the case that your book will only be found in a few stores. And, it's not unusual that a new book will find few booksellers willing to stock it. This is especially the case for a first work of fiction by a completely unknown writer.

The common lament of many authors is that they visit bookstores expecting to see stacks of their book for sale and are sorely disappointed when this is not the case. And, their complaints grow louder when they cannot find one copy of their book in visits to numerous stores. To add to the authors' plight is the fact that few publishers are willing to honor single-copy mail order sales direct to consumers.

This has spawned the birth of companies and services that sell books directly to the public. One widely used company is Book Call, 59 Elm St., New Canann, CT 96840. For information, call (203)966-5470. Basically, Book Call will honor single-copy orders for books they have stocked, and will accept major credit cards and mail orders. They ship worldwide 24 hours a day, seven days a week. (They say they honor customer orders for books they "have stocked," which means your publisher will have to have sold books to them.)

Another similar service is offered through the Doubleday bookshops. But, here again, your publisher will have to have sold your book to the chain. Therefore, if your book is available at their stores, interested customers can contact DBS Xpress™, 724 5th Ave., New York, NY 10019, (800)635-0045. They are open seven days a week, provide free gift wraping, accept all major credit cards, and will send books worldwide. They state they have access to over 100,000 titles.

If you look through the pages of those Sunday newspapers that carry a book review section you will see other similiar companies advertising. You can contact each to see what arrangement they can make in this regard.

Buying Your Book for Resale to the Public . . . .

If you are interested in personal appearances and/or public speaking and concurrently selling your book, as we've said in a previous chapter, the very first thing you must do is to carefully read the section of your contract addressing the question of how you can buy quantities of your book from your publisher and how much you will have to pay them.

Refer to that portion of your contract that is headed "Copies Purchased by Author" or the like. This section will provide details on the quantities of your book that you can purchase and at what discount. For example, you know your book will retail at $9.95 and that your contract allows you to purchase books at 40 percent off the retail price, so if you decide to purchase 100 copies you will pay your publisher $5.97 each. When you direct sell your book you will be able to keep the $3.98 profit. The pitfall here, however, is you either have to sell the 100 copies or be prepared to keep them.

Some authors, knowing for certain that they will be able to direct sell their book, arrange for direct selling even before their contracts are finalized. Before they receive their final contract—and knowing what the list price of their book will be—they inform their editor that in lieu of part or all of their advance they are asking for x number of copies of their book to be used in direct sales. Or they arrange, again before their contract is finalized, that they will take a smaller advance than had been discussed, and instead will receive x number of copies of their book in lieu of the heretofore-agreed-on amount of their advance.

If, prior to signing your contract you are interested in undertaking direct sales and prefer to leave your advance intact, or if you have no idea of how many books you can sell, you can still exercise your right to buy books at discount if your contract stipulates this. Therefore, before you sign your contract you should carefully read it through (this being just one of the points you want to look for).

If you decide to pursue this idea some time after your contract is in effect and your contract allows for this, you have the option of purchasing your books at the price and terms stated.

Librarians: The Writer's Best Friend . . . .

Did you know that public libraries' buying policies usually mean that you have at least one place where your books can live on and on?

Unlike consumer bookstores where books can be returned well after they are purchased, by and large, libraries usually buy books "for keeps." This means that when all else fails—if your books are not to be found in any bookstore—hopefully some libraries will have purchased your book.

Taking this optimistic forecast further, if you know that your books have been acquired by a library in your area, why not approach the librarians in charge of setting up speaking appearances and offer to speak to patrons? At the least you'll probably create a cadre of new readers, and at best you might interest the library in buying additional copies of your book.

It might be that in your area there are volunteer groups (sometimes known as "Friends of the Library" or "library boosters") who undertake arranging these events. Once you've established who to contact, keep in touch with that person.

Before you do this outreach you might want to read, *Library Programs: How to Select, Plan, and Produce Them* (John S. Robotham and Lydia LaFleur, published by The Scarecrow Press, Inc., 52 Liberty St., Box 656, Metuchen, NJ 08840, 2nd edition, 1981.) This book contains advice from, and for, librarians to help them plan book programs. You should find it instructive.

Specific Suggestions and Examples

You'll find some good ideas on library promotion tactics in the *Workbook Edition* of *How to Get Happily Published Handbook* (available for $27.50 from Sensible Solutions, Inc., 275 Madison Ave., #1518, New York, NY 10021). For example, it is suggested that early on (when your book is accepted by a publisher isn't too early) you find out if your publisher puts out a catalog specifically intended for librarians. If so, make certain to communicate with the person in charge of creating these catalogs. You want them to include your book in any library-oriented catalogs or mailers.

Also, if you receive good reviews in important media that are valued by librarians (such as those we discuss in this book) make certain your publisher immediately calls librarians' attention to these reviews. We would suggest that they either send out copies of the reviews with a cover note, or that they create a special mailer for librarians. If they place ads in publications that librarians read, ask that they include quotes from your good review in advertising your book.

Show and Tell Time?

Another excellent suggestion in the *Handbook* is that you offer to appear at library conferences—such as at the annual meeting of the American Library Association, or at any of the Association's regional meetings. If your publisher does exhibit at these or other professional association meetings, ask the person who sets up the exhibits for your publisher if they feel you should do an in-person appearance. Their answer might be in the affirmative if (1) your book dovetails with the theme they will take for the exhibit; (2) your work is of special interest to the members and attendees of the association; (3) they are specialist publishers and you typify their list; or (4) you have a particularly relevant subject.

You might, for example, learn that your publisher is bringing out a new group of ethnically themed children's books, and you have written a book of African folktales. Or, you might have written a seminal work on the Missouri Compromise for a regional publisher. If you are the author of a work on the First Balkan War in 1912-13, and the countries then involved are again making headlines, you might well be a likely person for an appearance. Or if you have written a novel that takes place in Alaska in 1897, you might be a good guest author at regional conclaves in this geographic area. Likewise if there is a regional meeting in Montana and you have written a young adult book on Custer's Last Stand at the Battle of Little Bighorn, you might be of interest to the publisher as a guest with a book of special interest to librarians in this locale.

Publicity and the Vanity Press . . . .

If you are considering having a book published by a so-called "vanity press"—that is, a company that you pay to publish your book—you should be aware of the problems you'll likely encounter in undertaking publicity.

First, it's quite rare for bookstores to stock vanity books, and it's rarer still (if not almost unheard of) for quality book review media to review these books. Understand that we are not referring to self-published books, nor those published by entrepreneurial authors and small, new publishing companies. We are speaking of those companies that publish solely for pay.

"Vanity" by Any Other Name . . .

Of late, one finds increasing numbers of such companies calling themselves "subsidy publishers," thus escaping the tarnished image of the term "vanity press." You should be aware that while some reputable commercial publishers do accept subsidies from authors for things like enhanced publicity and promotion campaigns, this is not what we're speaking of here.

Caveat Emptor Obtains

Several years ago, a widely read magazine ran a short article that presented a fairly positive picture of vanity houses. The article said in part:

> Typically, for about $5,000 you get 500 copies of a 32-page book (standard for poetry.) Spend upwards of $50,000 and you get 5,000 copies of a 500-page volume with color photos and a fancy jacket. [One vanity publisher said the average cost at his company was] "$12,000 for 1,000 copies of a 250-pager, sold in bookstores and by direct mail. . . . If the book sells out, the publisher prints more copies at its expense. Your royalty is 40 percent of the retail price. . . . About 10 percent of your cost goes toward a modest marketing effort—mailing review copies, running some small ads." [Another vanity house spokesperson said,] ". . . only 10 percent of our authors break even."

Even with the last, revealing, quote, this report was sanguine indeed!

It doesn't, however, accurately reflect the actual situation. Far too many authors tell heart-rending stories of how miserably they fared! One such author (whose anonymity we must preserve) suffered just such a fate . . . and at the hands of one of the companies mentioned in the article. According to his publicist:

> [He] managed to make every mistake it is possible for a first-time author to make—down to turning his manuscript, (and $5,000) over to a subsidy publisher so notorious as to now be under investigation by [the state in which he lives,] and the Federal authorities.

After You've "Signed on the Dotted Line"

If you have already contracted to have a vanity house publish your book, or are about to do so, carefully read that section of your agreement that relates to publicity and promotion. And realize that even if the agreement states the vanity publisher agrees to send *x* number of copies to the media for review consideration, or if you have assumed the cost of so doing, you should be prepared to be ignored by the media. This is not unfair or prejudicial treatment, but rather a long-held practice in book review circles. The belief is that vanity books are just what their name implies. However meritorious some of these books may be, they carry a stigma. Most book reviewers believe that if a book is worthy of being published, hence being reviewed, a commercial house or university press would have acquired it.

Further, given the fact that channels of distribution are almost uniformly closed to vanity books, the public cannot obtain such books in bookstores. Reviewers are uniformally loathe to touch these works as they feel they'd be doing their audiences a disservice; publicizing books that are unobtainable is bad practice. Even some small or new publishing houses have a hard time convincing media that they have sufficient national distribution to warrant coverage.

If you want *only* to have a book with your name on it in print, one that you can give away, and if you have no expectation of seeing your book in stores or reviewed by the media — and if you can afford to do so — then you might explore the vanity presses. But, to repeat, if you want the general public to know about your book and expect they will learn about it from the media, vanity publishing won't serve your purpose.

Even if the agreement offered you by the vanity publisher states they will send your book to major book review media, ask for details. Ask them to send you the following information: A complete list of the books they have published in the past several seasons, along with copies of all reviews from *recognized* book review media that have appeared on these works.

Ask especially to see reviews from any and all of the following: *Publishers Weekly, Library Journal,* The American Library Association's *Booklist, Choice, Kirkus Reviews, The New York Times Book Review,* and major U.S. newspapers or general interest magazines. Ask also to see a list of all major regional and national radio/TV shows that have interviewed authors on their house lists. This should be an instructive undertaking.

Remember that advertising space can be bought by anyone, so do not pay any attention — however impressive the ads they may show you — to their books' advertisements. (Which, in some cases, might well have been paid for by their authors!)

"Ah, But *Your* Book is of Special Interest"

If you are told by this type of publisher that as yours is a book of scholarly interest, the above criteria won't in any case apply, be mindful of your colleagues' opinions. By and large professionals (and that includes the professional journals in your field) recognize just what having one's book published by a vanity press means. Thus, think long and hard on the subject. Often having a scholarly work published by a vanity house will backfire and may cause a professional to "lose face" among his or her colleagues.

11

How to "Make" Your Own Luck

As the anonymous aphorism puts it: "Chance favors the prepared mind."

Writers often tell tales of serendipitous events that are instructive. To wit: Some years back, the author of a travel guide for disabled people sat next to a widely read newspaper columnist on an airplane. This chance meeting and friendly conversation led the writer to send the columnist an autographed copy of the book (along with the name and address of a specialized retail store from which individual copies could be ordered). The columnist used all the information in a column, and a huge response ensued. Orders for the book poured into the store.

Here again, we're *not* suggesting that every writer undertake hoopla or push their work upon people. Rather, we point to these instances as good examples of creative ways writers have drawn attention to their work.

Unusual Ideas for All Writers . . . .

There are many ways you can bring yourself to people's attention that will keep your name alive.

Card Smart

One creative writer had an outsized postcard made up bearing the words "Free-lance Writer" printed in large type, along with the Dewey system's decimal code for his type of writing. He sent this to editors adding a handwritten, personalized message.

One fairly inexpensive way you might want to investigate is to create a special business card notched to fit onto the popular rotary style telephone directory. These rotary directories are usually referred to as Rolodex directories.

To create the notched card, you will need to purchase a device called a "business card punch." I have seen these priced between $4 and $6. (See illustration page 160 for the punch made by Merrick Industries, Sunnyvale, California, and available through the Quill Company's catalog.) This special punch cuts two specially shaped slots at the bottom of your card so it can be placed onto the rotary directory. You would have a printer print all relevant information onto a plain business card which you then manually punch.

This "business card punch" can convert standard business cards to fit onto rotary type telephone directories.

Or, if you have a computer *and a laser printer* you can print your own pre-cut index cards for a rotary phone index. A company that sells packages of blank, die cut index cards for laser printing is Intergraphix Corporation, 260 Corporate Park, Oak St., Pembroke, MA 02359; phone (800)451-2515. At this writing, a twenty-five sheet package of these with eight cards to a sheet, costs $12.95 plus shipping and handling.

If you decide to send this type of card to editors, it should include your name, address, phone number, and — the whole point of mailing these cards — information on the type of writing you do. If space permits, you should also include a brief credentials list (major publications that have published your work and other relevant data).

That is, it might read:

> **Joan Johnson**
> 123 Your Street
> Anytown, U.S.A., Zip
> Area Code — Your Phone Number
> **Writes on:** Home repair; home remodeling, inexpensive do-it-yourself projects for home and apartment owners.
> **Has appeared in:** *Home Handyperson; Homeowners Save Money Tips; Do It Yourself Annual; Beautiful Homes; House & Homes Guide.* Author of *Homeowners Quick & Easy Fix-it Projects.* (Smyth Press, 1989, $5.95 pb.) Lecturer at Maryland College Extension Service on home repair.

If you decide to have your printer create these cards, you will probably want to work with an artist or the printer on copy layout.

Send each finished, notched card with a personalized letter explaining to each magazine editor that you hope they will place you in the "freelancers" section of their phone index.

Sticker It to Them

Authors take note: One good way to draw attention to your book is to sticker it. (Also sometimes referred to as "seals," these stickers bear printed messages and are affixed to a book's cover or jacket.) Generally these seals are self-adhesive and can be done in metallic or matte finish paper, and shaped into circles, squares, rectangles, or custom shaped. If your local printer cannot reproduce these in quantity, check the Yellow Pages for specialist printers.

You would have a message printed onto your sticker and then have it pasted onto the front cover of your book. Your sticker might read: "Local Author" or "Nominated for the Bancroft Prize" or "From the author of [Your Earlier Titled Novel]" or anything that you think would entice customers to pick up your book.

If your publisher is willing to do so, it would be most expeditious to have their warehouse people sticker your books. If they cannot do so, then you can try it on your own—but you will have to know which bookstores are selling your book. Don't dash into bookstores ready to sticker your books, without first obtaining the approval of the store owner or manager. Better yet, if you have established a relationship with local distributors or jobbers who have stocked your books, ask them if you can do this at their warehouse.

Banners, T-Shirts, and More

While not exactly low-key, you might consider having a banner made up announcing your appearance if you will be undertaking a major public speaking engagement, such as one at a large store in a shopping mall. These vinyl banners can be large or small, and could say something like:

"Meet Jane Smith, author of: *Books I have Loved,* here at Smiler's Bookstore on January 3rd and 4th, from 10 A.M. until Noon."

If you cannot locate a local supplier of banners, there are companies you can contact by phone or mail. Hale Sign Co. (2465 Russellville Road, Bowling Green, KY 42101; phone (800)626-7446) is a factory, and says it can deliver quickly and offer commensurate discount prices. Ask to see their free catalog of custom banners, flags, pennants, and banner frames. Another company offering similar products is Bannerland, 1039 West Barkely Ave., Orange, CA 92668; phone (800)654-0294 or fax (714)633-0984.

Another way to really blow your own horn—and, again, this is not for the shy among you—is to have custom-imprinted items made up bearing your message. We've all seen T-shirts with commercial messages made up by stores, but have you considered balloons, shopping bags, caps, jackets, aprons, or matchbooks made up that announce your message?

Numerous companies exist that create these items. Some will not work with individuals, preferring to work only with established business firms. Most, however, will be happy to fill your order—if you pay cash up front. So find out first. To locate such companies in your area, consult the Yellow Pages of your phone

*This outsize matchbook
was created as a promotional
device for a humorous book.*

book under "sales promotion" or "advertising specialties." Or refer to copies of magazines such as *Premium/Incentive Business*. Published by Gralla Publications, 1515 Broadway, New York, NY 10036, this magazine contains descriptions of promotional items. It's geared to business users, but you might find merchandise and companies you can work with.

To obtain information about promotional items, you can also contact B & B Advertising, P.O. Box 220, Scott City, KS 67871. Outside of Kansas, phone (800)835-0002; if you live in Kansas, they accept collect calls at (316)872-2340. B & B can create custom-imprinted caps and other imprinted items. (At this writing, eight dozen caps with one color printed message, would cost $2.43 for each cap.) You can obtain B & B's free descriptive material by contacting them at the above address.

Another company is: Active Concepts, %Motivators, Inc., 143 Madison Ave., New York, NY 10016, (212)889-5550. They too have a wideassortment of items including neat glow-in-the-dark pails, logo-bearing sneaker laces, lanyards, and eyeglass holders (union-made in the U.S.), plastic shopping bags, brass bookmarks, Mylar balloons, and lots more. Contact them for their splendid catalog.

Other things from promotion houses include items such as message imprinted calendars to use in lieu of Christmas cards, as well as key chains, metallic coasters (that can carry an imprinted message), miniature flashlights, desk accessories, pens, kinetic clocks and calendars of all kinds, even small "fuzzy bears" holding messages that can be worn as pins.

The small fuzzy bears are in a catalog put out by Impact Advertising, 124 E. 40th St., New York, NY 10016; phone (212)370-5590 or fax (212)697-5893. This company's catalog is especially helpful, as its index groups items by price category. For under 50 cents, for example, they list appliques, balloons, bottle openers, bumper stickers, buttons and badges, candies and gum, coloring books, first aid kits, flyers, foil seals, growth charts, lapel pins, luggage tags, magnets, paper clips, pens and pencils, plastic tumblers, self-exam cards, snack bag clips, shopping bags, toys, and visors.

If you send out Christmas, New Year's or Season's Greetings cards you might be interested in the colorful, clever rubber band-activated pop-up calendars and greeting cards sold by Graphics[3], Inc., 1400 Indiantown Rd., P.O. Box 937, Jupiter, FL 33468-0937; phone (407)746-6746 or fax (407)746-6922.

The 1990 pop-up polygon calendar was quantity priced — starting at 99 cents each for 250. (The price decreases with the number ordered.) These are available with the top and bottom imprinted with your message, and are ready for mailing.

Another company offering the pop-up custom printed, polygon calendar, with similar quantity prices, is Perrygraf, 19265 Business Center Dr., Northridge, CA 91324-3552; phone (800)423-5329, (818)993-1000, or fax (818)993-7572.

Button, Button

You can also create your own unusual promotional items, including buttons that can be customized to carry a personalized message or piece of artwork. A button could show a reduced version of a book's cover, a drawing, or bear a printed message. While not everyone would be comfortable handing out buttons with the message "Writer for Hire," bearing their likeness, there are numerous creative ideas that can be used for personalized messages or designs. For example, if you are promoting a specific magazine or newspaper article you could obtain permission to reduce the masthead of the publication and use that on a button along with a message about your article(s). Or, you could even put a brief poetic statement onto your button.

When my cookbook was published, we arranged to have bright green and yellow buttons made up bearing the message, "I'm *GOING BANANAS.*" In smaller type we printed the book's price, the publisher's name, and other essential information.

Instead of holiday greetings, create personalized buttons. And, don't think that the *only* holiday to mark is Christmas. You could use this device to create a unique button for any holiday. It's unlikely that many people will receive greetings marking Flag Day or Hawaii's "Lei Day."

To better understand button possibilities, you might contact Badge-A-Minit, 348 North 30th Rd., Box 800, LaSalle, IL 61301; outside Illinois phone (800)223-4103, inside call (815)224-2090. The company sells various button-making kits for 2¼-inch buttons. These include a three-part set, which can be used to create metal front and metal pinned-back buttons, and a five-piece mirror part set allowing you to create pocket and purse mirrors on one side of the button with the other side suitable for holding artwork. They sell magnetic back-button part sets with clear plastic covers that can be used to create magnets, as well as sets for pendants, key chains, and pinless, "sticky-back" button sets that are reusable. Additionally, you can purchase all the accessories you'll need — background papers and foils, dry transfer lettering, rosettes (to turn buttons into these more permanent items), preprinted rosette ribbons, and several hundred preprinted buttons. They also do custom design and printing of these items.

They have several "starter kits," ranging from $29.95 up to $71.95. The company says they have a forty-eight hour "turn around" time from receipt of orders, and they accept Visa and MasterCard.

Thinking BIG

If you will be making personal appearances or doing speaking engagements and want to draw attention to your appearance by using a poster, but are not artistically inclined or able to hire a sign maker, there's equipment available that can help you create large posters. PosterPrinter® can enlarge an 8½ × 11 inch sheet to up to eight times its size. You can use your computer printer or typewriter and create a poster as large as 23 × 33 inches.

The firm offers seven color combinations: pink, blue or yellow paper with black printed images, and white paper with black, blue, red, or orange printed images. At this writing the average cost on the East Coast, runs to about $25 for one poster. For information, call or write: PosterPrinter Division, Varitronic Systems, Inc., P.O. Box 234, Minneapolis, MN 55440; phone: (800)637-5461.

Sound It Out?

If you'll be doing personal appearances and want passersby to know about it, there's a clever electronic gadget being sold that "talks" to passing people using your voice. These "photo-electronic talkers" automatically "speak" to anyone passing within ten feet of them. It delivers your prerecorded sixteen-second message or announcement when activated by a passerby. These are pocket-sized, and can be used in a variety of ways. If you're doing a lot of personal appearances, for instance, you can record a message such as "Hi. Jane Smith is in the mall today at Readmore Bookstore. Stop in to chat about her latest book, *Mallwalking for Fun and Fitness*."

Check a full-service electronics store in your locale for details on this product. Or you can contact one company that recently advertised it, S.A.M. Electronics, 2701 Belmont, Chicago, IL 69618; phone (312)588-1020.

At this writing, one "Talker" sold for under $100.

The VNR

Advances in technology have given rise to another wrinkle in the industry: the VNR (Video News Release), a professionally produced, filmed publicity vehicle.

VNRs are not only too expensive for the average person to consider, they also meet with less than hearty approval from journalists and others in communications. Television people are often loathe to air what is held by many to be "free advertising." So, if you have considered having a VNR created to publicize yourself, your book, an article, or your writing in general—think long and hard. More to the point, call several of the television shows and stations you are considering as likely recipients. Ask them if, in fact, *they* feel you should undertake such a project. In other words, what is the likelihood of their airing your VNR?

Using Your Computer to "Spread the Word" . . . .

A computer and a modem can help you spread the word about your writing. Using your modem you can alert people via bulletin boards (or special computer "chat" services) of your article or book.

These electronic bulletin boards reach people all over America. You could send a message publicizing your work, and if interested, could dialog with other people. To find out about the commercial sources such as CompuServe, Delphi, and others, as well as many other fascinating aspects of this topic, you might want to read *The Modem Reference*, by Michael Banks, published in 1988 by Brady Books/Simon & Schuster. ($21.95 paperback edition.)

Though you would not consider investing in a modem for your computer solely to publicize yourself, it could be valuable for more than just broadening your potential readership. With a modem, writers can communicate with publishers, transmit copy, and (for a fee, of course) access varied on-line services, such as data bases and information retrieval services. This is especially helpful to those writers who are far removed from comprehensive libraries.

A Personal Newsletter

Have you ever considered sending editors a personal newsletter? Why not follow the lead of the professional direct mail experts and regularly circulate a newsletter to editors of publications you have written for, or to those you would like to write for in the future? Here again, you want to be remembered as someone who is an expert in his or her field.

If you have a computer and the capability to do desktop production of artwork, you can create a good-looking newsletter. If so, look into using what is called "clip art" software for the non-text portion of your piece. These programs are widely available and offer a large array of images: designs, borders, symbols, etc. And, you can also create all styles and sizes of type if you have the proper computer software and hardware.

There are many companies that sell these clip art software programs. You should find many advertised in computer magazines.

If You Don't Own a Computer

To save money, or if you will not be hiring a graphic artist to design a logo (symbol) and letterhead for your direct mailer, go to an art supply store where you should be able to buy paperback books with copyright-free art. These are also known as "clip art" books. Pick a symbol for your newsletter, such as a black-and-white picture that signifies the period of which you write, then paste it atop a sheet of your letterhead stationery. You've thus created your own "mechanical" (a page, including artwork, which is ready for printing).

If you do not have access to an art supply house, you can mail order clip art books. Many such companies advertise in books geared to graphic arts people. Two of these are Deuville Publications (611 South Canyon Dr., Suite 7-440, Palm Springs, CA 92264) and Artmaster Book Company (500 North Claremont Blvd., Claremont, CA 91711).

Another old-line company with a splendid array of these books is Dover Publishing, 180 Varick St., New York, NY 10014. Dover maintains a retail bookstore at this same address.

How to Proceed

Have your printer photo-offset a batch of these special newsletter letterheads. Each month, type relevant data below this logo letterhead. Remember to allow at least a one quarter-inch margin at the top and bottom of your paper to facilitate the printer's using this. And allow generous margins right and left. (Refer to other such newsletters as examples of how you can set up your material.)

For subsequent pages, type your copy on plain white paper and have your printer collate and staple your newsletter. If the printer can supply larger sheets of paper, you can type your copy so it will fit onto 11 × 17-inch paper, using as many sides as you'll need. (This large-sized paper is then folded.)

What Type of Information Should I Include?

Unless you write for highly specialized publications, you won't want to write on highly esoteric topics in your newsletter. Rather, you want to share information that will position you in the recipient's mind as a writer who is an expert in his or her field.

Each time you create your newsletter, do so mindful of your media audience's "lead time." For example, let's say that you write about world history with an emphasis on the 20th Century. In May you would write of the August date that marks the end of World War II and how it affected people on the U.S. homefront; if you write on interior design, in September you could explore what America's homes looked like when the December 1941 attack on Pearl Harbor occurred. Depending on your area of expertise, you have many possibilities for your personal newsletter.

If you are more ambitious, you can create an even more artistic newsletter and use it to regularly contact editors with information that you feel they will find interesting, valuable, *and possibly worthy of reprinting.* For example, if you write on home furnishings, you can send them informational data that you know is outside the mainstream of what they will receive from manufacturers and public relations people. Or, if you specialize in writing about the growth of interest in 18th century antiques, and on the growing number of spurious pieces for sale purportedly from this period, what you have to say will probably be of special interest since you have no commercial ax to grind. And it might very well be that your doing this type of informational mailing could result in your being called upon to write for the publication, or at least your being quoted in a column.

Advertise Yourself . . . .

Some freelance, nonfiction magazine and newspaper writers have tried an approach that you might like to emulate. Have you considered taking out a classified advertisement in publications read by editors? Your ad, which you would place in the "Positions Wanted" section of publications such as *Folio, Editor & Publisher,* or *Magazine Week,* for example, might read like this:

> FREELANCER
>
> Seeks trade/professional magazines with which to develop an ongoing relationship. I've written regularly for newspapers and magazines in [fill in your area of expertise here: e.g., personal finance, real-estate, retirement living, travel and gardening, etc.]
>
> Am a "quick study" and produce good copy on time and on budget. Will also ghost edit jargon-ridden manuscripts into readable copy for lay audiences. For sample clips etc. [Insert your name, address, phone number here.]

Another way that authors can promote themselves is by having their publishers try to have them included in Gale Research's *Contemporary Authors* (see our Reference/Resources Section for general information).

One approach that frustrated authors often take, and one we *don't* suggest, is buying space in the classified section of *Publishers Weekly* announcing they have written a book and are seeking a publisher. If this is something you've been contemplating, save your money; you would be much better off following traditional routes to finding a publisher. For example, start, as we'd suggested elsewhere, by subscribing to *PW.* Doing this means you'll be on top of publishing world activities.

An Example of Creatively Used Frustration . . . .

One writer turned his frustration at his failure to interest anyone in publishing his books into a creative event that elicited intense national publicity coverage.

The *New York Times* headlined his story "Writer Acts on a Craving for Publicity." They reported that Alan Ira Rosenberg had numerous mailings sent to the major New York-based media announcing that he intended to hold an auction of what he dubbed "the first futures market in literary memorabilia." He would sell off his tools and writings, he said, with the thought that someday they would become valuable (an idea born when he noticed that the Hemingway estate had created media interest when such a public sale was held after the writer's death).

What Mr. Rosenberg hoped to accomplish was not so much wealth as publicity. And in this regard he succeeded admirably. He retained the services of New York public relations counsel, Bob Perilla, and also hired an auctioneer. A hotel penthouse was the auction site, he served champagne, and to up the ante (as it were) he arranged to marry his fiancee that day. Thus, numerous publicity and photo opportunities were provided the attending media.

Among the items offered for sale were notes, pictures, letters, tapes, a computer, and Mr. Rosenberg's original manuscripts.

When members of the press and the invited guests arrived, they were greeted by a bevy of nearly one dozen aspiring actresses — all of whom were loudly reading excerpts of the latest of Mr. Rosenberg's work — all at once.

While it made no sense to listeners, the ensuing cacophone added to the media-worthiness of the event.

While the event may have been a bit extreme, it garnered Mr. Rosenberg extensive media attention all over the nation.

Media attention — and subsequent strong sales — were created for a novel by another unusual promotion. Leonore Fleischer, in her "Talk of the Trade" column in *Publishers Weekly* (April 29, 1989) described the "fragrant" campaign created by a publicist working on Jayne Ann Krentz's book, *Gift of Fire.* A special "Fire" perfume was created solely for the book's promotional campaign. It was sent to buyers at book wholesalers, to retailers, and to the press. Ms. Fleischer writes that one Philadelphia columnist's wife was so taken with the fragrance that she insisted he *buy* her a larger bottle . . . which, naturally, was not possible. This clever campaign helped propel the book to success. Book sales outstripped that of the author's earlier works. As Ms. Fleischer points out, this is indeed unusual in publishing circles, where sequels generally don't do as well as first books.

Another Unusual Story

Some seasons back I created an unusual event to publicize a fairly straightforward work of history, *The Jews in Old China,* which traces the history of the Jewish people in early China. Its author, Sidney Shapiro, was born in the U.S. but had lived for many years in the People's Republic of China. To mark his visit to America and to celebrate the publication of the book, we planned a party for press people and dignitaries.

Mr. Shapiro had an intriguing personal history, which included operating a bagel bakery while he lived in Beijing. (He said he did so to re-create a favored — and obviously unobtainable! — food of his Brooklyn childhood.) Thus was born the idea of having his publisher, Hippocrene Books, work in conjunction with the prestigious Asia Society on what we called a "Dim Sum *and* Bagel Brunch." Given the uniqueness of the book's subject, and the author's fascinating background — both of which we delineated in a press kit — along with the unusual fare we were serving and the elegant location for our event, the response was superb!

Coat-Tailing. . . . .

If you have written an article, book or books on a subject that is in the news or one that is the subject of a popular TV show or film, you have an excellent opportunity to employ what is called "coat-tailing." Plainly put, you can create a connection between your writing and something that has captured the public's interest. *Authors take note:* This type of self-promotion works equally well for new and older books.

Once you have determined what popular subject you will employ to coat-tail, this is how to begin.

To interest booksellers in placing your books in their window, offer to provide a relevant poster. (See samples at the end of this chapter.) Make certain, however, the poster you provide is of professional quality. If you will not be using a professional sign maker or graphic artist, then refer to page 94, for details on creating professional quality signs.

Here are some examples of how writers might coat-tail to take advantage of "names in the news":

• If you write nonfiction specializing in Asia in the pre-World War II period, and you read there is to be a forthcoming television mini-series set in Asia during this time, you have a good reason to approach your local bookstore. Suggest they consider doing a window display featuring your book, thus capitalizing on the airing of this series. If you write books or articles you could try your local media outlets. They might like to use you on one of their shows, to have a "local angle" on the upcoming TV series.

• If you have written a critical evaluation of the work of painter Pablo Picasso during his "blue period" and there is a motion picture out that portrays his life, this, too, would present you with a good reason to approach a bookseller or your local media.

• Or, if you have an inprint, nonfiction book detailing the history of beauty pageants in America, you could try to interest your local bookseller in featuring your book to capitalize on this subject in September—coinciding with the annual Miss America pageant.

• If you had written a book that explores the life of a noted writer, and her works have just been reissued in a new format, try to interest bookstore(s) in doing a window showing her books *along* with yours. In this instance, your poster would say something like: "Read the newly reissued version of Margaret Mitchell's *Gone with the Wind* and Joan Smith's biography of Ms. Mitchell: *Margaret Mitchell—A True Southern Belle.*" Note, however, if you live in a small town with more than one bookshop, *don't* approach all the book dealers at the same time with your idea.

• If you have authored a book on the subject on the Civil War and it is an anniversary of a Civil War battle, try to interest your bookseller in featuring your book as part of a window display on the period.

• If you write historical fiction and the period you cover in one of your books is in the news — the Centenary of the Johnstown Flood, for example — approach your local bookstore with that "timely" angle.

• Or, if you have written a spy story centering on the IRA in Ireland, or a mystery centered on the Middle East today and the troubles there, you have (sad to say) almost daily opportunities to approach a book dealer and/or media outlet. Employ techniques similar to those outlined above.

• The same applies if you write young adult fiction and your latest work is centered upon the troubling theme of teenage alcoholism.

Wherever you are published, whatever type of writing you do, and whatever time of year it is, there is always some reason to approach a bookseller or the media with this type of promotional idea. (If you are stumped as to what to do, turn to the *Chase's Calendar of Events* where you're likely to find help.)

If you're an author, undertaking this type of self-promotion can be of multiple benefit. Not only will your success bring you attention, but if the bookstore that you contact isn't presently stocking your books, they might feel this would be a good time to order! Following are some samples of copy for posters used to "coat-tail" your book.

Example #1. Background reading when watching the hit TV show, "From Trash to Treasure." Read *Treasures in My Attic?,* available here.
Autographed by the author: Sven Johnson - $16.95 in paperback

Example #2. Did You See the Oscar Winning Movie, *Bombs over Oregon?* Read the book, *Oregon at War,* by Jane Seyland.

Example #3. Learn more about Celtic Art . . . featured at the Stetson Museum . . . Read *The Art of the Celts,* by Barbara Jompole.

TIP: Paste your book's front cover onto your poster, and if you can obtain copies of colorful promotional material about the project you are "coat-tailing," also paste it onto your poster.

Product Plugs in Your Book? . . . .

Some writers feel that by including product "plugs" right in their books they'll receive added publicity. And, some in doing just that, have unleashed a storm of controversy as well.

The *New York Times* "Media Business" column reported that author Beth Ann Herman "raised hackles by putting her novel's protagonist in a Maserati." But that mention also gained her a $15,000 party at a Beverly Hills, California, Maserati auto dealership — which in turn produced media pickup by major national shows. Ms. Herman was also given a window display of her book at the posh Beverly Hills store Giorgio, as she'd prominently mentioned this shop in her novel.

While some authors blanch at this type of product mention, summoning her public relations work experience, Ms. Herman said she clearly understood the problems a first time author faced and felt that sprinkling such mentions throughout her book was the only way she could get major publicity. She said that her publicity background proved to her that, "Publishers are notorious for not giving their all."

But, the practice has many strong-minded opponents. Michael Jacobsen, executive director of the Center for Science in the Public Interest, wrote a *New York Times* "Op-Ed" article speculating on the negative implications of a novelist "obtaining such promotional help." He cited the example of having a major pharmaceutical company provide promotional help should a novel's infirm protagonist be written of as repeatedly taking the company's medications. But, Ms. Herman felt there is no breach of faith between writer and reader in doing promotional tie-ins in her book. She said, "The bottom line is I'm no James Michener or Joseph Heller." She did concede, however, that "the path to ethical compromise was a slippery slope."

Robert K. Massie, president of the Author's Guild and author of the Pulitzer Prize-winning work, *Peter the Great,* said flatly, "An author who does this is not only on a slippery slope, but over the precipice." Mr. Massie felt that it's specious to draw distinctions between forms of literature for the purpose of justifying Hollywood-type product placements.

Personally, I believe that if a mention of a specific product is important to your story, and if it makes sense, there's nothing particularly wrong with such a "plug." But if done gratuitously, or in a heavy-handed manner, with ulterior motives, it strikes a false note.

12

Should You Hire a Personal Press Agent?

Let's assume you are loathe to undertake personal publicity or promotion, even with the suggestions in this book. Or you want some professional assistance for a specific media campaign. You may be thinking, therefore, of professional public relations representation.

The First Questions to Ask Yourself . . . .

The first question to ask yourself must be: "Can I afford publicity representation?" Second, ask yourself: "Am I willing to undertake a professional PR/promotion program knowing that it might not pay off?" It is of paramount importance that you realize there are absolutely no guarantees that even the best public relations campaign will produce results. Plainly put, you "pays your money and takes your chances!" Unlike placing an advertisement, where even if the ad fails you have something tangible to show for the money you spend, sometimes even the most successful publicity campaign doesn't equate to an immediate, quantifiable "result." Hence, you might have nothing to show for your efforts.

Having said all of this, let's look at the varied options open to you.

But even before we begin it is important to clarify several issues:

• If you think an *advertising* person can do your publicity, please understand, as we said at the beginning, these are two distinctly different fields. While there are some advertising people who wear two hats, this is not always the case (especially in large cities where there are communications specialists of every stripe). Therefore, it is important that you first ascertain — if you are considering hiring an advertising person — that the person is also *actively* involved in publicity.

• *Authors take note:* You may discover there are no professional *book* publicists in your area. (And, you do need someone adept in doing book publicity.) If this is the case, and you are unable to conduct your search based on the recommendation of a writing colleague, you will find that *Literary Market Place* will prove helpful. This valuable book should be found on the reference shelf of your library. (See our Resource Section.)

• If you will contact publicists using resource directories such as *LMP*, *please do not*—as I've often seen—merely dash off a postcard saying, "Send me your information" and only provide your name without detailing the nature of your request. Any publicist worth his or her salt needs *detailed* information to help understand the type of campaign you would need. Namely, if you are an author: what your book is about, if it is a forthcoming title, when it will be published, who your publisher is, and the extent of—or lack of—the publicity campaign your publisher will undertake. Or, if you are seeking to publicize an in print work, having copies of review quotes would be helpful, as would all of the information we have just mentioned for a forthcoming book. You do *not*, and should not, however, have to send every prospective publicist a copy of your book or galleys. Magazine and newspaper writers should also spell out the nature of what they hope to accomplish.

 • You have to consider what type of public relations representation you will have. Depending upon where you live, you may not have all that many choices, but it is important that you know what choices you have.

Using a Public Relations Agency Versus a Freelancer . . . . .

Hiring a full-service public relations agency (or hiring the PR division of a local advertising agency) is usually well beyond the financial reach of the average person.

At public relations agencies, monthly retainers (fees paid to the agency for being your press representative) can be expected to range in the thousands of dollars. In major urban areas, for instance, it isn't unusual for such fees to run to three, four, or five thousand dollars—or more—monthly. Clients customarily sign a contract for a year, or half a year, though some agencies are willing to undertake three-month campaigns.

Clients usually also pay for expenses such as printing, photocopies, and phone calls made in their behalf. In addition to paying these expenses they are generally also billed by the agency for "production charges," which are based upon expenses the agency incurs. These might include charges the agency incurs for you in using a messenger service, doing printing, or sending faxes. These production charges can really skyrocket—at this writing, one frequently hears that public relations agencies charge 18.75%, and more, of the expense being billed.

By and large, therefore, using a public relations agency is not for those on a tight budget. You might find, however, especially in small cities and towns, that there are small, one- and two-person public reations agencies that might be willing to undertake a short-term program for you on a project (flat) fee basis.

Given the costs involved in hiring a full-service public relations agency, many people seek the services of public relations consultants who work on a freelance basis.

How to Select a Freelance Publicity Consultant . . . .

If you decide to hire a freelance publicist here are some suggestions that should help you select the right type of person: Any publicist who tells you, "It's not what you know, but who" – or who nudges you with his elbow, winks and says, "I can spread some money around and get you publicity," is one you want to avoid like the proverbial plague! As in other professions, there are ethics and regulations that prevent journalists (and others involved in promotional activities) from accepting such "grease" money.

Publicity is free, and anyone who tells you otherwise is either not a professional, is ill-informed, or is a charlatan. *Be warned!* Even if a press agent bribes people to take note of you and you receive publicity (or have promotional events arranged) in this manner, it will usually boomerang. Word will quickly get out that you have bought your way to prominence. Ethical journalists and others will likely henceforth avoid you and deny you your sought-after exposure.

Don't confuse advertising with publicity. FYI – and this is stated, *not* in the way of insult to our colleagues who labor in the vineyards of advertising, but merely as fact – *publicity* is any mention you do *not* pay for, and carries significantly more weight than that which you buy. If you place an ad that says you are the world's foremost authority on widgets, that simply does not compare to a newspaper or magazine article or the host of a radio or TV show saying this about you.

Who – and Who *Not* – to Work With

If a press agent "greases some palms" and buys your way into a promotional event (having you do a personal appearance somewhere for which you paid) then you've eroded any credibility you may have as someone people would be willing to see.

Work with a publicist who is skilled in doing personal publicity – preferably one who works, or has worked previously, with creative people such as yourself. Doing publicity for a company is significantly different from doing so for a creative individual.

Of Things Financial

You must immediately determine – *in a general sense* – what the publicist's fee scale is. As to what they might *specifically* charge you, please don't – in fairness to them or to yourself – expect to be given this information on the telephone before they've had a chance to evaluate what type of promotion/PR you need. Only after he or she has met with you and determined the type and extent of the program needed, should a publicist fairly estimate a fee. When you call to set up your initial appointment, ask if the publicist ever works on a "project basis" (that is, a flat fee) versus on a monthly retainer.

Freelancer's Fees and Other Topics . . . .

Most writers will find that a flat project fee, with a time limitation on when the publicist's work starts and ends, will be best for them. Paying a freelance publicist a monthly retainer is generally too costly a proposition for most writers.

If the publicist does work on a project basis, be ready to provide a brief statement of your goals. It is important you think about this before you even begin contacting publicists. Unless you are a professional PR or promotion person, you most likely cannot tell the publicist specific details on the type of exposure you seek. And do understand that while most writers would love to be asked to appear on major national television and radio talk shows and be interviewed by the most prestigious print publications, realistically, you have to build to that stage of prominence.

First Establish Your Goals. . . . .

In your initial call to a publicist, be prepared to give some idea of what you realistically hope to accomplish from a publicity and promotion campaign. Statements such as "I want to be famous" or "I want everyone in the country to know my name!" or "I want to sell a million copies of my new book" are to be avoided.

The old dictum prevails: Do, indeed, "know yourself." Acknowledge the realistic potential of your efforts and know what you are comfortable doing. If, for example, you are terrified by the thought of any in-person or television appearances, say so. Ditto on being interviewed by print journalists.

Ask the freelance publicist to honestly tell you if they feel you should undertake a PR/promo campaign. If the publicist hedges and has to think about this question, that's reasonable. To help them evaluate your potential in their sphere, offer to send the publicist your press kit. And do so, pronto.

Do raise the issue of money. Openly discuss your financial constraints, if you have any (i.e., if you are a magazine writer and have put aside just $500 for a publicity campaign, say so.)

If *you* don't raise the issue of finances, be prepared to be asked by the freelance publicist if you have established a budget for your project. If you know the maximum you have allocated for such activities, be ready to discuss it. (If you've given absolutely no thought to the subject you shouldn't be calling!) Authors, for example, after speaking with their publishers about what they can realistically expect in the way of company-generated publicity and promotion, often set aside a portion of their book advance for these purposes. (While not unheard of, unless one is a fairly prominent author, having the publisher include a specific amount in a book contract for freelance PR help is not routine.)

If you feel comfortable doing so, tell the publicist the absolute outside maximum amount you can spend. You might well be told (by more than one publicist) that the amount allocated isn't sufficient for them to undertake your publicity. But at least you're not setting yourself up for a huge shock later.

The Important Personal Meeting . . . .

If you want a publicist to undertake a publicity campaign for you, never commit yourself to hiring them via telephone. A personal meeting is important.

Before you call anyone, you might want to jot down the key points we've just listed so that you won't forget to raise any of them in your phone conversation. If all of the questions you pose are answered to your satisfaction, *then* set up an in-person meeting.

When you set up this meeting, ask the publicist to bring along samples, and extra copies for your later perusal, of materials they have written for previous clients. The publicist will be writing press releases, and other materials, for and about you, and you must make certain that you will be represented by someone who is literate and polished.

At your first personal meeting, (and for this one it's best *not* to let the publicist know in advance that you will want this information) ask him or her to describe publicity campaigns similar to your needs that they have previously created.

This serves several purposes. First, it will provide you with needed information. Second, it will graphically demonstrate to you the person's skills as a "presenter." (Much of a publicist's work is in verbally "selling" clients.) Finally, it will give you a good idea of their ability to think on their feet, the last of which is another important trait that a good publicist possesses.

Even if you had previously thought out some general ideas of what you want to accomplish, you might find that your initial meeting compounds your confusion. It's possible that you will be completely in the dark as to the specific type of publicity and promotion you need. After you have again briefly outlined what you feel comfortable, and uncomfortable, undertaking (such as personal appearances versus TV or radio interview shows) ask the publicist to suggest *directions*. But do this understanding that you cannot ask the publicist to develop an "action plan" or complete program for you until you are officially a paying client.

What you do want from them at this first meeting is simply an overview of the direction they might take. It is, therefore, vital that *you* at least know what you want to accomplish, and that you be able to concisely impart this information to the publicist. As do freelance writers, freelancer publicists value their time as money. Thus, an unfocused meeting that goes on and on and in which you attempt to get the publicist to give you specific details, or to tell you just how they will proceed then and there, and to give you advice is not only unproductive — it is simply unprofessional on your part!

Ask the publicist about how he or she expects to be paid. Some freelancers ask for one-half or two-thirds of the project fee before starting work and the balance on the date the project ends. And tell the publicist that if you do work together, for your mutual "protection," you will ask for an agreement form and a cover letter detailing the nature of your project. (Explanations and samples follow.)

Do not make a decision on whether to hire someone or not at your first meeting. Unless the publicist comes to you on personal or business referral, or on the recommendation of someone whose opinion you respect, you should ask for references and definitely check them. And, however much you are taken with a publicist, reserve your decision for a day or two. Check their references, sleep on it, then decide. Remember that being persuasive and a good "salesperson" are often the hallmarks of a PR person. Yet that particular publicist might not be right for your project.

Loose Lips Might Sink Your (PR) Project! . . . .

A note here: If you tell family and friends—who are unaware of what good PR/ promo can achieve *and what it costs* — about your plans, be prepared to hear that you're "crazy" or to hear other less than salutary remarks about your sanity. Most people don't understand publicity and promotion, especially as it relates to writers. In many cases you shouldn't even attempt to convince others about the wisdom of your undertaking. And unless the person rendering the judgment on your project holds the purse strings, explanations can often merely compound confusion. Thus, if you *must* consult with another concerned party before making this expenditure, share *all* that you have learned with them.

"Protection" Cuts Two Ways — Plus Other Advice . . . .

When you have selected the person you'll work with, before you begin paying and after you have clarified all aspects of your agreement, ask for the letter of agreement and something in writing: A letter or formal proposal detailing the nature of the work the publicist will undertake on your behalf.

Note: You might encounter a publicist who says you will only have to pay *if they succeed,* and further, that they *guarantee* you *x* number of interviews per city. While this sounds enticing, be aware that they might indeed provide you with a quantity of placements *but* the quality may be severely lacking. Merely appearing on radio or TV, or in print is a waste of your time and energies if the show or publication is not right for you, your book or article, topic or subject, or whose audience is not likely to find your topic of real interest.

Sample Agreement for Working with a Freelance Publicist . .

Your publicist should provide an agreement comparable to the one that follows on their letterhead. You should also be given an outline of the proposed project. See pages 178 and 179.

The Freelance Publicist and Your Upcoming Book . . . .

If you are the author of a book that will be published in the future, do not—*we emphasize, do not*—wait until your book is published, or just about to be published, to investigate the subject of hiring a freelance publicist. First, you will want to seek the services of a specialist, a PR person well versed in doing book publicity and promotion. This type of publicity and promotion is dramatically different from general publicity, and requires the services of a publicist who is skilled in doing book projects.

The reason we specify starting early on this is that it is vital that you—and

• SAMPLE FREELANCERS' AGREEMENT FORM •

Their Letterhead Here

It is agreed that (publicist places name here) will undertake the project outlined in the enclosed material for _____ (your name here) _____.

Project: _____ (name of project here) _____

Project fee: _____ (total fee here) _____

To be paid as agreed [either ½ or ⅔] upon signing this agreement, and the balance on completion of project.

Any out-of-pocket expenses (local and long distance phone calls, messengers, printing, photocopies, etc.) will be direct billed to you, without any production fees.

My responsibility will be to provide you with publicity (and/or promotion) as outlined in the attached.

You agree to indemnify and hold me harmless from and against all losses, claims, damages, expenses, or liabilities which I may incur based on information, representations, data, etc., with which you furnish me.

Please indicate your approval by signing the original copy of this agreement, dating and returning it to me. Attach to this agreement a check or money order in the amount specified herein.

Date: _____ **By:** _____ (sign here) _____

Residing at: _____ (insert your residence here) _____

Publicist's signature: _____

Date: _____ (publicist inserts date here) _____

• **SAMPLE LETTER SENT BY FREELANCER OUTLINING PROJECT** •

Their Letterhead Here

Mr. John Jones
12 Elm Street
Anytown, U.S.A. ZIP

Dear Mr. Jones:
As stated in the attached agreement, I will undertake a publicity and/
or promotion project for you. All fees, payment schedules, and terms
and dates of this project are described in the agreement.

Project: Securing publicity via radio and television appearances
and interviews for you on the subject of indoor home gardening. Also,
offering you as interviewee to major nationally circulated general
interest publications. (Here you would be available for phone interviews to help in another writer's article — you would be quoted as an
expert in the field of indoor home gardening.)

Promotion activities: Trying to arrange your appearance as a guest
speaker at annual gardening events in Anytown, U.S.A. Specifically,
I will try the following:

• Securing radio/TV interviews for you on the six locally produced
radio talk shows in Anytown, U.S.A., and also on the three locally
produced TV "morning" shows. (Lists attached.)

• I will try to secure interviews for you in both Anytown, U.S.A.
daily newspapers (*The Anytown Morning Herald* and *The P.M. ANY-
TOWN CLARION*).

• I will contact editors of the nationally circulated consumer magazines that have garden columns, offering you as "expert" in the field
of home gardening, offering editors the possibility of interviewing
you, and quoting you in any stories they have assigned in the subject
area.

• *Setting up personal appearances:* I will attempt to secure speaking
engagements for you at the two local department stores (SMITH'S
and R.J. MAX). In conjunction with the Anytown Flower Show, you
would deliver brief talks on indoor home gardening.

• I will offer you for interview to the three major television network "morning" talk shows (see media list attached) as an expert on
the subject of indoor home gardening.

I will begin work, as noted in the agreement, when you sign it and
return it to me along with a check or money order for the first part
of the payment for this project.

Sincerely,

Mary Smith

they—have as much "lead time" as possible. For example, if the publicist (versus the publisher) will be doing the earliest publicity—namely, working with the book trade media, as we discuss herein—these publications must have three to four months lead time to consider books for review. Therefore, the first thing you have to do is check with your editor or the company's publicist as to what your book's publication date will be. Your editor or the book publisher's publicity person should know your "pub date."

The "pub date," as it's widely known, is the official date your book is "born." That is, it's the date that finished books will be available for sale in bookstores and the date on which (optimally) newspapers and magazines would begin reviewing it. We say "should be in bookstores" and use the word "optimally" because, realistically, few books ever even make it to the shelves of trade (that is, consumer) bookstores. And reviews, if they are forthcoming, are often months and sadly even sometimes, years late in appearing.

Once you have determined your book's official pub date, you should immediately ask if your publisher will be sending out advance unbound galleys or preparing advance bound galleys. (For information on the uses of bound galleys refer to pages 141-142.)

If bound galleys will be done for your book, you should have this information if you decide to work with an outside publicist. You should know exactly who your publisher will be sending these to for review purposes. (In case they are reluctant to tell you, explain that you need this information for your publicist to prevent duplication of effort.) In many cases, you will probably be told they they will send galleys—in one form or another—to the major book trade journals for review consideration. You, to be better informed, should be familiar with these publications.

What to Avoid When a Publicist Is Working on Your Behalf . .

First and foremost, it's vital to keep all lines of communication open. If an outside publicist—especially one employed by a magazine, newspaper, or book publisher, or one you've hired—is working on publicity projects on your behalf, there are things *you* should avoid doing.

Understand that if a company publicist has, for example, set up a television appearance for you, unless you are told the contrary, they will handle the details and you should absolutely *not* second-guess them. (In some cases they will ask you to take over on some details, but always clarify ahead of time what you'll be asked to do.)

Also, if you are working on publicity appearances in conjunction with the publicist you should not attempt to use anything they set up as a fulcrum. That is, you mustn't try to convince competing shows or print media to interview you *concurrent* with the arranged-for appearance. Many writers enthused and excited by their publicist's success in securing interviews try to parlay that appearance to gain other appearances on shows or with publications that directly compete.

I have witnessed the results of such ill-placed enthusiasm, enthusiasm that completely destroyed our many weeks of effort. An excited author—whom we had placed for an interview on a major television show—gleefully called a competing, nationally aired, morning television show informing them of his upcoming appearance on the competing network's show. He offered to do both shows, for as he reportedly told them, "I'll be in New York City anyway . . . so I thought I'd do both your shows." His innocent excitement produced the following results: He was rapidly turned down by the second show, but not before he had called the first show—which learning of his scheme, told him he was uninvited! These highly competitive shows demand exclusivity on such interviews.

We had devised a carefully structured campaign for him. It was built so that after we had definitely secured his appearance on one of the major morning shows, we would then use it as a door opener to several of the local New York City TV shows, where "rules" of exclusivity of appearances are not that stringent.

Another time a writer wrought havoc with a carefully developed campaign. She directly called and asked the people at a major TV show what airline and hotel they had reserved for her for her flight into their city. She was insulted to learn that she had to bear the cost of her own transportation and accommodations. Her lack of understanding of how these shows work and her pushiness produced a cancellation! Understand that if your publisher is not paying for your publicity trip, you will have to bear these costs. Remember, unless you are a major writer, you absolutely cannot expect any show or publication to pay your way.

Most often, if you're a midlist author, your publisher will not pay for airfare and other transportation, nor will they pick up your hotel bills. They might pay for reasonable daily expenses. *But this absolutely must be agreed to ahead of time.* It's not prejudice, but budget! Budgets for touring midlist authors simply do not exist at most publishing companies.

If you have not discussed this with your publisher and you commence work with a freelance publicist and they successfully arrange publicity that requires your traveling, you (or they) should immediately inform the publisher and see what, if anything, can be done to cover your costs. Again—don't expect too much.

On a personal note. I would enjoy hearing what you have done in the area of self-promotion. If you would like to write to me, to share these ideas, please address your envelope:

Elane Feldman
Author of: *Writer's Guide to Self-Promotion and Publicity*
%Writer's Digest Books
1507 Dana Ave.
Cincinnati, OH 45207

If you include your return address, that would be appreciated. I might someday want to contact you about your sharing information of your efforts with other writers.

• APPENDIXES •

APPENDIXES

• BOOK PUBLICITY ACTION PLAN •

Well before your book will appear you should have an action plan ready to be used. The following gives a general idea of the types of activities you will want to lay out.

Time period: On signing your contract.
Action:

      1. Give completed author's questionnaire to your publisher.
      2. Make certain they want, and you provide, a black-and-white photograph of yourself.
      3. Try to set up in-person appointments with key personnel at the publisher's office.

Time period: After you've turned in your manuscript and/or one year ahead of time.
Action:

      1. Contact national organizations and associations about speaking engagements and lectures.
      2. Verify whether your publisher will send out advance copies, and in what form—i.e., bound or unbound galleys, copyedited manuscript, etc.
      3. When your publisher tells you that your book is in production or actually being *typeset*, consult your previously filled out author's questionnaire. Make certain all areas are "covered" and that everything that had to be done is being—or has been done. This includes:

            • Providing your publisher with names and addresses of advance review copy recipients—that is, your list of influential "names" who should be sent advance galleys to elicit their advance comment, or "blurbs." (Note: If your publisher will not be doing any advance galleys on your book, ask that they send out the final version of your *edited* manuscript for this purpose.)

            • Also make certain that you have sent the publisher lists of your media contacts—that is all "possible users," such as *book reviewers*—with complete names and addresses.

            • Send the publisher your home town media lists with all names and addresses.

            • Write tightly focused, descriptive material on your book for your editor and/or the publisher's publicists to use at the sales conference at which your book will be presented. (Generally, trade book house conferences are held twice yearly, in late fall and in early spring.)

As suggested in *The How to Get Happily Published*, Workbook Edition, (published by Sensible Solutions,) this material should include:

> . . . a handle for selling the book, a list of who will buy it and why, a copy of the table of contents or a paragraph summarizing the contents, a short excerpt that will whet the appetite for more, information on why you wrote the book, and where it's likely to sell especially well.

- Write publicity/marketing people to ascertain their plans.

Other things you should be doing *at this time*, alone or in tandem with the publisher's promotion people:

4. Start work on setting up in-store events—phase 1 only. That is, outreach to retailers (of all types) and libraries. (*Note:* Do not firm up any date for appearances until you know for certain when bound books will be available.)
5. Discuss the possibility of your publisher creating a direct mail sales brochure (*if* you have not maintained direct sales rights). If the publisher will be doing this, devise and provide them with suggested lists of potential recipients.

Time period: Four to six months ahead of the time your bound books will be ready.
Action:

1. Verify that the important advance book trade media have been sent galleys or some advance form of your book for review consideration, *and* that subsequently someone has called these major trade publication reviewers to see if your book *is* being reviewed.
2. When and if good advance trade reviews arrive, make certain all key people at your publisher's offices have them. (Production department people may use them on your book jacket or cover; promotion, publicity, and advertising people for catalog, brochure, and news release uses. Subsidiary rights and sales departments should immediately disseminate good reviews to all potential "sub rights" buyers and all company sales representatives. Copies should also be sent to book buyers at wholesalers, distributors, and national buying offices of the book chains.)
3. Make certain all possible "subsidiary rights" buyers have been contacted.

4. Verify whether your publisher will create a flyer to be sent to all buyers at bookstores, wholesalers, distributors, and national book chains to announce your book's publication. This should incorporate any and all good advance quotes.
5. Ascertain the extent of all advertising and promotion activity on your book.
6. Query the publisher on what advance trade and institutional (schools and libraries) sales have been made. (You want to ascertain the strength of the advance sale of your book.)
7. After verifying the projected arrival date of bound books, begin setting up in-store and library appearances. Always allow a "cushion" just in case your book's delivery runs later than projected. Thus, if you're told bound books are due January 15th, set up appearances *at least several weeks after that*.

Time period: About two to three months ahead of the time bound books will be ready.
Action:

1. Contact radio and TV shows if appearances are to be set up.
2. Create and distribute your bookmarks. If you (or your publisher) have decided to produce book marks, one month before your book is due out, make sure you have these ready to go to your list of retail bookstore managers and/or owners for giveaways to their customers.
3. If you'll be mounting a full-scale *media* campaign, about two months prior to availability of bound books, send out your Media Alert to all media that you have planned to approach. (*Note:* See sample Media Alert in Appendix 2.)

Time period: Approximately six weeks to one month ahead of time when (and if) advance bound galleys are completed. *Note:* If they do not plan advance bound galleys, ascertain that they *will* have some form of your book to send out.
Action:

1. Verify if any advance reviews and/or encomia have arrived and been used and disseminated.
2. Verify if they will send galleys to their important wholesalers and other publicity outlets.
3. Check whether the publisher has had any results on subsidiary rights sales (to magazines for excerpting, and if appropriate to your subject, to book clubs and to paperback reprint houses). If so, make certain these are being circulated or recycled.

Time period: Several weeks prior to your bound books being ready to ship to retailers, wholesalers, et al.
Action:

1. Make certain all press-oriented materials announcing your book's

publication to the general interest media are ready to be mailed (press kits and general and targeted news releases to all consumer and general interest media).

Time period: When your bound books are shipped and are in stores.
Action:

1. If you know you will be appearing on radio and TV and be interviewed by print journalists, start rehearsing! That is, role play your responses and reactions as outlined in relevant chapters. If booked to appear on radio or TV shows or for print interviews, refresh your memory on what your book states! (You may be interviewed two or more years after the time you wrote your work.)
2. Prepare all materials for media interviews.
3. Make sure that the book has been submitted for any appropriate prizes or awards.

Time period: After your official publication date has passed.
Action:

1. Determine what consumer media reviews or articles have appeared.
2. Prepare to "recycle" all good write-ups.
3. Check with your publisher on the results of any advertisements and mail order brochures.
4. Ask all of your publishers' departments for updates and status reports on subsidiary rights and other sales.
5. Whenever you visit a new area or town, remember to stop in to the local bookstores and libraries to introduce yourself.

• SAMPLE PUBLICITY FORMS •

• TIP SHEET •

To be sent to media in advance of event. This is effective if you want the media to announce your event to the public. Your goal is to have them publicize your event to their readers, listeners, and/or viewers. Send this out a full week before your event. A follow-up call to your recipients is recommended. This Tip Sheet gives editors concise advance data on what will take place, and who they can contact for additional information.

Note: Provide information on how the public would find your site if it is in a hard-to-find location.

Letterhead

Contact: Jane Niven
Address: 912 Chestnut Street, San Francisco, CA 94109
Phone Number (day) (415)447-9000, Ext. 32
                     (evening/weekend) (415)447-9876

PUBLIC INVITED TO FREE CONCERT OF TAHITIAN MUSIC AND DANCE MARKING FRANCE'S BASTILLE DAY CELEBRATION

Event: Jane Niven, whose article on Tahitian music and dance will appear in the Sunday, July 15th edition of the *Bay News,* will introduce a troupe of Tahitian dancers and musicians in a free two-hour concert.

Date & Time: Saturday, July 14, 1990, 1 P.M.

Location: Golden Gate Park Band Shell, San Francisco

• ADVANCE NOTICE •

If you want the media to attend your event and report on it, you can prepare an advance notice along the following lines. *Note:* This is *not* done in lieu of a news release, but only provides a sketchy overview to entice the media to attend. You would send this type of notice out seven days before your event. And, make certain to make a follow-up call to your recipients two to three days before your event. Remember, make this enticing—as your aim is to have *them* in attendance for the event *and to report on it.*

Letterhead

Date/Time: Sunday, July 14, 1990, 1 P.M.
Place: Golden Gate Park—Band Shell, San Francisco
Contact: Jane Niven, 912 Chestnut Street, San Francisco, CA 94109
Phone Number (day) (415)447-9000, Ext. 32
　　　　　　　　(evening/weekend) (415)447-9876

FREE CONCERT OF TAHITIAN MUSIC AND DANCE MARKING POLYNESIAN CELEBRATION OF FRANCE'S BASTILLE DAY

The Polynesian People's Cultural Center co-hosts, with *Bay News* travel writer, Jane Niven, a free two-hour concert featuring Tahitian music, dance, and singing to mark France's Bastille Day celebrations.

A troupe of authentically—and very colorfully—attired dancers, singers, and musicians will demonstrate traditional Polynesian favorites.

Jane Niven introduces each musical number providing brief background information on the history of each song and dance. She also explains the significance of each artist's exotic outfit.

Date & Time: Saturday, July 14, 1990, 1 P.M.

Location: Golden Gate Park Band Shell, San Francisco

• MEDIA ALERT •

This alert is to be typed on your (or your publisher's) letterhead stationery. This is not a "form" per se, but a suggestion on one way you can handle this. *Note:* Type the words "Media Alert" in all caps and center it, or if you have access to a photocopy machine that can enlarge, create a larger version of the two words and paste them onto your paper across the center at the top of the page.

Letterhead

MEDIA ALERT

WHAT: New book, *Travel Safety Tips,* by Richard Silvers to be sent you for review and author interview consideration

DATE WE WILL MAIL YOUR COPY: November 1, 1990

OTHER: Book to be published on November 15, 1990
Publisher: Iowa City Press
Price: $6.95 paperback

ABOUT THE AUTHOR: Richard Silvers is a lifelong resident of Iowa City, Iowa. He is a Contributing Editor to *Travel World* magazine, specializing in travel writing.

CONTACT FOR MORE INFORMATION: Richard Silvers, (123)756-4321. Or write: Richard Silvers, Unit #4, River Towers, 12 River Rd., Iowa City, IA 52556.

• CONFIRMATION SLIP •

This is the type of confirmation you want to send to media people to confirm interviews or other media appearances you have booked.

Letterhead

This confirms that _____(insert your name)_____ author of (or writer of)

_____(insert name of book or title of magazine article, and name of publication)_____

will appear at: _____(insert address and name of place set for your appear-

ance)_____ on _____(insert date and time) for _____(insert name of show or publi-

cation)_____ to be interviewed by _____(insert person's name)_____

I can be contacted at _____(insert address/phone numbers and dates where you

can be reached)_____

• RESOURCE SECTION •

A word of advice. Please understand that we list a wide number of groups, organizations, and resources for your information. But inclusion here doesn't constitute a blanket endorsement. Not all of those presented here may be right for you. Therefore, prior to buying any materials or joining groups we suggest you evaluate them carefully and speak to other writers about their experiences.

• Writers' Organizations •

If you are interested in any of the following organizations contact each directly for eligibility criteria, information on activities, and membership dues.

American Society of Journalists and Authors, Inc.

1501 Broadway, Suite 1907, New York, NY 10036; phone: (212)997-0947.

Founded in 1948, ASJA today numbers 700-plus freelance, nonfiction writers. Membership is "open to qualified professional writers of nonfiction, who can present evidence of sustained nonfiction writing, produced on a freelance basis." ASJA, a nonprofit literary and education organization, has regional chapters in the U.S., which hold varied functions, symposia, and conferences.

The Authors Guild, Inc. and The Authors League of America, Inc.

234 W. 44th St., New York, NY 10036; phone: (212)398-0838.

A national society of professional authors, representing over 6,500 writers of books, articles, short stories, poetry, and other literary works. Founded in 1921, their stated objectives include dealing with the business and professional interests of authors (copyright, freedom of expression, taxation, and other such issues). They hold symposia and provide members with a series of helpful reports and expert advice. Membership entitles authors to various services.

Council of Writers Organizations

Box 341200, Los Angeles, CA 90034; phone: (213)301-8546.

This national organization is a coalition of twenty-five professional writers' groups. They publish various items, including a newsletter.

The National Writers Club

1450 South Havana, Suite 620, Aurora, CO 80012; phone: (303)751-7844.

Founded in 1937, NWC has an international membership of 5,300 members. They have local chapters across America, put out several publications, including a bimonthly magazine, a newsletter, and a monthly for their "professional members."

They offer services including: professional consultation, marketing recommendations, agent referral, contests, member discounts on writing supplies and on writing-related books.

The National Writers Union

13 Astor Place, 7th Floor, New York, NY 10003; phone: (212)254-0279.

Founded in 1984, this activist organization (with membership numbering about 2,500) works in coalition with other artists' groups and unions in the U.S. and abroad to "build a progressive force for change, employing collective bargaining and united action" for fair treatment of writers. Locals in many metropolitan centers provide services such as contract advice, marketing support, and tax information. Membership dues are based on annual income.

PEN American Center

Division of International PEN, 568 Broadway, New York, NY 10012; phone: (212)334-1660.

This prestigious writers organization has some 10,000 members internationally, with centers on all continents. The American Center, with 4,200 members, is the largest of their 92 centers. Founded in London in 1921 PEN is well known for the activism of its members, working on social issues affecting writers and their works. They often attract worldwide notice for their international human rights campaigns on behalf of writers, editors, and journalists who are imprisoned or censored (for example, the Salman Rushdie case). Other PEN activities comprise public literary events, conferences, international congresses, and their very prestigious literary awards. PEN also offers assistance to writers in financial need.

• Special Interest and Genre Writers' Organizations •

Mystery Writers of America

236 W. 27th St., Room #600, New York, NY 10001; phone: (212)255-7005.

With 2,500 members internationally, MWA has eight U.S. chapters. Members receive national and regional newsletters and hold meetings in varied locales, including their major annual meeting each spring in New York City, at which the coveted Edgar Allan Poe Award is given.

MWA maintains a New York City-based mystery library (for members use only) and provides contract advice to member-writers of works of suspense, mystery, and crime.

Poetry Society of America

15 Gramercy Park, New York, NY 10003; phone: (212)254-9628.

With 1,700 members and regional chapters open throughout the U.S. the Society holds readings, workshops, and lectures and sponsors contests—some open to book publishers. A major annual awards ceremony/meeting is held in NYC. You must send them an SASE if you want membership or other information.

Poets & Writers, Inc.

72 Spring St., Room 301, New York, NY 10012; phone: (212)226-3586. (*Only* call between 11:00 A.M.-3:00 P.M. EST.) In California write: 1862 Euclid Ave., Box 292, Berkeley, CA 49709; phone: (415)548-6618.

Founded in 1970, this nonprofit organization provides services and publications for poets and fiction writers throughout the United States. They have four programs: Publications, Information Center, Readings/Workshops, and Writers Exchange.

Poets & Writers Magazine is described later in this section, as are some of *P&W's* helpful lists, books, and guides. A mailing list of near 40,000 writers, readers, and literary organizations is available on either Cheshire or pressure-sensitive labels. (To purchase this list contact their Marketing Director.)

The Information Center keeps data on U.S. poets and fiction writers who are currently publishing. The Center staff is also able to provide help on finding writing workshops and conferences, the pros and cons of using a literary agent, and on ascertaining if a press is a vanity house. (*Note:* Telephone information is generally free, but there's a $1 per address charge for written requests.)

Persons interested in being listed with the organization should write for application forms. (There's a one-time-only application fee of $5.)

Romance Writers of America

5206 FM, 196 W, Suite 208, Houston, TX 77069; phone: (713)440-6885.

RWA has some 3,500 members and holds national and regional meetings.

Science Fiction Writers of America, Inc.

Box 4236, W. Columbia, SC 29171.

This organization has 1,000 members throughout the nation. It's open to writers, artists, editors, agents, and publishers working in sci-fi and fantasy genres.

Society of American Travel Writers

1100 17th St., N.W., Suite 1000, Washington, DC 20036; phone: (202)785-5567 or fax (202)659-4991 – ATTN: SATW.

With 800 members, this national organization has a writers' referral service and a job bank. They hold an annual meeting.

Society of Children's Book Writers

Box 296, Mar Vista Station, Los Angeles, CA 90066; phone: (818)347-2849.

SCBW, founded more than twenty years ago, now numbers over 4,000 members and is a national professional organization that acts as a network for exchange of knowledge for all those involved with young people's literature. They hold a four-day annual conference (generally in mid-August), and also sponsor meetings and workshops throughout the country and present awards for outstanding young people's book and magazine work. They make financial grants and publish a bimonthly bulletin.

The Children's Book Council

67 Irving Place, New York, NY 10003; phone: (212)254-2666.

Members are major children's book publishers and editors. This group has valuable information including three free brochures:

• "Writing for Children and Young Adults" with information on where you can examine current children's books (for SASE with one first-class stamp).

• "Illustrating Children's Books," (for SASE with one first-class stamp).

• "Member's Publishing Programs," (for SASE with two first-class stamps).

Western Writers of America, Inc.

1753 Victoria Station, Sheridan, WY 82081; phone: (307)672-2079.

Founded in 1953, WWA now has over 600 members—poets, journalists, novelists, scholars, scriptwriters, and others involved in the dissemination of works about the American West, fictive and nonfictive, set in the past or the present. The WWA holds an annual convention (generally the last week in June) culminating with the Spur Awards Banquet. They publish the quarterly magazine, *The Roundup*.

• Books For Writers •

The following five titles are published by Writer's Digest Books, which has scores of books for writers of every type, including those specializing in certain subjects/ areas. Their catalog is available free of charge by writing: Writer's Digest/North Light Books, 1507 Dana Avenue, Cincinnati, OH 45207.

Children's Writer's & Illustrator's Market

Published annually. Presents key aspects of writing for children, pre-schoolers through teenagers. Introduction on how to freelance, followed by 500 detailed publisher listings. Includes special markets: comic books, coloring books, and greeting cards. Resource section has listings of and data on agents, clubs, and workshops. $14.95 Paperback.

Novel & Short Story Writer's Market

Also an annual, this popular directory contains facts and information on getting short stories and novels published. Has approximately 1,750 detailed listings of commercial books and magazine publishers, small presses, and little/literary magazines. Includes some 300 pages of fiction writing and marketing techniques, plus advice on—and listings of—agents who handle fiction. $17.95 Paperback.

Poet's Market: Where & How to Publish Your Poetry

Updated each year, this annual lists close to 2,000 mass circulation and literary magazines, trade book publishers, small presses, university quarterlies, etc. Each listing bears an authoritative critique with detailed market analyses; each is coded as to type of market (beginner, specialized, etc.) This directory also contains names of people to contact, submission policies, payment rates, if any, and other helpful advice for poets. Also includes opportunities in writing poetry for greeting cards, posters, and on contests and awards, workshops, and organizations. $18.95 Hardcover.

Writer's Yearbook

Containing the "Top 100 Nonfiction Markets," this annual is compiled for aspiring and established writers, and reflects the current status of the marketplace with practical, how-to articles and other information. $3.95 Magazine-format.

Writer's Market

This annual contains listings of over 4,000 places for freelancers to sell articles, books, fillers, greeting cards, novels, plays, scripts, etc. Includes market information with editors' names and addresses, pay rates, editorial needs, submission requirements, information on literary agents, and awards and contests. Also, has articles on the profession of writing and other insider information.

Books About Publishing
The Awful Truth About Publishing
By John Boswell (Warner Books).

Subtitled, "Why they always reject your manuscript and what you can do about it." This provides details on how *not* to wind up in the "slush" pile. Includes essential points necessary to a book proposal, finding the right working title, information on targeting the right publisher, and understanding what each department does. $14.95 Hardcover.
A Writer's Guide to Book Publishing
By Richard Balkin (E.P. Dutton).

A fine reference to many phases of the author-publisher relationship, from manuscript submission and contract negotiation through editing, book design, publication, and marketing. $11.95 Paperback.
How to Market Your Books: For Publishers & Authors
By John Kremer. Ad-Lib Publications, 51 N. 5th St., P.O. Box 1102, Fairfield, IA 52556-1102; phone: (515)472-6617. $19.95 Hardcover; $14.95 Softcover.

Includes scores of ideas, tips, and suggestions on every phase of book marketing.

• General Reference Books •

From Gale Research
The following *six* directories are from Gale Research, best known as publishers of books for libraries. Their catalog is a particularly helpful resource, which you might find on file at your library. Call or write Gale for more information and for all current prices: Gale Research, Inc., Dept. 77748, Detroit, MI 48277-0748; phone: (800)877-GALE; in Michigan, Alaska, Hawaii and Canada: (313)961-2242; fax: (313)961-6083.
Encyclopedia of Associations
Described in detail in Chapter 7 on page 80.
Trade Shows and Professional Exhibits Directory
Over 4,500 scheduled exhibitions, trade shows, association conventions, and other similar events with dates, locations, sites, contacts, and other exhibit features. Covers U.S. and Canada and over sixty other countries.

Standard Periodical Directory

This annual includes over 65,000 U.S. and Canadian periodicals, listed under 230 major subjects. Includes listings for newspapers, consumer magazines, trade journals, newsletters, government publications, house organs, and directories.

Gale Directory of Publications and Broadcast Media

A three-volume set published annually, this directory lists major magazines, newspapers, radio and television stations, and cable companies in the U.S. and Canada. Periodicals are indexed according to subject and special interest, and radio stations by format.

Publishers Directory

Over 20,000 Canadian and U.S. book publishers are included in this annual volume: major and small houses, literary presses, art and science museums, religious institutions, and departments of universities and corporations.

Contemporary Authors

Published three times yearly, this directory contains personal information on scores of authors, including home and office addresses, lists of their works, and works in progress. Also includes essays about each.

Holidays & Anniversaries of the World

Covers 366 days of the Gregorian year, with data on U.S. state and national holidays, international holidays, special events and their sponsors, birthdates of famous people of all historical periods, saints days, holy days and other religious days, historic events, etc.

From R.R. Bowker

There are *many* invaluable books put out by R.R. Bowker, and their catalog is another treasure trove for writers and well worth scanning. For information on any of their titles, contact R.R. Bowker, P.O. Box 762, New York, NY 10011; phone: (800)521-8110; in New York, Arkansas, and Hawaii (212)337-6934; in Canada (800)537-8416.

Literary Market Place

This is the "bible" of publishing. This annual contains detailed information (13,000-plus entries in over 80 categories), includes listings of all major book publishers (those who issue three or more titles yearly), distributors, book clubs, literary agents, suppliers (including consultants in public relations and promotion), contests, literary awards, writer's conferences, associations, and writers' organizations. $110 Paperback.

American Book Trade Directory

An R.R. Bowker annual, this Directory includes names and addresses for key personnel at almost 25,000 bookstores in the U.S. and Canada, as well as antiquarian book dealers, and close to 1,500 book and magazine wholesalers, distributors, and jobbers, all organized geographically by state and city. Retailers are separately indexed by bookselling category; wholesaler entries indicate businesses that handle audiocassettes, software, and other sidelines. $169.95.

• References Covering Agents and/or Legal Issues •

Pamphlets

For a free descriptive listing of American literary agents, send SASE to: Society of Authors' Representatives, 3rd Floor, 10 Astor Place, New York, NY 10003; phone: (212)353-3709.

For a membership list, copy of ILAA's "Code of Ethics," and overview of services in a free pamphlet, send SASE to: Independent Literary Agents Association, 55 5th Ave., New York, NY 10003.

Books and Magazines

Literary Agents: How to Get and Work with the Right One for You

By Michael Larsen. This Writer's Digest Book offers a frank discussion with answers to some thorny questions. Complete details on knowing when a writer needs an agent, finding the right one, and how best to make contact. You'll learn what to expect of agents, negotiations, agreements, and more. $9.95 Hardcover.

How to Understand and Negotiate a Book Contract or Magazine Agreement

By Richard Balkin. Also from Writer's Digest Books. $11.95 Hardcover.

Literary Agents of North America: The Complete Guide to U.S. & Canadian Literary Agencies

From Author Aid/Research Associates International, 340 E. 52nd St., New York, NY 10022; phone: (212)758-4213.

This annual is a definitive reference listing of over 850 literary agents. $27.95, including shipping and handling, or $31.95 for first-class shipping and handling. Softcover.

It includes good articles on the subjects of agents, agenting, contracts, and copyright, by New York lawyer-publishing specialist, Mark L. Levine. He also writes regularly for the bimonthly, *Small Press Magazine,* Meckler Publishing, 11 Ferry Lane W., Westport, CT 06880; phone: (203)226-6967. Subscription $29.50.

How to Get Happily Published

By Judith Appelbaum. From Harper & Row. $17.95 Hardcover. From New American Library. $9.95 Paperback.

This splendid work, newly revised, is deservedly a perennial top seller. It belongs on every writers' shelf.

The Unabashed Self-Promoter's Guide

By Dr. Jeffrey Lant. Jeffrey Lant Associates, 50 Follen St., Suite 507, Cambridge, MA 02138; phone: (617)547-6372.

More than 350 pages of heavy-hitting advice, including a section on "The Obligatory Obituary" wherein he says, "Remember, just because you have clipped under the daisies, your self-promotional activities should not prematurely abate." $34 plus $3 for shipping and handling.

• Especially For Poets and Fiction Writers •

The following are just some of the references, source books, and guides available from the Poets & Writers organization, which is geared to the interests of poets and writers of fiction. Write them for a catalog at 72 Spring St., Room 301, New York, NY 10012.

Resource Lists

New York City Workshops
Annotated list of free and fee-charging poetry and fiction workshops in the New York metropolitan area. Issued three times a year. $2 with SASE.

California Resources List
In three sections: magazines—particularly those looking for work from California writers; bookstores and California arts organizations; and literary landmarks. $2 with SASE.

High School Writers Resources List
Literary and writing opportunities for young writers—those in grades nine through twelve. Includes information on magazines that accept high school writing; also contests, awards, conferences, reading series, and information centers. $2 with SASE.

Writers' Conferences
Detailed listings for 200-plus U.S. and overseas conferences. New edition each March. $4 + $1.50 shipping and handling.

Books (also available from the Poets & Writers organization)

The Writing Business: A Poet's & Writer's Handbook
Practical advice for writers, dealing with the business side of being a writer. $11.95 + $2.50 shipping and handling. Paperback.

Literary Agents: A Writer's Guide
Information on finding an agent, what agents do, and how to work with one. Also includes interviews with agents, information on rights and fees, plus an annotated list of agencies interested in handling literary work. $6.95 + $1.50 shipping and handling.

A Writer's Guide to Copyright
Revised and updated, this is a concise summary of copyright law. The first edition was highly recommended by *Library Journal, ALA Booklist,* and *Law Books in Review.* Illustrated with sample forms, glossary, etc. $6.95 + $1.50 shipping and handling.

Becoming a Writer
By Dorothea Brande (Tarcher). Originally published in 1934, "shows that if you want to write, you can—and shows you how." Humorous work blending philosophy and how-to. $6.95 + $2.50 postage and handling. Paperback.

The Art of Fiction: Notes on the Craft for Young Writers
By John Gardner (Vintage). Identifies seven basic matters of technique for writers; also, common errors novices make. A general discussion of the theory

of fiction. Also: thirty writing exercises. $5.59 + $1.50 postage and handling. Paperback.

Author & Audience: A Readings and Workshops Guide

A list of over 600 American organizations that present readings or workshops, alphabetically arranged by state. With introductory text on how to organize and promote readings and workshops, and specific instructions for both presenters and writers. $6.95 + $2.50 postage and handling.

Poets take special note:

The Triggering Town: Lectures & Essays on Poetry and Writing

By Richard Hugo (Norton). Essays recalling Hugo's writing teacher, Theodore Roethke, his experiences in WW II, and more. $6.95 + $2.50 postage and handling. Paperback.

• Commemorative Days, Events, Holidays •

Chase's Annual Events

Contemporary Books, Inc., 180 N. Michigan Ave., Chicago, IL 60601; phone: (312)782-9181. $27.95 Hardcover.

A Dictionary of Days

By Leslie Dunkling.

Facts on File

460 Park Ave. S., New York, NY 10016; phone: (212)683-2244.

Selected by *School Library Journal* as one of the best reference books of 1988, contains information on named days found on calendars for most English-speaking countries. *Viz:* "When is Pig Face Sunday? What was October 31st called before it was Halloween? Is Twelfth Night the eve or evening of Twelfth Day?" An excellent reference tool. $19.95 Hardcover. $10.95 Paperback.

The Day by Day Series

(The price for these hardbound reference works ranges from $125.00 for one volume editions, to $195.00 for the two-volume editions.) Chronological reference volumes to events day by day, at this writing, for the period from the 1940's to 1970's. Each illustrated volume contains front page news for the day cited covering foreign affairs, national politics, government, science and technology, culture, and the arts.

• Media Directories •

If purchasing any of the following, it's imperative that you contact each company listed to verify availability, current price, taxes, and shipping and handling charges.

Bacon's Publicity Checker

From BACON'S—*Publicity Checker*, 332 S. Michigan Ave., Chicago, IL 60604; phone: (800)621-0561.

Two annual volumes about newspapers and magazines, sold only as a set. Updated listings sent to purchasers. Excellent detailed listings of newspapers (daily/weekly), Sunday supplements, national newspapers, feature services, news syndicates, and more. Lists all daily papers in the U.S., with details including specific editors' names and departments. Also more than 7,500 weekly papers and weekly publisher groups, Canadian daily papers, the African-American press, feature news services and syndicates, and special lists of daily papers by circulation groups and demographically important markets.

Second volume of almost 5,000 magazines by category (trade, farm, business, industrial, and general consumer interest) covering the U.S. and Canada. Listings provide editors' names, publications' addresses, phone numbers, frequency, and circulation figures. $160 for set. Spiral-bound paperback.

Broadcast & Cable Yearbook

Broadcasting Publications, 1705 de Sales St. N.W., Washington, DC 20036; phone: (202)659-2340; fax (202)429-0651; or to order toll free (800)638-7827.

Detailed, updated annual including information on every U.S. and Canadian radio, cable, and television station, (including cross-directory for university and college stations), satellites, technology, programming, and more. *The* place to find the decision makers, learn formats, power information, find a guide to U.S. Arbitron/radio rating, and see market designation and size. The compendium for the entire electronic broadcast industry. $100. Large format, softcover.

From Public Relations Plus

New York Publicity Outlets

Public Relations Plus, Inc., P.O. Drawer 1197, New Milford, CT 06776; phone: (800)999-8448.

This is a valuable guide to national and local media based in the greater New York metropolitan area (i.e., New York City and all boroughs therein; all of Long Island; Westchester; Putnam and Rockland counties; Northern New Jersey and Southwest Connecticut). It's published in two revised, reprinted editions published at six month intervals. There are usually over 400 pages with thousands of detailed listings for print and broadcast media contacts: daily and weekly newspapers, consumer magazines, news services, feature syndicates, Sunday supplements, broadcast and cable TV networks, local TV stations and systems—with details on specific TV programs. Also black and ethnic publications, radio networks and local radio stations, with specifics on radio shows and lists of selected trade publications. The listings are fully indexed. $99.50, prepaid by check, money order, or charge card. Loose-leaf pages in binder.

Metro California Media

This 350-plus page book covers print/broadcast media contacts for the entire state of California. It contains essentially the same type of listings as the New York volume, with the addition of California-based syndicated writers. Published in two revised, reprinted editions at six-month intervals. $99.50 prepaid by check, money order, or charge card. Loose-leaf pages in binder.

From Hudson's Directories

The following three volumes are all available from Hudson's Media Directories, Box 311, Rhinebeck, NY 12572; phone: (914)876-2081.

Hudson's Washington News Media Contacts

For those seeking to publicize news of national or political interest via the Washington (DC) press corps. Includes detailed listings of correspondents for wire services, news bureaus, newspapers (by state), syndicates, radio and TV, magazines, and newsletters, as well as photographic services, freelance writers, and special Washington services. Hudson's provides buyers of this directory with updates in April, July, and October. In 1989 Hudson's added the fax numbers of news outlets with fax machines. $119. Spiral-bound paperback. Mailing label, magnetic disk service also available.

Hudson's State Capitals News Media Contacts Directory

Correspondents for the nation's state capital-based wire services, news bureaus, newspapers (both local and out of town), radio, television, magazines, and newsletters. $80. Spiral-bound paperback.

Hudson's Newsletter Directory

Information on worldwide subscription newsletters by subject category with editors and publishers; also includes reviews of major events in publishing, conferences, seminars, awards, and suppliers. $99. Spiral-bound paperback.

From Resource Media

The following directories are available from Resource Media, Inc., Box 307, Kent, CT 06757; phone: (800)441-3839 or (203)927-4616; fax (203)927-4800.

National Radio Publicity Outlets

The title of this directory amply describes the book. $179.50. Paperback.

All TV & Cable Outlets

$179.50. Paperback. *Note:* If Resource Media's radio and TV directories are purchased together there is a special discount price of $343 at this writing, but check with the company for current prices.

Feature News Publicity Outlets

Previously known as the *Family Page Directory,* in 1989 this was expanded to include new information, including fax numbers, of the feature departments of the top 500 U.S. newspapers, plus data on Sunday circulation. Also listed are the beauty, fashion, food, and home furnishings editors, and the top editors in charge of the family or women's pages (also called "lifestyle" or "living" pages). $75 + $5 shipping and handling for two issues. Spiral-bound paperback.

From Oxbridge Communications

The following three directories are published by: Oxbridge Communications, Inc., 150 5th Ave., New York, NY 10011; phone: (212)741-0231.

National Directory of Magazines
Annual directory containing 1,800 pages of U.S. and Canadian publications. $225. Softcover.

Standard Periodicals Directory
Lists U.S. and Canadian magazines, journals, newsletters, directories—70,000 publications in 100 fields with 230 subject areas. $395.

Oxbridge Directory of Newsletters
17,000 U.S. and Canadian newsletters. $195.

From R.R. Bowker

Ulrich's International Periodicals Directory
These three annual volumes contain detailed data on over 110,000 regularly and irregularly issued serials; 66,000-plus revised entries; over 7,000 cessations; and addresses for over 61,000 publishers from almost 200 countries. Free quarterly supplement. $300.

From Bowker in CD-ROM Format

Ulrich's Plus ™
Lists around 11,000 top periodicals, 135,000 active and ceased periodicals, and serial and annual (regular and irregular) periodicals published internationally. Available on CD-ROM (Compact Disc Read-Only-Memory). For IBM PC, XT, AT, PS/2, or compatible computers or a Macintosh Plus, SE, II, IIx, or equivalent. For information call (800)323-3288.

Books in Print Plus
Almost 1 million in-print books; call up all available titles by topic in any entry in the database. Eighteen search categories include: author, title, publisher, ISBN, price, publication date, and grade level.

Books in Print with Book Reviews Plus
Contains thousands of unabridged book reviews from *Publishers Weekly, Library Journal, School Library Journal, Choice, Research Book News,* and *Sci-Tech Book News.*

Books Out-of-Print Plus
Close to a half million titles declared out of print (O.P.) or out of stock indefinitely (O.S.I.) since 1979. If your library has this and you can access, you might find this of real help. Rather costly for the average person.

From National Research Bureau

Working Press of the Nation
National Research Bureau, 310 S. Michigan Ave., Chicago, IL 60604; phone: (800)456-4555.

The five volumes, issued annually are excellently detailed compendiums, one volume each devoted to: newspapers (weekly and dailies), magazines, radio and TV, writers, and internal publications. $290 for all five, or $135 each volume.

• Trade Show Catalogs •

The Folio Show & Magazine Publishing Congress
Seminar Registration, 6 River Bend Center, 911 Hope St., Box 4232, Stamford, CT 06907-0232; phone: (203)358-9900; fax (203)358-0594.

Book Pub. World
% Cahners Exposition Group, 999 Summer St., P.O. Box 3833, Stamford, CT 06905-0839; phone: (203)964-0000.

• Book Trade Publications and Review Media •

Note: To verify current subscription rates, refer to a current issue of each publication or to the *National Directory of Magazines* (listed here).

Publishers Weekly
Editorial Offices: 245 W. 17th St., New York, NY 10011; phone: (212)645-0027.

Subscriptions: $97 annually. Contact *Publishers Weekly,* P.O. Box 1979, Marion, OH 43302. Or call (800)842-1669. New York residents: (212)337-6934. Alaska and Hawaii, call collect: (212)337-6934. Canada: (614)382-3322.

Library Journal
Editorial Offices: 245 W. 17th St., New York, NY 10011; phone: (212)645-0027.

Subscriptions: $69 annual/20 issues. Contact *Library Journal,* P.O. Box 1977, Marion, OH 43302. Or call (800)842-1669. New York residents: (212)337-6934. Alaska and Hawaii, call collect: (212)337-6934. Canada: (614)382-3322.

School Library Journal
Editorial Offices: 245 W. 17th St., New York, NY 10011; phone: (212)645-0027.

Subscriptions: $59 annually/12 issues. Contact *School Library Journal,* P.O. Box 1978, Marion, OH 43305. Or call (800)842-1669. New York residents: (212)337-6934. Alaska and Hawaii, call collect: (212)337-6934. Canada: (614)382-3322.

The Booklist
The American Library Association, 50 E. Huron St., Chicago, IL 60611; phone: (312)944-6780; (800)545-2433; or in Illinois, (800)545-2444; fax (312)440-0901.

Sent to ALA members.

Choice: Books for College Libraries
Association of College and Research Libraries, 100 Riverview Center, Middletown, CT 06457; phone: (203)347-6933.

Sent to ACRL members.

The Kirkus Reviews
200 Park Ave. S., New York, NY 10003; phone: (212)777-4554.

$295 — Institutional rate for twenty-four issues.

The Sunday New York Times Book Review

229 W. 43rd St., New York, NY 10036; phone: (212)556-1234; toll free *for subscription only*: (800)631-2580.

Weekly, mailed one week before newsstand appearance. $31.20 in U.S.

• Newspaper, Magazine, Radio and TV Industry Periodicals •

Broadcasting Magazine

Available from Broadcasting Publications, 1705 de Sales St. N.W., Washington, DC 20036; phone: (202)659-2340; fax (202)429-0651; or to order toll free (800)638-7827.

Leading newsweekly of the electronic media: radio, TV, cable TV, and satellite. Includes programming information and FCC actions. Also, fast-breaking news, analysis of happenings in news gathering and the dissemination of electronic news, and personnel changes, $35 for six month subscription; $70 for one year; $135 for two years.

Editor & Publisher

11 W. 19th St., New York, NY 10011; phone: (212)675-4380; fax (212)929-1259.

Published weekly. Subscription $40.

Folio: The Magazine for Magazine Management

Cowles Media, 6 River Bend Center, 911 Hope St., Box 4232, Stamford, CT 06907-0232.

Monthly. Subscription $58.

Magazine Week

Lighthouse Communications, 233 W. Central St., Natick, MA 01760; phone: (508)650-1001 or fax (508)653-3624.

50 weeks a year. Subscription $178.

• Magazines for Writers •

Poets & Writers Magazine

72 Spring St., Room 301, New York, NY 10012.

Bimonthly magazine. In addition to helpful articles and interviews, contains information on grants and awards, state grants, and more. $18 for one year subscription; $32 for two years; $46 for three years. Note: Reduced rates are available for writers listed in the *P&W Directory*.

Writer's Digest

F&W Publications, 1507 Dana Ave., Cincinnati, OH 45207; phone: (513)531-2222; toll free for subscriptions only: (800)333-0133.

A freelance writer's monthly magazine, covering varied phases of writing with practical, instructive articles on subjects such as how to get published, writing and selling fiction and nonfiction, poetry, and scripts. Also includes author profiles, new sales markets and other such information. $21 for one year subscription.

The Writer

120 Boylston St., Boston, MA 02116; phone: (617)423-6157.

Monthly magazine containing articles on writing for publication: fiction, nonfiction, poetry, etc. $23 for one year subscription.

For Genre and Fiction Writers

The following are all published by Romantic Times and can be obtained by addressing the *specific* publication at 163 Joralemon St., Brooklyn Heights, NY 11201. Telephone hot line for writers and to subscribe: (718)237-1097.

Fiction Writers Magazette

(Formerly *Fiction Writers Magazine*). Now in a trade book format, this quarterly can now also be found in bookstores at $12.95.

Romantic Times

This bimonthly magazine is geared to the interests and needs of romance writers. $14.95 for one year subscription.

Rave Reviews

A bimonthly magazine covering topics for writers of all forms of *genre fiction*. $14.95 for one year subscription.

For Travel Writers

Travelwriter Marketletter

Robert Scott Milne, Editor, Waldorf Astoria Hotel, 301 Park Ave., Suite 1850, New York, NY 10022; phone: (212)759-6744.

This monthly newsletter — geared to the travel market — provides fine information about traditional and off-beat markets, (and those to avoid), as well as information on pay scales, editors, and also free trips for professional travel writers and photographers. $60 for one year subscription; $115 for two years.

• For Finding Scholarly Publications •

Both directories listed below are from the Association of American University Presses, Inc., One Park Ave., New York, NY 10016; phone: (212)889-6040.

Advertising & Publicity Resources for Scholarly Books

Lists 3,200 general and scholarly periodicals in forty-eight categories, with 1,000 cross references. Names, addresses of book review editors and other contacts, and publication descriptions. 850 pages. $200 Softcover.

AAUP Directory

A 200-page directory of members of this organization of university presses. Includes data on all U.S. university presses, and also international presses. Provides names of editorial people and information on each presses' preferred subject areas. $12.95 Softcover.

• Publications About Book Fairs and Exhibits •

In addition to the two Gale directories *(Encyclopedia of Associations* and *Trade Shows & Professional Exhibits Directory)* listed on page 197, there are several other such references:

Book Fairs: An Exhibiting Guide for Publishers

By Dan Poynter. Para Publishing, P.O. Box 4232-117, Santa Barbara, CA 93140-4232. Phone: (800)PARAPUB; fax: (805)968-1379.

Written for publishers, this will also help you understand how to select, arrange, and operate a book fair booth. With tips on "how to work a fair to your maximum advantage, whether you are staffing a booth or working the floor." $7.95 Paperback + $1.50 shipping and handling, or + $3 air mail.

The Exhibit Review

Alpha Publishing Group, Inc., 10200 S.W. Nimbus Ave., G-7, Portland, OR 97223; phone: (503)620-2554.

Trade show information in directory format with listings indexed by industry, location and date; updated every three months. Also: articles on effective sales techniques, reviews of shows and convention centers, and contact names and phone numbers. $50 U.S.; $70 in Canada (U.S. currency).

• INDEX •

advance notice, 80, 190
advertising
  for bookings, 124-125
  vs. publicity, 3
  yourself, as a freelancer, 167
agents
  literary, 3-4
  press, 172-181
  see also public relations agents
answering machines, 18
appearances
  see public appearances, television
autograph parties
  at bookstores, 90-95, 152-153
  for magazine writers, 94-95
  media coverage, 91

background sheets, 6-8
  sample, 7
backlist
  defined, 140
banners, 161
blurbs, 142-143
book marks, 153
book meetings, 129
book publicity action plan, 185-188
bookings
  advertising for, 124-125
  for radio, 108-110
  for television, 98-99
books in print, 1
booksellers
  contact with, 149-151
  getting stocked by, 154
bookselling
  nontraditional, 84-85
  examples of, 84-85
bookstore appearances, 90-95, 152-153
bulk mailings, 22-23, 153
business cards, 16, 18, 159-160
buttons, 163-164

calendars, 20
clip art, 166
clip files, 56
coat-tailing, 169-170
  examples, 170
columnists, 57-58
  syndicated, 61
computers, 19, 74
  and publicity, 165
conferences
  publishing, 73, 141
  writers, 70-72
confirmation slip, 97, 192
consignment, selling books by, 82
contact people, in media, 36
contests, 68-69

datebooks, 20
direct mail, 15
direct sales, 81-82, 154-155
  examples, 82-83
donations, 68

editors, 48-55
  letters to, 51-52
  meeting, 48-51
  keeping in contact with, 52-55
enclosures
  with news release, 37
endorsement,
  by well-known people, 142-143
envelopes, 17-18, 21-23
  stuffing, 22-23
expert
  getting known as quotable, 59

facsimile (FAX) machines, 20-21
flags, 19
folders
  for press kits, 13-15
  example, 14
follow-ups

to pitch letters, 46
  examples, 46-47

galleys
  sending for reviews, 141-142, 180
graphic artists, 15, 16

headlines
  for news releases, 36
hooks, 26
  examples, 26-27

ideas
  stolen, 50-51
income
  average, for writers, 1
independent publicity, 152-153, 172-173
interviews
  see also radio, television
  taping, 123-124
inverted pyramid, 35

KISS formula, 26, 34-35, 111

layout
  for news releases, 36
lead sentences
  for news releases, 44-45
lead time, 52
letterhead
  for newsletters, 166
  for stationery, 16-17, 21-22
libraries
  promotions at, 155-156
lists
  media, 28, 32
  of publicity successes, 149-151
localizing submissions, 53-54

magazine writers
  public appearances by, 85-86
mailing labels, 18, 21
mailings, 22, 153
markers, 20

media
  alert, 154, 191
  appearances, 96-126
  "golden rules," 96-97
  information services, 32-33
  lists, 28, 32
  needs, 27
  see radio, television
midlist authors
  defined, 151
  and publicity, 151-152
  on radio and television, 181

news releases
  enclosures, 37
  examples, 37-44, 120
  headlines for, 36
  layout, 36
  for press conferences, 88-89
  for radio, 119-121
  using reviews for, 147-148
  writing, 34-36
newsletters, 165-167

offprints
  of publicity, 8
op-ed articles, 62-63
organizations for writers, 193-196

packaging, 6
panel discussions, 103-104
photocopies
  in press kit, 8
photographs, 8-13
  captions, 10-11
  examples, 11, 12
  group, 13
pitch letters, 28-29
  examples, 29-32
  follow-ups, 46
  how to make timely, 52-54
plans
  for generating publicity, 27, 152
plugs
  for books, 121-123

for products, 170-171
poetry, 69
portfolios, 50
post-cards, 21, 23-24, 159
    return, 146
posters, 94, 164, 170
press conferences, 87-90
press kits, 6-15
press releases
    see news releases
promotional gimmicks, 161-164
    examples, 167-168
pub date, 180
public appearances, 82-83
    for magazine writers, 85-86
public relations agents
    agencies vs. freelance, 173
    contracts, 175
    example, 178
    fees, 174
    letters
        example, 179
    meetings, 175
    selecting, 174
public speaking, 60-61, 79-81
    bureaus, 80
    groups, 79
    potential places for, 79-80
    sponsors, 80-81
publication
    parties, 138-139
publicists, 172-173, 180
publicity
    action plan for books, 185-188
    advance, 138
    forms, 189-192
    independent, 141, 152-153, 172-173
    letters, 75-76
        example, 76
    programs, 140-141, 172-173
published works
    in press kit, 8
publishing companies, 127-128
    conferences, 141
    contracts, 130-131

promotion from, 128-139, 140-141
    working with, 130-131

questionnaires, 131-137
    example, 133-136
quotable
    getting known as, 59
quotes
    from book reviews, 143

radio
    stations
        big-city, 109-110
        small-town, 111-112
        local, 109
    interviews
        booking, 108-110
        phone-in, 112
        pitch letters, 111
        examples of material to provide
            for, 113-115
        of midlist authors, 181
        preparation for, 112-113, 115-117
        difficult, 118-119
research, recycling, 63-64
    examples of, 64-67
resources for writers, 193-208
reviews,
    of books, 143-149
    editors, 144-145
    of galleys, 141-142, 180
    getting, 143-144
    quotes from, 143
    recycling, 146-149
        examples, 147-148
    writing, 67

sales reps, 153
scholarly and special interest books,
    56
seminars, 72-73
stationery
    letterhead, 16-17
    for news release, 35
    paper, 17

computers, 21-22
stickers, 161
store appearances
  other than bookstores, 84-85
  see also autograph parties, book-
    store appearances
stuffing envelopes, 22-23
submissions, 52-54
  localizing, 53-54

T-shirts, 161
taglines
  see hooks
tags, 20
talkers, 164
taping interviews, 123-124
television
  personal appearances on, 104-108
    booking, 98-99
    remaining calm, 107
    clothes, 104
    eye contact, 107-108
    interviews, 97-108

stations
  contacting, 96-98
  working with, 106-107, 181
visual aids, 100-102
  examples, 101, 102
thematic promotion, 86-87
time, 24-25
tip sheet, 80, 189
touring, 124-126
trade journals, 129-130
typewriters, 74

vanity press, 156-158
  contracts, 157-158
video network release (VNR), 164
visual aids
  see television

workshops, 72-73
writers conferences, 70-72
writers groups, 73-75
workshops, 72-73

Other Books of Interest

Annual Market Books

Artist's Market, edited by Lauri Miller $21.95

Children's Writer's & Illustrator's Market, edited by Connie Eidenier (paper) $15.95

Humor & Cartoon Markets, edited by Bob Staake (paper) $15.95

Novel & Short Story Writer's Market, edited by Robin Gee (paper) $18.95

Photographer's Market, edited by Sam Marshall $21.95

Poet's Market, by Judson Jerome $19.95

Songwriter's Market, edited by Mark Garvey $19.95

Writer's Market, edited by Glenda Neff $24.95

General Writing Books

Annable's Treasury of Literary Teasers, by H.D. Annable (paper) $10.95

Beginning Writer's Answer Book, edited by Kirk Polking (paper) $13.95

Discovering the Writer Within, by Bruce Ballenger & Barry Lane $16.95

Getting the Words Right: How to Rewrite, Edit and Revise, by Theodore A. Rees Cheney (paper) $12.95

How to Write a Book Proposal, by Michael Larsen (paper) $10.95

Just Open a Vein, edited by William Brohaugh $15.95

Knowing Where to Look: The Ultimate Guide to Research, by Lois Horowitz (paper) $15.95

Make Your Words Work, by Gary Provost $17.95

On Being a Writer, edited by Bill Strickland $19.95

The Story Behind the Word, by Morton S. Freeman (paper) $9.95

12 Keys to Writing Books that Sell, by Kathleen Krull (paper) $12.95

The 29 Most Common Writing Mistakes & How to Avoid Them, by Judy Delton $9.95

The Wordwatcher's Guide to Good Writing & Grammar, by Morton S. Freeman (paper) $15.95

Word Processing Secrets for Writers, by Michael A. Banks & Ansen Dibell (paper) $14.95

Writer's Block & How to Use It, by Victoria Nelson $14.95

The Writer's Digest Guide to Manuscript Formats, by Buchman & Groves $17.95

Nonfiction Writing

Basic Magazine Writing, by Barbara Kevles $16.95

The Complete Guide to Writing Biographies, by Ted Schwarz $19.95

Creative Conversations: The Writer's Guide to Conducting Interviews, by Michael Schumacher $16.95

How to Sell Every Magazine Article You Write, by Lisa Collier Cool (paper) $11.95

How to Write Irresistible Query Letters, by Lisa Collier Cool (paper) $10.95

The Writer's Digest Handbook of Magazine Article Writing, edited by Jean M. Fredette (paper) $11.95

Writing Creative Nonfiction, by Theodore A. Rees Cheney $15.95

Fiction Writing

The Art & Craft of Novel Writing, by Oakley Hall $17.95

Best Stories from New Writers, edited by Linda Sanders $16.95

Characters & Viewpoint, by Orson Scott Card $13.95

The Complete Guide to Writing Fiction, by Barnaby Conrad $17.95

Cosmic Critiques: How & Why 10 Science Fiction Stories Work, edited by Asimov & Greenberg (paper) $12.95

Creating Characters: How To Build Story People, by Dwight V. Swain $16.95

Creating Short Fiction, by Damon Knight (paper) $9.95

Dare to Be a Great Writer: 329 Keys to Powerful Fiction, by Leonard Bishop $16.95

Dialogue, by Lewis Turco $13.95

Fiction Is Folks: How to Create Unforgettable Characters, by Robert Newton Peck (paper) $8.95

Handbook of Short Story Writing: Vol. I, by Dickson and Smythe (paper) $9.95

Handbook of Short Story Writing: Vol. II, edited by Jean M. Fredette $15.95

How to Write & Sell Your First Novel, by Collier & Leighton (paper) $12.95

One Great Way to Write Short Stories, by Ben Nyberg $14.95

Manuscript Submission, by Scott Edelstein $13.95

Plot, by Ansen Dibell $13.95

Revision, by Kit Reed $13.95

Spider Spin Me a Web: Lawrence Block on Writing Fiction, by Lawrence Block $16.95

Storycrafting, by Paul Darcy Boles (paper) $10.95
Theme & Strategy, by Ronald B. Tobias $13.95
Writing the Novel: From Plot to Print, by Lawrence Block (paper) $10.95

Special Interest Writing Books
Armed & Dangerous: A Writer's Guide to Weapons, by Michael Newton (paper) $14.95
The Children's Picture Book: How to Write It, How to Sell It, by Ellen E.M. Roberts (paper) $18.95
Comedy Writing Secrets, by Melvin Helitzer $18.95
The Complete Book of Scriptwriting, by J. Michael Straczynski (paper) $11.95
The Craft of Lyric Writing, by Sheila Davis $19.95
Deadly Doses: A Writer's Guide to Poisons, by Serita Deborah Stevens with Anne Klarner (paper) $16.95
Editing Your Newsletter, by Mark Beach (paper) $18.50
Families Writing, by Peter Stillman $15.95
How to Write a Play, by Raymond Hull (paper) $12.95
How to Write Action/Adventure Novels, by Michael Newton $13.95
How to Write & Sell A Column, by Raskin & Males $10.95
How to Write and Sell Your Personal Experiences, by Lois Duncan (paper) $10.95
How to Write Mysteries, by Shannon OCork $13.95
How to Write Romances, by Phyllis Taylor Pianka $13.95
How To Write Science Fiction & Fantasy, by Orson Scott Card $13.95
How to Write Tales of Horror, Fantasy & Science Fiction, edited by J.N. Williamson $15.95
How to Write the Story of Your Life, by Frank P. Thomas (paper) $11.95
How to Write Western Novels, by Matt Braun $13.95
Mystery Writer's Handbook, by The Mystery Writers of America (paper) $11.95
The Poet's Handbook, by Judson Jerome (paper) $10.95
Successful Lyric Writing (workbook), by Sheila Davis (paper) $18.95
Successful Scriptwriting, by Jurgen Wolff & Kerry Cox $18.95
Travel Writer's Handbook, by Louise Zobel (paper) $11.95
TV Scriptwriter's Handbook, by Alfred Brenner (paper) $10.95
The Writer's Complete Crime Reference Book, by Martin Roth $19.95
Writing for Children & Teenagers, 3rd Edition, by Lee Wyndham & Arnold Madison (paper) $12.95
Writing the Modern Mystery, by Barbara Norville $15.95
Writing to Inspire, edited by William Gentz (paper) $14.95

The Writing Business
A Beginner's Guide to Getting Published, edited by Kirk Polking (paper) $11.95
The Complete Guide to Self-Publishing, by Tom & Marilyn Ross (paper) $16.95
How to Sell & Re-Sell Your Writing, by Duane Newcomb $11.95
How to Write with a Collaborator, by Hal Bennett with Michael Larsen $11.95
How You Can Make $25,000 a Year Writing, by Nancy Edmonds Hanson (paper) $12.95
Is There a Speech Inside You?, by Don Aslett (paper) $9.95
Literary Agents: How to Get & Work with the Right One for You, by Michael Larsen $9.95
Professional Etiquette for Writers, by William Brohaugh $9.95
Time Management for Writers, by Ted Schwarz $10.95
The Writer's Friendly Legal Guide, edited by Kirk Polking $16.95
Writer's Guide to Self-Promotion & Publicity, by Elane Feldman $16.95
A Writer's Guide to Contract Negotiations, by Richard Balkin (paper) $11.95
Writing A to Z, edited by Kirk Polking $19.95

To order directly from the publisher, include $3.00 postage and handling for 1 book and $1.00 for each additional book. Allow 30 days for delivery.

Writer's Digest Books
1507 Dana Avenue, Cincinnati, Ohio 45207
Credit card orders call TOLL-FREE
1-800-289-0963
Prices subject to change without notice.

Write to this same address for information on *Writer's Digest* magazine, *Story* magazine, Writer's Digest Book Club, Writer's Digest School, and Writer's Digest Criticism Service.

POETRY LIBRARY
SOUTH BANK CENTRE
ROYAL FESTIVAL HALL
LONDON
SE1 8XX